God's Future for Animals

"Scholarly without being stodgy, biblically rooted and well informed by the Christian tradition, widely sourced and comprehensive in scope, *God's Future for Animals* offers a very persuasive argument for why Christians ought to rethink their view of animals. Raymond Hausoul is especially good at offering detailed and insightful readings of the Bible that call into question many assumptions we have about animals and their place in the world. Most importantly, this book clearly shows that God loves animals, covenants with animals, and includes animals in God's good future. *God's Future for Animals* is a welcome contribution and timely addition to the field of Christian environmental theology and ethics. I highly recommend it."

—**STEVE BOUMA-PREDIGER**
Professor of Religion, Hope College

"The future of God's kingdom—the epitome of Christian hope—encompasses all of creation and is not limited only to humans or the earth alone; rather, it includes the whole vast cosmos. This is the proper framework for a contemporary eschatology—even though, as mentioned, this most expansive horizon has not been at the center of Christian theology so far. Raymond Hausoul seeks to convince his readers that eschatology involves the complete transformation of the world by a radically new act of God, beginning at Easter and continuing into the future. The demand for such a comprehensive and all-embracing eschatology is challenging. From the perspective of the evangelical movement, the author's own constituency, this kind of constructive work is pioneering."

—**VELI-MATTI KARKKAINEN**
Professor of Systematic Theology, Fuller Theological Seminary

"In this honest, probing book, the author argues convincingly—drawing on a detailed analysis of a wide range of biblical sources—that all animals, not just humans, are included in creation, covenant, redemption, and future expectation. This highly accessible yet thoughtful book will challenge, encourage, and stimulate the reader to think differently and more positively about the place of animals in salvation history."

—**CELIA DEANE-DRUMMOND**
Director, Laudato Si' Research Institute, University of Oxford

"Raymond Hausoul offers an engaging and thoroughgoing study of the relationship between the Creator and animals. It turns out that the Scriptures have quite a bit to say about animals. In addition to surveying the biblical texts, the author brings into the discussion many other voices, including Jewish and Christian commentators, church fathers, philosophers, and theologians. The author is to be commended for highlighting the place of animals in both the creation and the promised new creation."

—PAUL R. RAABE
Professor of Biblical Studies, Grand Canyon University

"Raymond Hausoul has written a fascinating and wide-ranging study of the place of animals in God's world. Although his ultimate goal is to explore the possibility of animals in the eschaton, along the way the book mines Scripture (Old and New Testaments) and the Christian tradition for their teaching about animals and their value to God. Without dogmatism and with a healthy dose of humility, yet with immense learning, Hausoul has prepared a wonderful treat for those interested in this topic."

—J. RICHARD MIDDLETON
Professor of Biblical Worldview and Exegesis,
Northeastern Seminary, Roberts Wesleyan College

God's Future for Animals

From Creation to New Creation

RAYMOND R. HAUSOUL

Foreword by Veli-Matti Kärkkäinen

WIPF & STOCK · Eugene, Oregon

GOD'S FUTURE FOR ANIMALS
From Creation to New Creation

Copyright © 2021 Raymond R. Hausoul. All rights reserved. Except for brief quotations in critical publications or reviews, no part of this book may be reproduced in any manner without prior written permission from the publisher. Write: Permissions, Wipf and Stock Publishers, 199 W. 8th Ave., Suite 3, Eugene, OR 97401.

Wipf & Stock
An Imprint of Wipf and Stock Publishers
199 W. 8th Ave., Suite 3
Eugene, OR 97401

www.wipfandstock.com

PAPERBACK ISBN: 978-1-6667-0340-5
HARDCOVER ISBN: 978-1-6667-0341-2
EBOOK ISBN: 978-1-6667-0342-9

07/19/21

Unless otherwise indicated, all Scripture quotations are from the New Revised Standard Version Bible, Copyright © 1989, Division of Christian Education of the National Council of the Churches of Christ in the U.S.A., and are used by permission. All rights reserved. Emphasis added.

Contents

Foreword by Veli-Matti Kärkkäinen | ix
Preface | xiii

1 **God Loves Animals** | 1
   1.1 Christian Animal Quest | 2
   1.2 The Bible Starts with Genesis | 3

2 **Paradisiacal Conditions** | 7
   2.1 Majestic Creation Epic | 7
       2.1.1 The Artificial Structure of Genesis 1 | 7
       2.1.2 Three Days of Separation | 10
       2.1.3 Three Creation Days of Filling | 14
       2.1.4 The Seventh Day: Blessed Rest | 18
   2.2 Foundation for God's History of Salvation | 20
       2.2.1 God's Promise | 20
       2.2.2 The Relationship between Heaven and Earth | 22
       2.2.3 Eschatological Perspective | 23

3 **Manage and Subdue** | 30
   3.1 God's Commission to Humanity | 30
       3.1.1 Assignment with Negative Resonance | 30
       3.1.2 Assignment with a Positive Connotation | 34
       3.1.3 Representatives of the King | 36
   3.2 Names to the First Animals | 38
       3.2.1 In God's Footsteps | 38
       3.2.2 Wild and Field Animals | 42
       3.2.3 Speaking Animals | 45

4 **Death in Original Creation** | 49
    4.1 God's Creation and Animal Suffering | 49
        4.1.1 The Awareness of Pain and Sadness | 49
        4.1.2 God's Ethical Choice for Evil | 51
    4.2 Suffering as an Intruder | 56
        4.2.1 Genesis 3 and Suffering | 56
        4.2.2 Death to All through One Human | 57
        4.2.3 Animal Suffering in Genesis 1–2 and Genesis 6 | 58
    4.3 The Tree of Life and Carnivores | 60
        4.3.1 Mortal Humans on a Battlefield | 60
        4.3.2 The Origin of Meat Eaters | 63
        4.3.3 Descent from Harmony to Suffering | 65

5 **Humans and Animals** | 70
    5.1 Animal Skins for the First Humans | 70
        5.1.1 A Pessimistic and Optimistic Approach | 70
        5.1.2 Nudity or Clothes? | 72
        5.1.3 Clothes Make the New Self | 76
    5.2 Humans Use Animals | 78
        5.2.1 Animals and Earlier Life | 78
        5.2.2 Animals and the Old Rulers | 81
        5.2.3 Animals in the Later Roman Empire and Europe | 83

6 **God's Covenants with Animals** | 89
    6.1 God's Sorrow over Evil | 89
        6.1.1 Destruction on Earth for Humans and Animals | 89
        6.1.2 God Offers Deliverance in an Ark | 93
        6.1.3 The Raven and the Second Adam | 96
    6.2 God's Covenant with Animals and Humans | 99
        6.2.1 God's Blessings for Noah and His Sons | 99
        6.2.2 God's Covenant with Creatures | 103
        6.2.3 The Promise of God's Covenant | 105

7 **God Stands Up for Animals** | 108
    7.1 Rest, Respect, and Protection for Animals | 109
        7.1.1 God Gives Rest and Food to Animals | 109
        7.1.2 God Calls for Respect for Parents | 111
        7.1.3 God Gives Protection to Animals | 114

    7.2   Connectivity between Humans and Animals | 115
          7.2.1   Judgment about Animals and Humans in the Torah | 115
          7.2.2   Animals in Egypt | 116
          7.2.3   Animals in Nineveh | 118

8   **God's Peace for Animals** | 121
    8.1   God's Renewal for Animals | 121
          8.1.1   Wolf Finds Shelter with Lamb | 121
          8.1.2   Image and Reality | 122
          8.1.3   Humans and Animals in Peace | 127
    8.2   Jesus and the Wild Animals | 129
          8.2.1   Christ Was with the Wild Animals | 129
          8.2.2   Legends about Jesus and the Animals | 131
          8.2.3   Legendary Stories of Animal Peace | 132

9   **Prophetic Images** | 136
    9.1   Taking a Closer Look at Prophetic Speaking | 136
          9.1.1   The Physical World and Biblical Images | 136
          9.1.2   Concepts and Metaphors | 140
          9.1.3   Positive Progress and Negative Removal | 142
    9.2   Continuity and Discontinuity | 143
          9.2.1   Discontinuity in Continuity | 145
          9.2.2   Continuity of Discontinuity | 150
          9.2.3   The Grain and Ear of Corn | 153

10   **Jesus, Firstborn and Protector** | 157
    10.1   The Firstborn and the New Creation | 157
          10.1.1   Christ as Firstborn of the New Creation | 157
          10.1.2   Plea for the Cosmos | 158
          10.1.3   Body, Space, and Time | 161
    10.2   The Messiah and the Protection of Animals | 165
          10.2.1   Jesus Stands Up for a Groaning Donkey | 165
          10.2.2   Jesus and the Battle between Pigs and Demons | 166

11   **Revelation: Creation Destroyed?** | 170
    11.1   God's Dealings with Creation in Revelation | 170
          11.1.1   The Book of the Birth Pangs | 170
          11.1.2   God's Judgment through Intermediaries | 174
          11.1.3   The Lamb That Frees Creation | 177

11.2 The Disappearance of the Sea | 179
    11.2.1 The Sea as a Physical Element of Nature | 180
    11.2.2 The Sea as a Source of Evil | 180
    11.2.3 The Sea as Primeval Flood | 182

12 **Animals in the New Creation** | 184
  12.1 Relationship between Humans and Animals | 184
    12.1.1 Life and Death | 184
    12.1.2 Hero Francis of Assisi | 186
    12.1.3 Reflections on a Systematic Approach | 188
  12.2 Biblical-Theological Reflections | 190
    12.2.1 Cosmological Reflections | 191
    12.2.2 Eschatological Reflections | 193
    12.2.3 Soteriological Reflections | 199

13 **Vegetarian Meals in the Eschaton** | 203
  13.1 Vegetarians and the Bible | 203
    13.1.1 Christians and Vegetables in History | 203
    13.1.2 Biblical Arguments | 206
    13.1.3 Was Jesus a Vegetarian? | 211
  13.2 Vegetarians and the Future | 215
    13.2.1 Luxury Meals in the Past and Future | 215
    13.2.2 Isaiah and God's Future Meal | 219
    13.2.3 Jesus' Words at Holy Communion | 221

Epilogue | 224
Bibliography | 227

Subject Index | 247
Author Index | 249
Ancient Document Index | 255

Foreword

THE DOMAIN OF SYSTEMATIC theology has been traditionally limited to what is considered to be the classical doctrines. As important and central as that may be, it has also resulted in the neglect of a number of themes and issues with weighty theological significance. These include race, environment, animals, ethnicity, inclusivity, violence, and colonialism. It is refreshing to note that Raymond R. Hausoul in this fine study, based on his doctoral dissertation, makes an effort to address one of these challenging contemporary topics, namely the place of animals in creation and new creation.

In twentieth-century theology, the centrality and comprehensive nature of eschatology has been rediscovered, including the personal and the communal dimensions of the Christian vision of the "End." But even then, a fundamental weakness still remains, namely the lack of a cosmic orientation. After Karl Barth rediscovered the centrality of eschatology to theology, Karl Rahner, Jürgen Moltmann (both of whom Hausoul examined in his dissertation), and Wolfhart Pannenberg rediscovered the implications and significance of a cosmological eschatology. From this perspective, a consistent systematic-theological engagement of the destiny of animals is a part of a comprehensive, cosmological eschatological vision.

The future of God's kingdom, the epitome of Christian hope, encompasses all of creation and is not limited only to humans, nor the earth alone; rather, it includes the whole vast cosmos. This is the proper framework for a contemporary eschatology—even though, as mentioned, this most expansive horizon has not been at the center of Christian theology so far. Instead, the focus on the human destiny has been the focus of Christian hope as, quite early in the history of theology, the wider context of the kingdom of God was marginalized. Its meaning was reduced to a hope for a personal "sweet by and by" exit from this world! The biblical testimonies of a new earth were forgotten because the wide and inclusive domain of the hope for the coming of God's kingdom was replaced by merely personal redemption.

As in his doctoral dissertation, in this book Hausoul points to the final consummation in which matter (physicality) and time are not so much "deleted" as they are transformed. As a result, the relationship between the individual and collective hope will not be separated from the destiny of the universe in light of the fact that the Christian hope of the eschatological consummation includes the whole of God's creation. It is nothing less than the integration of the real history of human beings with the whole of creation. This holistic and earthly eschatological vision is wonderfully developed and highlighted in this programmatic book on *God's Future for Animals*. Because the new creation is based on the resurrection of Christ and consummated through the Spirit of God, it also reshapes the physical world in its transformation of the whole cosmos. It is a transformation of the present nature beyond what "natural" emergence has brought about.

Rightly, Hausoul doesn't view the new creation as a replacement of the present creation. New creation is not a second *ex nihilo* or a working out of the natural processes of the cosmos. He interprets the new creation as a transformation of this present creation. Doing so, he seeks to convince his readers that eschatology involves the complete transformation of the world by a radically new act of God, beginning at Easter and continuing into the future.

The demand for such a comprehensive and all-embracing eschatology is challenging. From the perspective of the evangelical movement, the author's own constituency, this kind of constructive work is pioneering.

Speaking about the new heaven and the new earth requires also a proper methodology—particularly when the final hope encompasses the future of animals. A part of the methodological considerations is the search for a suitable language and rich imagination. As Alister E. McGrath notes in the beginning of his *A Brief History of Heaven*, "From a Christian perspective, the horizons defined by the parameters of our human existence merely limit what we can see; they do not define what there is to been seen."[1] Theological imagination, as much as it has to be anchored in the wider human pursuit of truth, should bravely, though also carefully, rush in where angels fear to tread. Modern and contemporary theologians

---

1. McGrath, *Brief History of Heaven*, 1.

have tended to be so overly cautious that they may have also missed the rewards of the discovery of the radically new and unanticipated.

For the theologian, the guiding tradition is the biblical-historical and contemporary theological wisdom, the deposit of faith. However, that tradition is neither a straitjacket that limits the creative pursuit of knowledge nor a basis for mere repetition and defense. A sympathetic critique of tradition is also a part of the task. As I have argued in my five-volume series, A Constructive Christian Theology for the Pluralistic World, "Systematic theology is an integrative discipline that continuously searches for a coherent, balanced understanding of Christian truth and faith in light of Christian tradition (biblical and historical), the context of the historical and contemporary thought, cultures, and living faiths. It aims at a coherent, inclusive, dialogical, and hospitable vision."[2] It is easy to see that Hausoul's book aims at a similar kind of comprehensive vision of theology in which eschatology encompasses not only the human destiny but also makes space for a proper hope for animals, God's creatures. This book shows the way towards a more holistic, multifaceted, and progressive vision of Christian doctrine of the "End."

—Veli-Matti Kärkkäinen
Professor of systematic theology at
Fuller Theological Seminary
(Pasadena, California),
and Docent of ecumenics at the
University of Helsinki, Finland.

2. Kärkkäinen, *Creation and Humanity*, 1.

Preface

ONE BEAUTIFUL SUMMER EVENING, I talked with friends about my research on the new heaven and the new earth. While enjoying a refreshing glass of red wine, the thought arose to write a book about animals in the present and the new creation.

Motivated, I realized that this was a very challenging subject. It was a subject about which not much had been written in Christian literature. However, in recent years several works have appeared on the relationship between the environment and Christianity. Nevertheless, in these publications, the place of the past and future of animals was only touched upon briefly. Scholars draw our attention to other relevant themes about animals, such as dealing with growing environmental problems and the bio-industry. As far as I know, books that focused on God's treatment of animals in the original creation were not much available in the present time of that creation and the future new creation. That observation has not changed since I completed the manuscript for this book.

This book was a pleasant relaxation for me. It was an oasis in which I could regularly indulge myself in addition to my busy work as a pastor, researcher, and lecturer. Writing it demanded genuine creativity when it came to exploring new paths in Christian doctrine. At the same time, caution was needed to stick to the biblical history of interpretation. I hope to have found a healthy balance in this. May the final result encourage new discussions about this in the Christian congregation and doctrine.

I am grateful for my friends Els Devoldere, Déborah Giampietro, Lisanne van Dam, Arjen van Trigt, Dimitri Vanderheede, and Nathan Vanharen. They all provided comments on an earlier edition of this book and helped to make the clarity stronger. Of course, I am fully responsible for the final result. Finally, a sweet "thank you" to my wonderful wife, Belinda, and my sons Adriël and Ilja. All of you gave me the time to fascinate and bore them for hours with all kinds of discoveries in the search for the animals in God's present and future creation.

Ieper/Ypres, Spring 2021
Raymond R. Hausoul

1

God Loves Animals

PERHAPS YOU ARE ONE of the many earthlings who had to learn all kinds of fascinating details at school from an early age. Countless mathematical and linguistic formulas and charts still haunt our minds when we are older. Yet, far fewer people ask questions about the *big picture* of the world. The focus on fine details in mathematics, physics, geography, history, biology, and so forth threatens to overshadow the perspective on the *big picture*. In recent years, we have become increasingly aware in science that we have such highly specialized knowledge that no one can get an overall view of the greater whole.

Fortunately, Christians have a growing desire to look again at Christian doctrine from the *big picture* perspective. One of those related questions is the crucial question of God's way with the animals in the history of salvation. This book wants to give an impetus to this. It intends to reflect from a new approach on the place of the animals in the story of creation (chapters 2–3), in the drama of the first human disobedience (chapters 4–5), in its further consequence in the story of salvation (chapters 6–7), and in the future completion of the new heaven and the new earth (chapters 8–13).

In plain language, we could formulate the critical questions as follows: How does God treat animals? Do animals also have a place in Christ's work of salvation? Will there later be animals on the new earth? These are questions about which there is not much discussion in Christian literature. In Christian theology, the world of animals is considered a *terra incognita*—an unknown territory. Thus, it is a great challenge to reflect on these questions more responsibly and offer openings for a constructive follow-up discourse. That is the goal I have in mind with this book and to which I invite the reader warmly. It will be an adventure in search of the animals in God's plan of salvation.

1.1 CHRISTIAN ANIMAL QUEST

Over the last few years, there has been a growing focus on animal welfare. This attention does not only take place in our media. There is also more attention to animals and the environment in theological reflection than before. We live in a time when there is a positive reflection on the relationship between humans and animals. In churches and conferences, preachers pay more attention to the special blessing God has for animals.

Of course, this does not mean that there was little attention for the animal in the past. The Greek philosopher and mathematician Pythagoras of Samos (~570–510 BC)—yes, this is the famous discoverer of the theorem $a^2 + b^2 = c^2$—is known to have been a great lover of animals. When Pythagoras went to the market, he liked to buy several living animals to give them their freedom. He held the animal in high esteem. During a barbecue, this mathematical genius would only have enjoyed a tasty vegetable burger. Meat did not enter his mouth. The impact of Pythagoras's choice was so significant in his time that people called anyone who did not eat meat a "follower of Pythagoras." From the nineteenth century onward, our society introduced the new term "vegetarian" for people who followed the "diet of Pythagoras."

From the second half of the twentieth century onwards, there has been a powerful urge to treat nature and its creatures responsibly. Many are touched when they hear how millions of animals suffer because of what people do. Whales are exterminated for the sake of "scientific research." Elephants are killed to sell their ivory tusks. Kangaroos are slaughtered and processed into dog food, sneakers, and souvenirs for tourists. Shark fins are cut off while the animals are still alive. Young seals are skinned alive. Chimpanzees are caught and used in the laboratory, not to mention the many chickens, cows, pigs, sheep, and other animals that are industrially modified to provide better eggs, milk, and meat.

Besides, several indicators are pointing in the direction of an impending global environmental crisis of unprecedented proportions. Concepts such as "sustainable agriculture," "environmental terrorism," and "bio-industry" have become part and parcel of the social debate. What role does the Christian faith have in all of this? Do we find indications in the Christian tradition and biblical traditions that support our reflection on this?

In addition to the many good media sources and various other popular and scholarly publications, let us be motivated to contribute on the topic of animals from a Christian perspective. These reflections on God's view of animals are essential. This becomes visible when we realize that the idea sometimes arises that the Christian faith is a crucial cause of today's environmental problems (cf. chapter 3). For example, studies of religion assume that the rejection of the idea that everything is god (pantheism) or that everything has a soul or spirit (animism) is one of the environmental crisis's foundations. For this reason, activists in ecological ethics are fiercely critical of "Christians and their faith." They feel strengthened by the fact that Christian doctrine does not pay much attention to God's vision of animals or nature. "Animals can rightly feel slighted by the lack of attention they receive from commentators," writes Australian Old Testament scholar John Olley.[1] The medieval theologian Thomas Aquinas (~1225–74) even dares to state that a wrong view of creatures leads to a false conception of God and leads people away from God.[2]

Anyone familiar with the biblical testimony realizes that in the tremendous Judeo-Christian themes of creation, covenant, redemption, and future expectation, animals do not play merely a peripheral role. God creates land animals and humans on the same day as partners, side by side. Noah fills his ark with animals and people to find salvation during the flood. Moses talks about humans and animals in his teaching. The prophets follow him in their picturesque panoramas of the future by not losing sight of the animals.

1.2 THE BIBLE STARTS WITH GENESIS

It sounds like kicking down an open door when I say that the Bible does not start with the liberation of God's people in Egypt, but with the creation in Genesis. Anyone who reads the Bible from the first pages cannot get rid of the impression that God has a particular interest in this creation. The first two chapters of Genesis colorfully describe how God

---

1. Olley, "Mixed Blessings," 131.
2. Aquinas, *Summa Contra Gentiles*, II.3.

created the earth and planted a garden in the land of Eden. From the beginning, God longs for a planet on which a multitude of people reflect his glory. Therefore, our salvation is part of the higher plan that God has with creation. Speaking about God's grace and justification precedes talking about creation. As such, salvation expresses itself in thankful words about creation, such as, "My help comes from the Lord, who made heaven and earth" (Ps 121:2). In this respect, creation and salvation belong together.

Still, it is striking that Christian doctrine focuses mainly on the redemption of God's people. Very often, the themes we encounter in the Bible, such as Jesus Christ, humanity, God's Spirit, the church, the future, are mainly related to the topic of salvation and deliverance. That gives the impression that the Bible is not much interested in its opening theme, creation. An example of this can be found in the work of the German theologian Walter Zimmerli. In his often reprinted *Old Testament Theology in Outline*, the theme of creation is only dealt with in the fourth part. The reason for this is that in the Old Testament, the exodus from Egypt is the central point of orientation.[3] This is a bizarre observation, on which the Heidelberg Old Testament scholar Rolf Rendtorff (1925–2014) consciously wants to focus the attention of his colleagues:

> The Hebrew Bible begins with creation. Old Testament Theologies usually do not. How is that? The answer is obvious: because of the theology of the respective authors of Old Testament Theologies.[4]

So the cause lies in the fact that there is an excellent reflection in Christian doctrine about God's way with people and that there is a minimal reflection about God's way with creation as a whole.[5] Christian doctrine is thus indirectly read back into the biblical testimony so that even for the Old Testament scholar—who knows that his Bible begins with Genesis 1—it seems only to be about God's way with humanity. The nonhuman world all too often falls outside the radar of Christian and theological reflection.

In my book *The New Heaven and the New Earth*, I have shown how complexly and unconsciously the influence of theological presuppositions

---

3. Zimmerli, *Old Testament Theology*.

4. Rendtorff, "Some Reflections on Creation," 204.

5. Kärkkäinen, *Hope*, 16; Kärkkäinen, *Creation*, 59–60. An example of a Christian doctrine that subordinates creation to the doctrine of salvation is Barth, *Creation: The Work*.

flows into biblical reflection.[6] It suffices here to mention seven different points which cause thoughts on God and creation to remain in the background of our proclamation.

1. The idea that God cares mostly for humans and that animals are given a subordinate place therein, serving only as illustrations or scenery.
2. The association of biblical creation stories with other creation stories, wherein the biblical storyline is not taken theologically seriously.
3. The assumption that the theme of creation belongs to the natural sciences and only causes controversy.
4. The idea that ecclesiastical sacraments and services are meant for people and not for other creatures or creation as a whole.
5. The emphasis on the spiritual, non-physical reality of life, and the lesser appreciation of the corporal and physical reality.
6. A variety of end-time scenarios, in which God is often presented as the Destroyer of this creation and the Creator of a new creation.
7. The little attention paid to the Old Testament testimony in the theological proclamation.

In this book, we want to put the reflection on creation high on the list. We will primarily focus on the core question, "What can we say about God's way with animals in the light of biblical revelation and Christian doctrine?" We will start with the original creation and continue our research in the direction of the new heaven and the new earth. In doing so, the first and last two chapters of the Bible are connected. What God creates, in the beginning, finds its completion in the new heaven and the new earth. Anyone who reads the vision of the new creation in Revelation 21–22 will discover many references to the first creation in Genesis 1–2.

This relationship once again shows that God's salvation is part of the greater whole, the *big picture*. What God does in redemption is related to creation. Therefore, theologians typified the salvation time between Genesis 1–2 and Revelation 21–22 as "continuous creation" (*creatio continua*). After all, God creates new things in his work of salvation as well. For example, Jesus testifies to the learned Nicodemus about new birth

---

6. Hausoul, *New Heaven*.

(John 3:3), and Paul writes that whoever is in Christ is a new creation (2 Cor 5:17).

Because these new things use what *already exists* in salvation, some prefer not to use the term "creation" because it is not *radically new*. Instead, they speak of God's providence and use the word "creation" only for something completely new.[7] The Bible does not make this distinction. Terms from the first creation return in the age of redemption and the realization of the new creation. The prophet Isaiah, especially, likes to do this. So God "created" Israel in history (בָּרָא, *bārā'*, Isa 43:1–2), just as God "created" the first creation (בָּרָא, *bārā'*, Gen 1:1). God "formed" the people (יָצַר, *jātsar*), as well as God "formed" Adam and the animals (Isa 45:12; Gen 2:7, 19). God announces the redemption of Israel as something "new" (חָדָשׁ, *chādāsh*, Isa 42:9) and typifies the redemption of all creation (people, animals, and land) as something "new" (חֲדָשָׁה, *chādāsh*, Isa 43:19). Jeremiah also maintains this language and calls a husband's love for his wife something "new" (חֲדָשָׁה, *chādāsh*, Isa 31:22). God remains the Creator in this and will not be relegated to a Manager of the first creation. The work of salvation is a unique dimension of God's action as a Creator. The past does not entirely determine the present and future. God brings about new things in this creation. Animals are also crucial in this and are part of the grand plan that God has prepared for creation. So, what did that original state of creation look like when God created the animals in Genesis 1?

---

7. Westermann, *Genesis 1–11*, 175; Gunton, *Triune Creator*, 88–89.

2

Paradisiacal Conditions

2.1 MAJESTIC CREATION EPIC

2.1.1 The Artificial Structure of Genesis 1

GENESIS OPENS THE BIBLICAL story impressively. The story of creation is filled with beauty and glorious exaltation. It testifies to a God who reveals himself royally to this world as a loving Creator. Through the living Word, all things are created in power and wisdom. All living beings receive living space. The creation story in Genesis 1 is characterized by beautiful composition and magnificent compactness. It offers a colorful introduction to the biblical drama. It is useful to dwell at the beginning in more detail on this event because we will refer back to this early beginning of the biblical story several times in this book. The story of creation is the beginning of everything that God makes and everything that God continues. It is not only about humanity but also about the incredible story of God with animals. A complete overview of this description is thus appropriate in this chapter.

In the story of creation, it becomes clear how everything finds its place and time. We read about the known reality of our life on earth: earth and heaven, light and darkness, water and land, plants and trees, the sun, moon, and stars, fish and birds, terrestrial animals, and people. The only unknown is the "dome" or "firmament" on the second and fifth days. We can daily observe everything else. It is all related to each other and exists only through the choices God makes at that moment.

The seven creation days in Genesis 1 can be divided into a pattern of six plus one: six days and one day of rest. The six creation days can be divided into two blocks of three days. These two blocks form a parallel with each other through the pattern: light, water, land. The first block is characterized by separation, while the second block is characterized by filling the created spaces.[1]

On the first day, God *separates* darkness from light. On the second day, God *separates* water below and water above the "dome." On the third day, God *separates* water and land. On this third day, God causes the earth to produce all kinds of plants and trees. In the next three days, the different areas created in creation are filled with all sorts of objects that can move in front of us. On the fourth day, God *fills* the heavens with the sun, moon, and stars to indicate day and night. Their fixed careers characterize the sun and moon. On the fifth day, God *fills* the sky with birds and the water with fish. They enjoy even greater flexibility than the celestial bodies and can also reproduce. They are blessed by God right away, which is the very first time this happens. "Let the earth bring forth living creatures of every kind: cattle and creeping things and wild animals of the earth of every kind," it sounds from God's mouth (Gen 1:24). On the sixth day, God lets the earth *be filled* with living land animals, which the land brings forth. Then God creates humans, which may be characterized by procreation and even greater flexibility. Compactly this can be placed in the following structure.

Day 1: Light	darkness	Day 4: Light carriers
1. Separation between light and darkness.	1. Big light, small light, stars.
Day 2: Water	water	Day 5: Water animals and birds
1a. Water under the firmament.	1a. Aquatic animals.
1b. Water above the firmament.	1b. Birds flying along the firmament.
Day 3: Land	water	Day 6: Terrestrial animals and people
1. Water and land are separated.	1. Land summoned to produce flora.
2. Land summoned to bring forth fauna.	2. Creation of humans.

Day 7: Day of rest

Creation process complete. A new weekly rhythm starts.

---

1. Goldingay, *Old Testament Theology*, 94, relates this separation in Genesis 1 to the later priestly task. In Leviticus, divorce is the first task mentioned after the priests (Lev 10:10; 11:46–47). Furthermore, the priest is responsible for filling God's temple with the dynamics of worship (firstfruits, etc.). Separation and filling belong together.

This schematic representation expresses several parallels. On the first and fourth days, God acts at once: light. On days two and five, two steps belonging together are recognizable (1a + 1b). On the third and sixth days, two separate actions are present (1 + 2). This creates a confirmation of the pattern of 2 x 3 days + 1 day = 6 days + 1 day.

We see this pattern of 6 + 1 again when Moses ascends Mount Sinai to receive the Torah: "The glory of the Lord settled on Mount Sinai, and the cloud covered it six days; on the seventh day, he called to Moses out of the cloud" (Exod 24:16). For the last time in the Bible, we come across this pattern in the book of Revelation. The seven seals, the seven trumpets, and the seven bowls are there divided into the same model of 6 + 1. Between the first six stamps (Rev 6:1–17) and the last stamp (8:1), there is an interlude (7:1–17). Between the first six trumpets (8:6—9:21) and the seventh trumpet (11:14–19), there is an interlude (10:1—11:13). And between the first six bowls (16:1–12) and the last bowl (16:17), there is another interlude (16:15). In this way, the first week of world history, as described in Genesis 1, is a model for God's way with creation as a whole. With its seven-day week cycle, this calendar was already known to the western Semitic peoples of Mesopotamia. Their monthly calendar mentioned the seventh, fourteenth, twenty-first, and twenty-eighth days of the month. This calendar was based upon the different phases that the moon carried on as an indication of time.

Because of this background, the days in Genesis 1 have been conceived as defined weekdays, as we still know them.[2] Each day begins in the evening, goes into the morning, and ends in the evening. The evening then is the beginning of the next day. This method of determining times is still common in Jewish culture. Sunset determines when a new day begins, and after six working days follows the Sabbath, which is inspired by the pattern of Genesis 1 (Exod 20:11; 31:17). In our Western culture, the day starts at midnight and continues for twenty-four hours. Several Jews and Christians chose not to interpret the days in Genesis 1 as days of twenty-four hours.[3] For example, the French-Jewish interpreter Rashi (1040–1105), who was officially born as Shlomo Yitzchaki, believed God had created everything in one day. The reason for this was Genesis 2:4, were it was said that God made heaven and earth "in the day" (בְּיוֹם, be-jôm). According to Rashi, the creation happened on the sixth day of the

---

2. McCabe, "Defense of Literal Days," 113–20.

3. Samuelson, *Judaism*, 139; Williams, *Systematische Theologie*, 1:146–54; Lewis, "Days of Creation," 452.

Jewish month of Sivan. According to Jewish tradition, this sixth day of Sivan was also the day Moses received the Torah on Mount Sinai. Therefore the other days in Genesis 1 were only different "segments" of this one day.[4] A much earlier rabbi, called Nechemiah (~150 AD), already stated that God made creation in one day. In the days that followed, the earth produced just what God had already made.[5] The principles that God had laid down in it became visible.

2.1.2 Three Days of Separation

Day 1: Light Comes, Darkness Departs

On day one, the first command of God is heard in Genesis 1. God calls out "light," and "darkness" departs. As a servant, light takes the place that God as King commands. Traditionally, readers of the biblical story of creation realize that this light was already there. It existed before the celestial bodies, such as the sun and the stars, gave their shine. Therefore, the light of the heavenly bodies is not seen as the source and cause of all light. Sun, moon, and stars do not receive the high position in the Bible that they get in many religions. There is a light that existed earlier than that of the stars.[6]

The light in the story of creation contrasts with the darkness of the primeval flood. God's Spirit floated like a dove over the water of this flood. Although the translation "God's wind" is also possible in Genesis 1:2, the combination with the vivid "floating" and the Person of God pleads for "Spirit."[7] The Spirit of God stroked over the ink-black primeval flood, which was characterized by baldness and emptiness. The earth was

---

4. Ben Jitschaki (Rashi), *Complete Tanach*. Cf. Buber, *Midrash Tanhuma*, 1; Kara, *Yalkut Shimoni*, 6.

5. Zlotowitz, *Bereishis 1:1—28:9*, 30.

6. Jewish tradition believes that God created the celestial lights on the first day and did not give them their place in the vault of heaven until the fourth day. Cf. Neusner, *B. Hagigah*, 12a; Zlotowitz, *Bereishis 1:1—28:9*, 39. This explanation presupposes that God created creation in one day. The earth produced what God had created in the next six days (see chapter 2.1.1). From Genesis 1:15 it can be concluded that God "made" the heavenly bodies only on the fourth day, so he did not merely "place" them there.

7. Zlotowitz, *Bereishis 1:1—28:9*, 38; Ben Jitschaki (Rashi), *Complete Tanach*; Ouro, "Earth of Genesis 1," 59–67. See for the translation of "God's wind": Neusner, *B. Hagigah*, 12a; Wenham, *Genesis 1–15*, 16–17; Von Rad, *Genesis*, 49–50. Cf. Tg. Onq. on Genesis 1:2.

as ferocious as a desert. It was an inhospitable place that had not yet received the orderly form that God wanted to give it. That is why God said, "Let there be light" (Gen 1:3).

In this light of the first day, Jewish interpreters thought inextricably of the Messiah. "This is the light of the Messiah," it is written in their sources.[8] Accordingly, that meaning carries the light also in texts like, "Arise, shine; for your light has come, and the glory of the Lord has risen upon you" (Isa 60:1), and, "In your light we see light" (Ps 36:9b). Possibly this is also the background of statements such as, "God is light and in him there is no darkness at all" (1 John 1:5), and Jesus' own words, "As long as I am in the world, I am the light of the world" (John 9:5).

Christians gladly joined this Jewish view of the light in Genesis 1. From the heavenly city in Revelation, we learn, "And the city has no need of sun or moon to shine on it, for the glory of God gives it light, and its lamp is the Lamb" (Rev 21:23). The light of the Messiah is far above the light of the celestial bodies. Is this why the light is already there on the first day, and the heavenly bodies appear only on the fourth day? Does this mean that everything God created could only be organized because this light was placed in the first place? From a Christian perspective, I would answer these questions with "yes." There is no creation without putting the Messiah first and highest. The light of Genesis testifies of the Firstborn of creation. This idea corresponds with Paul's thoughts of the Messiah:

> He is the image of the invisible God, the firstborn of all creation; for in him all things in heaven and on earth were created, things visible and invisible, whether thrones or dominions or rulers or powers—all things have been created through him and for him. He himself is before all things, and in him all things hold together. (Col 1:15–17)

The light in Genesis 1 comes first and is the first who receives God's "it was good." Consequently, Jewish and Christian interpreters rightly distinguish this light from heaven's light in their works and relate it to the light of God's new creation. The light of the first day already bears witness to the light of the coming century.[9] The light of Genesis challenges us and gives us vision.

---

8. Freedman and Maurice, *Midrash Rabbah: Genesis*, 62.1; Samuelson, *Judaism*, 117.

9. Hausoul, "Protologie," 11–29.

Day 2: Segregation of Water

On day two, God makes a "dome" (NRSV), "vault" (NIV), "expanse" (ESV, NASB, NIV84) or "firmament" (NKJV, Vulgata). The Hebrew term רָקִיעַ/*rāqi'a* is used elsewhere for thin adhesive material, such as "hammered out gold leaf" (Exod 39:3) or "expanse" (Ezek 1:22; 10:1). It is also compared to a cast mirror (Job 37:18) or a window of the heavens, which God can open for the flood (Gen 7:11–12). These indications emphasize the solidity of the material rather than its flatness.[10] Some related this plane of heaven to a tent, "You stretch out the heavens like a tent" (Ps 104:2), and "Who stretches out the heavens like a curtain, and spreads them like a tent to live in" (Isa 40:22). Creation then takes the form of a palace, which God builds and provides with a protective roof.[11] From this background, many saw in the creation story the description of a sizeable macrocosmic temple that later found its miniatures in the microcosmic temples on earth.[12] This relationship between God's sanctuary on earth and his sanctuary in heaven is also expressed in the call, "Praise God in his sanctuary; praise him in his mighty firmament!" (Ps 150:1).

So on the second day, God creates an immovable surface of heaven that protects the earth from the water like a dam. This surface of heaven separates the original mass of water from the primeval flood. Heaven is then connected to the water mass above it. According to the Jewish Talmud, the Hebrew words for "heaven" and "water" are therefore connected. "Heaven" (שָׁמַיִם, *shāmajim*) can be dissected in "water" (מַיִם, *majim*) and "there" (שָׁם, *shām*).[13] The meaning of heaven then is "there is water." The psalmist even calls this water to praise God: "Praise him, you highest heavens, and you waters above the heavens!" (Ps 148:4).

In the interpretation of Genesis 1, the mention of this celestial surface raises questions. Does the writer claim that there is a hard dome in the sky that blocks the rainwater? Although details about heaven's character are missing, the story of creation mentions that the surface above is called "heaven" by God (Gen 1:8). The psalmist also uses this synonym, "The heavens are telling the glory of God; and the firmament proclaims

---

10. Zlotowitz, *Bereishis 1:1—28:9*, 45; Ben Jitschaki (Rashi), *Complete Tanach*.

11. Skillen, "Seven Days," 126; Van Leeuwen, "Cosmos, Temple, House," 72–77; Jaki, *Genesis 1*, 9, 22–23, 26–27, 279.

12. Goldingay, *Old Testament Theology*, 84–89; Kline, *Images*, 21, 39; Fisher, "Creation at Ugarit," 319.

13. Neusner, *B. Hagigah*, 12a.

his handiwork" (Ps 19:1). The first part of this verse says the same as the second part of it. In concrete terms, biblical scholars interpret the Hebrew רָקִיעַ/rāqi'a in Genesis 1:6 as the clouds of heaven or the atmosphere.[14] The reason for this is that nothing remains of a solidity, vault, firmament, or dome in the sky. The plane of heaven then dissolves into the air.

A challenge in explaining the Hebrew רָקִיעַ/rāqi'a with the celestial clouds or atmosphere are the celestial bodies attached to the רָקִיעַ/rāqi'a (Gen 1:17) and the birds that fly along with the רָקִיעַ/rāqi'a (v. 20). Birds fly miles below the atmosphere, and celestial bodies are miles above the atmosphere. Birds "along" and celestial bodies "on" the vault are then out of the question. After all, creation is not an aviary with hanging lamps, where birds whiz along the roof. Even those who look up can see with the bare eye a big difference in distance between birds and stars. So this explanation remains a challenge.

After God has separated the water, no evaluation takes place on the second day. An "it was good" is missing in the Hebrew text. Only on the third day do we hear it. Then it even sounds twice, "It was good" (Gen 1:10, 12). The work that began on the second day is thus finished on the third day. Then the water beneath the plane of heaven gets its definitive name. On the second day, the earth is still covered with water and does not yet offer enough space for life.

Day 3: Solid Ground and Sea

On the third day, the water is given its fixed place. All the water flows to one place so that the dry land appears. The land is freed from the sea. Jewish tradition connects this event with the future: also, in the new creation, God will deliver the land from the sea.[15]

The land must then produce young green. This gives the earth a mediating role in the creation of the flora. Plants and trees appear and testify for the first time to the freshness of life on earth. According to Rashi (1040–1105, Shlomo Yitzchaki), the flowers, plants, and trees were then very clean in appearance. Their "ugly" deformities would only come as a

---

14. Hilbrands, "Veraltetes Weltbild," 193; Zlotowitz, Bereishis 1:1—28:9, 47; Seely, "Firmament," 227–40.

15. Freedman and Maurice, *Midrash Rabbah: Leviticus*, 27.4; Freedman and Maurice, "Midrash Rabbah: Ecclesiastes," 3.15. The same thought appears in Egyptian tradition: Clifford, *Creation Accounts*, 102–4.

result of human disobedience in Genesis 3.[16] The later Jewish philosopher Maimonides (1135–1204) thought God created only fruit-bearing trees on the third day. Trees that do not bear fruit appeared after the events of Genesis 3.[17]

Then, for the second time, it sounds on the third day that "it was good" (1:10, 12). This "double goodness" is for Jews a reason to marry on the third weekday (cf. John 2:1). By the way, I wanted to do the same. However, this had nothing to do with Jewish culture, but with my Dutch "economic" culture. Marrying on a Tuesday was free in Vaals (Netherlands). Still, my wife and I had to choose a Friday, so that our guests from faraway Germany could make it a weekend. In the end, it turned out to be a day of "double goodness."

2.1.3 Three Creation Days of Filling

Day 4: Hanging Lamps and Hanging Clocks

Day four is also characterized by light. This is not the Messiah's light, as on the first day, but the light of the celestial bodies. God made the great light, the small light, and the stars. They helped distinguish between day and night, giving seasons, days, weeks, months, and years. Like a celestial calendar, these lamps, in the vault of the sky, indicate when days of rest and other feasts take place.

Consciously the biblical story of creation speaks of a "great" light and a "small" light. The terms "sun" and "moon" are not used. Presumably, because many peoples on earth worshiped the sun and moon as gods—some examples of this are the ancient Indian Vedas in which Surya is the sun god, the Mesopotamian religions in which Shamash is the sun god, ancient Egypt in which Aten and Ra are sun gods, and where we also find the city of Heliopolis ("city of the sun"), the many European gods, such as the Norwegian Sól and Heimdal, the Germanic Sunna or Sigel, the Irish Lughm, the Celtic Belenos, the Roman Phoebus Apollo, and the Greek Helios, who were all worshiped as sun gods. In these cultures, we also know several moon gods, such as the Indian Varuna, the Mesopotamian Utukku, the Sumerian Inanna, the Akkadian Nanna, the Babylonian Sin, the Egyptian Thoth, the Phoenician Aphrodite, the

---

16. Ben Jitschaki (Rashi), *Complete Tanach*.
17. Zlotowitz, *Bereishis 1:1—28:9*, 53.

Greek Selene and Artemis, the Roman Luna, the Celtic Cailleach, and the Norwegian Máni. Sun and moon were thus awarded sacrilegious worship from ancient history up to the present time. However, in the story of creation, the sun and moon are merely hanging lamps on the vault of the sky. There, as servants of God, they fulfill the function of hanging clocks to indicate the times. In this capacity, they show people and animals in which part of the day we find ourselves. Day and night, animals derive their rhythm of life from it. The fifth day concerns them.

Day 5: Aquatic and Aerial Animals

On the fifth day, God fills the water, far below the plane of heaven, and God supplies the air space, close to the plane of the sky, with animals. In the water, living creatures must swarm, and above the earth, along with the celestial vault, birds must fly. Although plants and trees are also characterized by life, "living beings" is only used for animals and humans in the story of creation (Gen 1:20–21, 24, 30; 2:7, 19).

As animals of water and air, fish and birds represent the two extremes of the earth. As a result, the sea's deepest point and the sky's highest point stand side by side. Elsewhere in the Bible, birds and fish are typically placed together side by side (Gen 1:26, 28; Ps 8:9; Ezek 38:20; Hos 4:3; Zeph 1:3).

God creates the great sea creatures, all other aquatic animals, and various birds (Gen 1:21). The "great sea creatures" (ESV, NIV, NKJV) were traditionally seen as "great sea monsters" (NASB, NRSV). One of these sea monsters is the mythical Leviathan, which threatens the waters.[18] Jewish tradition states that God did not want this Leviathan to multiply. That is why God killed the female partner of this monster. According to this legend, the flesh of this animal is kept for the righteous. They will consume it in the new heaven and the new earth.[19] The biblical story of creation does not tell us anything about these things. It does not force us to think of the "great sea monsters" as winding mythological creatures. With the "great sea monsters," we think of the giants of water, which we as humans fear. An example of this can be found in *Moby Dick* (1851),

---

18. Neusner, *B. Baba Batra*, 74b; Samuelson, *Judaism*, 126.

19. Zlotowitz, *Bereishis 1:1—28:9*, 62; Ben Jitschaki (Rashi), *Complete Tanach*. Cf. 4 Ezra 6:52; 2 Baruch 29:4; Neusner, *B. Baba Batra*, 74a–75b; Neusner, *B. 'Abodah Zarah*, 3b; Neusner, *B. Hullin*, 67b; Freedman and Maurice, *Midrash Rabbah: Genesis*, 7:4; 11:9.

the old novel by the American writer Herman Melville (1819–91). In this novel, the keen captain Ahab hunts fanatically the white whale, Moby Dick, because he lost his leg in an earlier confrontation with this animal.

The text in Genesis leaves no ambiguity that enormous sea creatures such as whale sharks, basking sharks, orcas, and whales are nothing but creatures of God. They do not deserve human worship any more than the sun and moon do. They are all beautiful creatures. Today, we are still witnesses to these numerous birds and fish that exist on earth. The life of each of them is a discovery in itself. Birds and fish know what it is like to travel miles and live their lives on earth efficiently. God blesses them in this life. Also, they are the first creatures to have the honor of hearing God's voice: "Be fruitful and multiply and fill the waters in the seas, and let birds multiply on the earth" (Gen 1:22). That blessing is desperately needed for a life in the (later) endangered waters and air.

Day 6: Land Animals and Land Dwellers

On the sixth day, God speaks the most, out of all the creation days in Genesis 1. First of all, God creates terrestrial animals on this day. They are allowed to walk on the green-red "colorful robe" that God brought out on the third day. The animals are distinguished into the domestic animals, the crawling animals, and the wild animals. They consist of recognizable groups and multiply within those groups according to their nature.[20] "God made the wild animals of the earth of every kind, and the cattle of every kind, and everything that creeps upon the ground of every kind. And God saw that it was good" (Gen 1:25).

Speaking of "species" can raise questions. Does this mean that the species are not allowed to mix? For example, is crossing two species like a donkey and a horse into a mule forbidden? Are biotechnological interventions prohibited? Is the extermination of species wrong? We must be careful not to interpret "of every kind" or "according to their nature" as a precept. After all, nowhere does the story of creation require us to preserve the visible order of species or see it as immutable. An answer to whether biotechnological interventions are unlawful is not explicitly to be found in the biblical text. We only read that every living creature has the same right to life as humans. The Jewish rabbi Nathan the Babylonian (second century) made an exception only for mosquitoes, insects,

---

20. E.g. Neville, "Differentiation," 209–26; Mathews, *Genesis 1–11:26*, 153, 157.

fleas, and other irritating animals. He stated that God did not create these animals on the sixth day. After all, nowhere in the entire Bible are they mentioned as "living creatures." According to Rabbi Nathan, together with many other nasty animals, they only came into being after humans' disobedience in Genesis 3.[21] As a result, the original creation in Genesis 1 looked very different from today. What the absence of those insects meant for the edible flowers and plants is a good question. A soil without insects is terrible for plant development, and without insects, there is no fertilization possible for many flowers.

However, God did not only want to be surrounded by galaxies, seas full of fish, primeval forests full of birds, and rainforests full of chimpanzees and crocodiles. That is why God created humans in his image and likeness. This gives humans a unique privilege. No star, tree, or animal except the human is the representative of God on earth. God did not create people as soloists or loners. God chooses to create humanity, both masculine and feminine. Man and woman are equal to each other.

God took the risk that humans could choose for or against their Creator. The great Jewish scholar and mystic Rabbi Akiva ben Josef (40–137 AD) point to the words "image" and "likeness" in Genesis 1:26. He states that every person is an image-bearer of God, but not every person chooses to resemble God. The image comes from God. The likeness lies in the hand of humans. The fact that humanity faces this choice between blessing and curse is reflected in the lack of evaluation. An evaluation does not appear after the creation of the first humans. On the sixth day, we only learn that God calls the creation of the tame, crawling, and wild animals "good" (Gen 1:25). This is lacking in the creation of humanity. It is all the more striking when we realize that the sixth day is related to the third day, where precisely this double "good" is present (1:10, 12).

In the end, it does sound like a blessing to humans. They may be fruitful, multiply, populate, and subdue the earth. Thus humans receive control "over the fish of the sea and over the birds of the air and over every living thing that moves upon the earth" (Gen 1:28). This command for multiplication puts a red line through the thought that the first humans only had sexual contact with each other after Genesis 3. God blessed Adam and the great fathers, like Noah and Abraham, explicitly with fertility (Gen 1:28; 9:7; 15:5). He also added that productivity would be a characteristic of the promised land (Lev 26:9, 21–22). Everything

---

21. Samuelson, *Judaism*, 121.

that lives is characterized by fertility as early as Genesis 1. This fertility is reflected in the very first blessings God expresses in the story of creation. According to the Torah, there would not even be infertile women left in Israel by obedience to God (Exod 23:26; Deut 7:14). Jewish tradition based on this blessed fertility the thought that Adam and Eve went to bed and got up with two or five kids in the morning.[22] Sexual intercourse in the garden of Eden was a very fruitful event because God's blessing was connected with it.

The terrestrial animals lack this blessing of fertility on the sixth day. Rashi suspects that this is because a terrestrial animal in Genesis 3 stirred up humanity against God. The trick of the serpent then forbids blessing the animals.[23] At the same time, the terrestrial animals are closely related to humans on the sixth day. In contrast to other Mesopotamian creation stories, both are very close to each other. They are created on the same day as humans (Gen 1:24), use the same food (Gen 1:29), are called living creatures (2:7, 19), receive both God's breath of life (Gen 2:7; Ps 104:30), share space in the garden (Gen 2:19), and share the same fate in dying (Pss 49:13, 21; 104:29; Eccl 3:19–21). In the Bible, animals and human beings are never separated. They are only distinguished. Both are part of God's creation. This connection is also shown by the fact that the Old Testament has no separate word for "nature" or "creation." A modern Hebrew word like טבע/*teva'* for "nature" was unusual at that time. So there is no abstract word for the separate collection of animals, plants, and climatological and geological data in creation. The term "creation" always includes this collection and human beings.[24] Also, the idea of "creation" (modern Hebrew: יצירה, *yetzirah*) does not exist in the Old Testament. The biblical texts only speak of "heaven," "earth," and "God's works" (cf. Gen 2:4; Ps 145:4, 9).

2.1.4 The Seventh Day: Blessed Rest

The creation story finds its climax on the seventh day. God rests on this day from his work of creation. God blessed and sanctified this seventh day (Gen 2:3), traditionally calling it the "crown of creation." God created

---

22. Neusner, *B. Sanhedrin*, 38b; Freedman and Maurice, *Midrash Rabbah: Genesis*, 22:2.
23. Ben Jitschaki (Rashi), *Complete Tanach*.
24. Allen, "Hebrew View," 81.

the world for his glory. Therefore, the Bible never uses the term "crown" for humans. It takes some getting used to because Christians like to use "crown" for humans. Although God created humans beautifully and exaltedly, the Bible testifies that the crown in this creation can only be achieved if humans choose to live with God. Thus, a human being who wants to live without God is not a crown on creation. He is a fool in the eyes of God and others (Ps 14:1).

In the Age of Enlightenment, humanity left this biblical testimony far behind, and a misrepresentation arose. Human beings then saw themselves as the "crowning glory" of creation. They were only too happy to abuse this idea to control things independently of God. Humans became autonomous, and the seventh day's testimony was set aside as the climax of God's work of creation. However, the seventh day is the climax of the story of creation. It is a day of rest with God. While the previous six days always talked about "evening" and "tomorrow," this description is missing on the seventh day. Day seven has no end in the story of creation. The day testifies of an open invitation, which allows Genesis 1 to work on itself. Every day had its twosome in the form of separation or addition: light–darkness, water–water, water–land, sun–moon, fish–birds, terrestrial land animals–people. Only the seventh day had not yet found a partner. Thus an invitation sounds to every human being: Do you want to be God's partner on the seventh day? Will you accept that the relationship between God and humanity may find its most profound intimacy on the seventh day?

In later passages of the Bible, this day of rest is related to the new creation. It is an extension of the original creation in Genesis 1. It is the ultimate and definitive completion of God's work of creation and redemption, which, like the seventh day, has no end.

The day of rest offers a foretaste of this new creation, which the Israelites must maintain with respect. On that day, people will realize that the goal of God's creation is not creation itself or the work that people do in it. God's desire is a creation in which people can have an intense relationship with God. Jews and Christians realized this. They saw the day of rest as a beautiful moment to have time together with God and with their family members. It was a day of relationships.

The importance of intimacy between Creator and creation on the seventh day is also evident in how God deals with the Sabbath. Thus God took rest when he provided food for the people in the wilderness. Six days a week, heaven gave manna. On the seventh day, there was rest, and no manna fell from the sky. The people were then allowed to enjoy the double blessing they received the day before. Indeed, on the sixth day, a double portion of heavenly food fell (Exod 16:22–30). God honored and rested the seventh day. This is a testimony of the serenity of God's future new creation. We also see this in the life of Jesus Christ when he chooses to heal the sick on the day of rest, against the strict religious beliefs in his time. By Christ, the sick may also taste the tremendous peace that God wants to give creation.

2.2 FOUNDATION FOR GOD'S HISTORY OF SALVATION

2.2.1 God's Promise

God's choice for the story of creation is an inspiration for the biblical heroes of faith. It reveals that what God says happens. The calling of God brings about creation. As in a stately procession, the creation story of Genesis 1 features ten times the saying, "God said" (Gen 1:3, 6, 9, 11, 14, 20, 24, 26, 28, 29). Of these ten times, God speaks the last three times to humans (1:26–29). Furthermore, God pronounces three blessings (1:22, 28; 2:3), and we hear that everything God commands happens (1:3, 7, 9, 11, 15, 24, 30). The whole creation is entirely subservient to what God says.

The psalmists connect this speaking of God with respect: "Let all the earth fear the Lord; let all the inhabitants of the world stand in awe of him. For he spoke, and it came to be; he commanded, and it stood firm" (Ps 33:8–9); "Let them praise the name of the Lord, for he commanded and they were created" (148:5). Without the word of God, there is no creation. God's creation is expressed by it. This is what the Jewish tradition says: "An artist achieves nothing without hard work, but God makes all things only by the breath of the word."[25] In this emphasizing of the speaking Word, the biblical creation story differs from other creation stories.

This speaking of God is fundamental. The patriarch Abraham was allowed to recognize that God "calls into existence the things that do not exist" (Rom 4:17b). That was the basis for his belief in the promise of a son. Also, in the Letter to the Hebrews, we read, "By faith we understand that the worlds were prepared by the word of God, so that what is seen was made from things that are not visible" (Heb 11:3). Everyone is allowed to witness that whatever God says will happen. God stands at his word. Simultaneously, the story of creation shows that God's Spirit must

---

25. Bar Nafha and Buber, *Midrash Tehillim*, 18.26.

not be separated from this process. The Spirit hovers over the primordial flood in Genesis 1:2 and is present at the beginning of new life. The same place is given to the Spirit in salvation. We are born again of God's Spirit (John 3:8). Creation and redemption are therefore closely connected, as we noted earlier (chapter 1.3).

Although we often say that God created everything "out of nothing," the biblical prophets and apostles consistently use the expression that God created everything "through the word." The apostle John writes at the beginning of his Gospel:

> In the beginning was the Word, and the Word was with God, and the Word was God. He was in the beginning with God. All things came into being through him, and without him not one thing came into being. What had come into being in him was life. (John 1:1–4a)

The Word is the beginning and the end. This testimony continued in Christian confessions, such as the Nicea-Constantinople confession. There it is confessed that the Son is "of the same Being as the Father, by whom everything in heaven and on earth is made." One can also think of the Belgic Confession, "We believe that through his Word, which is through his Son, the Father did not create heaven, earth and all creatures out of him."[26]

Historically, the expression that God created everything "out of nothing" comes from 2 Macc 7:28. There a mother says to her son, "Recognize that God made these things out of nothing." In doing so, she responds to the ancient notion that creation has no beginning. The church father Irenaeus of Lyon (~140–202) caused a wide spread of the expression "out of nothing" (Lat. *ex nihilo*). The reason for this was that in his time, many claimed that God did not create matter. God had left this "dirty work" to a so-called "demiurge" (craftsman). Irenaeus opposed this and emphasized that God had made the creation "out of nothing."[27] A "demiurge" was not involved. Nothing preceded creation.

From the beginning, people were able to maintain God's creation and rework the available material. They had to realize that God was also the Creator of the animal world. According to many, this indicated that we also had to take care of animals. In our time, many Christians base the

---

26. "Belgic Confession," 58 (§12).

27. Delio, "Is Creation Eternal?," 281; Bonting, "Chaos Theology," 324–26; Gunton, *Triune Creator*, 65–96.

ethical treatment of animals on the story of creation. Nevertheless, the fact that God is Creator is not the primary reason for biblical writers to take care of animals. For example, there is no biblical text that motivates a responsible treatment of animals because God is their Creator. Slightly, the accounting treatment is based on the respect of humanity towards animals. It is primarily a choice based on love for the other creature. We will discuss this further in chapter 7.

2.2.2 The Relationship between Heaven and Earth

In Genesis 1, heaven and earth are put to each other. While the first and fourth days focus on the heavenly light, the third and sixth days talk about flora and fauna on earth. In between are the second and fifth days. These days discuss both the area above (water above the celestial plane and birds along the celestial plane) and the area below (water below the ethereal plane and the aquatic animals therein).

The higher celestial spheres are not separated from the earth or described as existing outside the cosmos. Heaven and earth are in harmony with each other, as "visible matter" and "dark matter" seem to be nowadays. Later, people realized that the place where they are can be a gateway to heaven (Gen 28:16–17) and that heaven is invisibly present (2 Kgs 6:17). So, the term "heaven" is used for the visible heaven above and the invisible place of God and the angels. This connection between heaven and earth is reflected in the idea of interpreting creation in Genesis 1 as a macrocosmic temple. This macrocosmic temple can be recognized in the microcosmic temples on earth (chapter 5.1).

Researchers tried to find out to what extent the testimony of Genesis 1 was unique. Did the biblical creation story have parallels with other creation stories? Some thought this was the case and looked for similarities between the biblical creation story in Genesis 1 and creation stories in Mesopotamia, Babylonia, and Egypt.[28] A parallel discovery was suspected to be found in the Mesopotamian creation report *Enuma Elish*. Although there are parallels with this report, those are of such a small amount that researchers acknowledge that there is more difference than similarity with Genesis 1.

---

28. Tsumura, *Earth*; Johnston, "Genesis 1," 178–94; Cohn, *Cosmos*, 3–56; Currid, *Ancient Egypt*, 27–32; Walton, *Ancient Israelite Literature*, 19–42.

The conclusion is that there is no parallel between Genesis 1 and other extrabiblical creation stories from antiquity until now.[29] The testimony of Genesis 1 is unique and extraordinary. It resists the usual ancient representations of humans as subjugated slaves of the gods. It also opposes the old idea that only the king or lord represents the deity on earth.[30] Nor is it impossible to read the extrabiblical mythological representations of birth or development of the Creator or a battle between the gods in the biblical story of creation.[31] The creation in Genesis 1 does not arise because God overpowers an enemy power, as the *Enuma Elish* mentions. Although these conflicts are present in other mythical accounts of creation, Genesis lacks any reference to them. First and foremost is the love of God and not the battle between a multitude of primeval powers. This difference results in a different view of creation. It frames the choices a human being makes towards nature and his fellow human beings.

Nor does God, as in many other creation stories, describe humans as helpless creatures. Humans are not produced by blind magical-godly forces or pushed forward in the inevitable rhythm of the world of the gods. Nothing is beyond the control of God in creation: not the dark beginning, not the wild or threatening animals, not the ominous celestial bodies, not the dark powers. The Bible opens with a creation story that presents humans as worthy, free, and responsible for controlling God's creation. God gives people a fantastic beginning. However, what is God's purpose with all creation?

2.2.3 Eschatological Perspective

Darkness and Light, Sea and Land

Several elements can be derived from the biblical story of creation that point to a future fulfillment. Jews, for example, think that the light that is called on day one nearby refers to the coming of the Messiah and is concerning God's glory.[32] The light also refers in the Old Testament to the glory

---

29. Garrett, *Rethinking Genesis*, 192.

30. For the idea of Genesis 1–11 as an ideological critique of Mesopotamian representations of regency, creation, and religion, see Middleton, *Liberating Image*, 185–231. Cf. Stek, "What Says the Scriptures?," 231.

31. For such a battle of the gods, see texts like Ps 74:13–14; Isa 27:1; and 51:9, where the context is not the creation of the world, but the redemption of God's people.

32. Philo of Alexandria, "Creation," 31, 35. See 4 Ezra 6:40; 2 En. 25:3.

of God (Exod 34:29; Ps 104:2; Ezek 1:26–28; cf. Isa 58:8; 60:1, 19). At the beginning of creation, the coming of the Messiah is, of course, still in the future. It finds its completion only in the new heaven and the new earth, where the Messiah is the light of the city garden (Rev 21:23). The light of the first day thus already bears witness to the light of the coming century.

In the age to come, the light will triumph over darkness. In Genesis 1, that darkness is placed before the light. According to the Jewish Talmud, it is one of the first things that God created, and that cannot exist without God's will.[33] This thought follows the testimony of the prophet Isaiah: "I am the Lord, and there is no other. I form light and create darkness" (45:6b–7a). Still, God chooses in the story of creation to speak first about the day and then about the night. This may indicate that the day has the highest priority.[34] It is during the day that most people prefer to enjoy life. When the sun shines, we like to walk along the sea and visit different places. At night most of us avoid walking in nature or inhabited areas and prefer to stay inside and rest. During the first six days of creation, the day's dawn indicates that creation is moving forward towards the coming of the great day of God. There is a progression in salvation history from the total darkness to the light of the new creation.

In Genesis 1, God calls the light "good" but does not say anything about the darkness. This is also the case with primordial water. After God separates the water above and the water below the firmament on the second day, no expression follows that it was "good" (Gen 1:2). The second day is the only day in which God does not say that something was good. Those familiar with the biblical story realize that darkness and the sea often have a negative connotation in the further course of God's plan of salvation. From that perspective, we can already see in Genesis 1 the potential of creation to develop in two directions. There is one direction that does creation good (pro-creation), and there is a direction that turns itself against creation (anti-creation). This theme of pro-creation and anti-creation is discussed several more times in biblical history. We will further reflect on this in chapter 7.2.2.

---

33. Neusner, *B. Tamid*, 32a.
34. Levenson, *Creation*, 123.

Beginning and End

Another facet that points to the future in the story of creation is the first letter of the first word in Genesis 1:1. In the Hebrew text, it is the word בְּרֵאשִׁית/*bərē'shît*, where the first letter, the *beth* (בּ), is displayed larger in Hebrew Bible editions. In Jewish literature, there is much attention given to the initial *beth* (בּ). At an early stage, interpreters stated that this letter offers prospects in terms of form.[35] Here we realize that the Israelite reads the sentences from right to left and not, like us, from left to right. When we look to the form of the *beth* (בּ), we see that a person has ground under his feet, a roof over his head, and cover in his back. Everything else is focused on the opening on the left side of the letter. That is the reading direction of the Israelite. There is an open future present from this first letter. Humans do not have to think about what is above or below the earth; neither should they think about what happened before the world existed. Instead, as human beings, we are allowed to focus on what lies ahead of us.

At the end of the first week of creation, this perspective of the future emerges again. This perspective is expressed by the fact that the seventh day will not be closed. The expression "there was evening, and there was morning" is missing on that day (Gen 1:5, 8, 13, 19, 23, 31). The seventh day ends only with the remark that God "rested from all the work that he had done in creation" (2:3). The Jewish philosopher Norbert M. Samuelson (b. 1936) writes in his extensive reflection on creation that

> the conclusion of creation itself points to the fact that the first thirty-four verses of the Pentateuch are only a first tale that initiates a series of tales.[36]

In this reflection, the expression "to make" (לַעֲשׂוֹת, *la'ăsôm*) in Genesis 2:3 is also used worth mentioning. Translators often do not know what to do with this word and see it as a Hebrew redundancy. For example, the expression "make" is absent from the ESV and NIV. The NKJV chooses to associate the term with "creation" and translates, "that he had created and made" (ESV, NASB). But that is not in the primary text. NASB also places a footnote for its readers that the source text reads literally "God had created to make." Therefore, a solution could be from the Hebrew text that God created his work so that humanity would continue with it and complete it.

---

35. Freedman and Maurice, *Midrash Rabbah: Genesis*, 1.10.
36. Samuelson, *Judaism*, 163. Cf. Lane, *Hebrews 1–8*, 100.

Sabbath and Other Celebrations

At the end of the biblical story of creation, the day of rest points to the future rest that God has in store for his creation; the seventh day is related to the Sabbath institution. When God reveals his Ten Words on Mount Sinai, the Sabbath institution is associated with the seventh day of the story of creation and the remembrance of the salvation process that God's people went through. This practical institution of the Sabbath points forward to the new heaven and the new earth. There God's creation enjoys its eternal rest. It is a foretaste of the "day of the holy kingdom for Israel."[37]

Similarly, the biblical feasts testify of God's plan of salvation with this creation. Passover, the Feast of the Firstfruits, and the Feast of Weeks are already related in the New Testament to the work of messianic redemption. During Passover, the Messiah gives his life of deliverance as a perfect Lamb. During the Feast of the Firstfruits, the Messiah rises from the dead as Firstborn. At the Feast of Weeks/Pentecost, the Israelite gives his tithes as gratitude for the harvest to God, and God gives his Holy Spirit as the fruit of his work of salvation. Bible interpreters are not afraid to relate even the other biblical feasts to God's plan of salvation.[38] The interpretations differ. However, a much-heard explanation is: During the Day of Atonement, the people recognize the work of reconciliation that the Messiah has done for them. During the Trumpet Feast or New Year, the people prepare to meet God as the beginning of a new century. During the Feast of Tabernacles, the people of God experience entry into the messianic realm of God.

In the story of creation, God places the sun as a great light and the moon as a small light in the sky. "Let them be for signs and for seasons and for days and years" (Gen 1:14b). Literally, instead of "season," there is talk of "times" (מוֹעֵד, *mûʿēd*). Traditionally, these times have been seen as an allusion to the later biblical feast.[39] From the very beginning, the heavenly bodies help us to remember the biblical feasts that bear witness to God's complete plan of salvation. Thus, the sun and moon are servants who indirectly look forward to completing this plan of salvation. This completion will realize God's new creation, the coming of the new heaven and the new earth. Then the sun and moon will no longer be

---

37. Jub. 50:9.

38. Van der Poll, *Sacred Times*.

39. Wenham, *Genesis 1–15*, 23; Roop, *Genesis*, 29; Freedman and Maurice, *Midrash Rabbah: Genesis*, 6.1.

necessary as lights in the darkness because the creation will only know the total light (Isa 60:19–20).

The Threefold Mission

If God creates humans, male and female, they receive the command, "Be fruitful and multiply, and fill the earth and subdue it" (Gen 1:28). These three assignments have yet to be completed. From the very beginning, people realize that God has a fantastic task for them. The new life in the garden of Eden offers a starting point for the subjugation and earth-population. From the beginning, the soil outside the garden is part of the humans' sphere of activity. For this reason, the biblical writers several times compare the future of the land of God's people with the fertile Eden: "For the Lord will comfort Zion; he will comfort all her waste places, and will make her wilderness like Eden, her desert like the garden of the Lord; joy and gladness will be found in her, thanksgiving and the voice of song" (Isa 51:3); "And they will say, 'This land that was desolate has become like the garden of Eden; and the waste and desolate and ruined towns are now inhabited and fortified'" (Ezek 36:35; cf. Gen 13:10).

The garden in Eden is a perfect starting point for world history. God's presence in Genesis 1–2 is only connected with the garden in the land of Eden. His glory does not yet fill the entire creation. That will be the case in the future. The beginning of Eden may result in the process of glorification that the Messiah eventually realizes. His new creation is of a higher and more definite form. It is the unfolding and crowning of that on which creation was built from its beginning. Jesus Christ is "the origin of God's creation" (Rev 3:14), for whom it is already at the beginning of creation.

From the above observations, it can be concluded that the biblical story of creation already makes the reader curious about the future of God's creation. The record shows how God creates the world because of his eternal plan. That is the creation of God's desire. In this way, the seven days of the creation story come to us as the first seven beginning days of God's kingdom. From this perspective, it is fascinating to see that later biblical testimonies refer back to these early seven days. The biblical writers describe events in such a way that one is reminded of the beginning of Genesis.

God's Battle for Creation

The eternal plan that God has in mind for this creation does not only include humans. Light, water, and land are mentioned in the prophetic images of the new creation (cf. Rev 21–22). When reading such prophetic testimonies, we realize that God has his whole creation on the future program. Precisely from the Hellenistic philosophies came significant criticism of these biblical images. The prophetic descriptions of a future concrete earthly reality were sensitive. For example, many thought that the physical was just an undervalued child. In their opinion, what was at stake was the spirit and the mind. As a result, with its brilliant thinking abilities, the head came to be at the center of the human universe. Everything physical was seen as an unwanted bastard, created by a "subordinate being" (*demiurge*). Had it been up to God, these people claimed, there would only have been souls without bodies. Thus, the creation was of lower quality and could not be related to a highly exalted God. Ultimately, the earth would be demolished and destroyed. Because of the influence of the serpent, this had already begun. Therefore, this animal was more rational than the other animals of the field (Gen 3:1). From these considerations, people chose not to allow any room for faith in a future redemption of the physical reality. Those who believed in the body's resurrection were portrayed as idiots and were allowed to return if they got bored in philosophy (cf. Acts 17:32). As a result, creation was torn away from God and only seen as a temporary backdrop to its disappearance.

The biblical testimony is opposed to this. Not only humanity, but the whole creation is precious in God's eyes and wanted by him. God has a higher purpose in mind from the beginning and therefore bears witness to a new heaven and a new earth. Creation does not dissolve itself in the future either. Animals also belong to that higher purpose with creation. The former Roman Catholic pope Benedict XVI, Joseph Ratzinger (b. 1927), rightly characterizes the extrabiblical Greek-gnostic systems of thought mentioned above as a movement that radically denies God's work of creation and goes against the testimony of the New Testament.[40] To this, the message of the Old Testament can be added. The New Testament, however, gets a special mention because it is precisely this work that radically opposes these gnostic ideas. The followers of Jesus insisted adamantly that the heavenly Messiah became physically human, died physically on the cross, and rose bodily from the dead. Jesus had no

---

40. Ratzinger, *In the Beginning*, 96–97.

apparent body, and the resurrection of his physical body was a proven fact: "In him the whole fullness of deity dwells bodily" (Col 2:9), and "If Christ has not been raised, then our proclamation had been in vain and your faith has been in vain" (1 Cor 15:14).

God created this world with a purpose, and he does not forsake the work of his hands. He gives his beloved Son to accomplish that goal, that much creation is worthy of him. Therefore, from the beginning of his gospel, John consciously chooses to speak of the salvation of the "world" or "creation" (κόσμος, kosmos). "Here is the Lamb of God who takes away the sin of the *world* [κόσμος, *kosmos*]!" sounds from the mouth of John the Baptist (John 1:29). "For God so loved the *world* [κόσμος, *kosmos*] that he gave his only Son, so that everyone who believes in him may not perish but may have eternal life. Indeed, God did not send the Son into the *world* [κόσμος, *kosmos*] to condemn the *world* [κόσμος, *kosmos*], but in order that the *world* [κόσμος, *kosmos*] might be saved through him" (3:16–17).

Easily we read in these well-known verses the word "people" instead of "world." We then think of ourselves, humanity, in the work of salvation. The apostle, however, testifies that the work of Christ has a much broader scope. The Son did not only come to free people from the forces of evil. He came to free the cosmos, creation, the world from these powers.

> For the creation was subjected to futility, not of its own will but by the will of the one who subjected it, in hope that the creation itself will be set free from its bondage to decay and will obtain the freedom of the glory of the children of God. (Rom 8:20–21)

Not only humans are part of this creation, but also fish, birds, and land animals. On the sixth day, God even creates the land animals together with the first humans. Man and woman are then summoned on the same day with the words:

> Be fruitful and multiply, and fill the earth and subdue it; and have dominion over the fish of the sea and over the birds of the air and over every living thing that moves upon the earth. (Gen 1:28)

Nevertheless, what exactly is meant by the words "subdue it"? There was fierce debate about this in the twentieth century. The central question was whether this biblical statement was not the cause of all the misery that humanity observed in environmental issues. Was the Christian faith at the root of so many natural disasters on earth? The statement "subdue it" evoked the necessary rejection. That is reason enough to ask ourselves in the next chapter how we should interpret this biblical commission.

3

Manage and Subdue

3.1 GOD'S COMMISSION TO HUMANITY

3.1.1 Assignment with Negative Resonance

Christian Arrogance about Nature

In Genesis 1, God calls upon humanity to exercise dominion over animals: "Then God said, 'Let us make humankind in our image, according to our likeness; and let them have dominion over the fish of the sea, and over the birds of the air, and over the cattle, and over all the wild animals of the earth, and over every creeping thing that creeps upon the earth.'" (Gen 1:26). Traditionally, in Western theology, this call has been referred to with the Latin expression *dominium terrae*, "reign over the earth." What is meant by this *dominium terrae*?

Translators choose to translate Hebrew רדה/r-d-h with expressions such as "dominion" (NRSV, ESV, NKJV), "have power" (GNB), "reign" (NLT), or "rule" (NASB, NIV, NCV). Nevertheless, often all these words leave a negative sound in people's minds. Having dominion is then understood as "controlling" or "being the boss." You then get the taste of "kicking down," as is the case with this expression in Joel 3:13b, "Go in, tread [רדה, *r-d-h*], for the wine press is full." This kind of meaning is gladly thought of in Genesis 1.

Throughout history, Genesis 1:26–28 has often been used to approve violent acts against plants and animals. This application of the text could not remain without consequences. Lynn T. White (1907–87), professor of medieval studies at Princeton, Stanford, and UCLA, is associated with the indictment of the misuse of this biblical text. In 1967, he referred in a reflection on the ecological crisis to Western Christianity as one of the leading causes of environmental problems. Western Christianity was "the most anthropocentric religion the world has seen."[1] It carried a heavy burden of guilt. There was "Christian arrogance toward nature."[2] Because Christianity undervalued nature and the animal world, it laid the foundation for centuries of animal abuse. This abuse manifested itself mainly from the Middle Ages onwards. Western society emphasized humanity's exaltation over creation from the first Crusades and early discoveries during the periods of the Renaissance and Enlightenment. Humans had to "rule" creation and be in control of it. This ruling of creation was written in the Bible. Numerous "cultivations," which the European population carried out in other countries, were therefore seen as the fulfillment of God's commission in Genesis 1.[3] But that attitude was nothing more than an absolute human madness. It had nothing to do with God and Christ.

Soon others echoed Lynn White's statement about Western Christianity. Often White's article was no longer consulted. This negligence caused White to be portrayed as an enemy of the Christian faith. This is not the case. In his article White nuances his thought by mentioning that he focuses mainly on the developments in Western Christianity. As a historical scholar in medievalism, he knows that these developments originate from more than an expressive succession of Genesis 1.

Cultural and Social Views

Theologians were challenged by whether the Western world had abused Genesis 1:26–28 for its selfish purposes. When it came to the abuse in Western civilization of Christianity, White was right. Western Christianity had degenerated and lost track. But did the Judeo-Christian faith lay the foundation for the over-exploitation of nature?

The British theologian James Barr (1924–2006) reacted against that thought. In the context of various factual and methodical objections, he called on theologians to make an objective analysis of the expressions "rule" and "subject." This was of great importance since he discovered that

---

1. White, "Historical Roots," 1204.
2. White, "Historical Roots," 1207.
3. Cf. Giamatti, *Earthly Paradise*; Sanford, *Quest for Paradise*.

Bible interpreters quickly included erroneous social ideas about "reigning" in their explanations. Thus Hermann Gunkel (1862–1932), professor of Old Testament at the universities of Berlin, Halle, and Giessen, refers to the blessing of Genesis 1:28 as "great words; the program of an entire cultural history of humanity."[4] We have to realize that Gunkel was a much-praised Protestant interpreter of the Bible. His interpretations of Genesis are among the best to be found in the twentieth century. His colleague and equally famous contemporary Otto Procksch (1874–1947), who was associated with the universities of Greifswald and Erlangen, also wrote as an evangelical theologian that the words in Genesis 1:26–28 indicated that humanity had control over the lives of animals.[5] So it is up to human beings to decide whether or not to kill an animal. Life is in our hands, and we are free to select. These interpretations by Gunkel and Procksch show how strongly cultural-social views can determine biblical understanding. Their decision at that time, to explain the text in this way, would have been imitated by many of us. Had Gunkel and Procksch written their arguments today, they would have dealt with the biblical text in a different way. They were, like us, children of their time.

In older rabbinic literature, we also find that animals were only created to benefit humans.[6] Presumably, this thought came from the ancient Greek and Roman philosophy into Judaism and Christianity.[7] In the philosophical current of Greek stoicism, it was assumed that animals were irrational, and people were rational. Therefore, there would be no unjust treatment of animals. Animals had no rights, as people knew them. Animals were there to benefit humans.

Nowadays, we realize that there are numerous animals on earth that have no immediate, clear benefit for humans. Also, nowhere in Jesus' teaching do we come across the idea that people have no ethical responsibility towards animals. Instead, the idea is that both humans and animals are creatures of God and express how God deals with his creation. In later times, interpreters argue against using these expressions as a license to exploit nature. There is instead an exaltation of humans over animals because they were created in God's image. The idea that the Judeo-Christian faith and the biblical story of creation encourage humans to elevate

---

4. Gunkel, *Genesis*, 113.
5. Procksch, *Genesis*, 432–33.
6. Neusner, *B. Qiddushin*, 82b; Neusner, "M. Qiddushin," 4.14.
7. Aristotle, *Politics*, I.8; Cicero, *Nature of the Gods*, §2.

themselves above animals could not stand up. Instead, the exploitation of nature took place as Enlightenment thinking began to take people away from biblical values and norms. For example, the London philosopher and Lord Chancellor Francis Bacon (1561–1626) stated that nature was the slave of humankind. Humans had to fight nature and subdue it in order to fulfill God's mission.[8] The French mathematician and philosopher René Descartes (1596–1650) gave his audience the impression that the animal was nothing more than a soulless machine.[9] From this, it was deduced by his followers that animals were numb. As Lynn White rightly acknowledges in his article, all these insights and the associated negative consequences of growing technology and industrialization were a catastrophe for creation.[10] Almost one century before White, the German philosopher Ludwig Feuerbach (1804–72) already made in his *The Essence of Christianity* (1841) the remark that "nature, the earth, has no value or interest in Christianity. Christians think only of themselves and the salvation of their souls."[11] Western Christianity was unconsciously drawn into a Greek worldview. Creation was nothing more than a temporary backdrop close to destruction. What remained was a hardrock anthropocentrism that placed only humanity at its center. Nevertheless, the Bible is not about what the American philosopher Francis Schaeffer (1912–84) wrongly called "the upper story," namely saving souls to go to heaven and let go of the earthly forever.[12] It is far more than that.

A New Awakening

In later times, a new awareness of this degeneracy would make a different sound in the explanation of Genesis 1:26–28. This difference can be seen in the reflection on Genesis 1:26 by Claus Westermann (1909–2000), professor of Old Testament at the University of Heidelberg:

> Dominion over the animals certainly does not mean their exploitation by humans. People would forfeit their kingly role

---

8. Bacon, *Valerius Terminus*.

9. Descartes, *Descartes*; Matthews, "Augustine"; Harrison, "Descartes on Animals."

10. White, "Historical Roots," 1204. See further on these negative consequences: Gindi, *Greening the Torah*, 40–47; Bernstein, "(Mis)Reading Genesis," 33.

11. Feuerbach, *Essence of Christianity*, §25.6.

12. Schaeffer, *Pollution*, 40.

among the living (that is what רדה refers to) were the animals to be made the object of their whim.¹³

Parallel to this are the words of Victor Hamilton (1941), professor of Old Testament at Asbury University: "Man is created to rule. But this rule is to be compassionate and not exploitative."¹⁴ Genesis 1 encourages us to take an interest in God's creation and to value it highly. Therefore, it is wrong for Christians to give others the impression that their faith has no meaning for creation.

The idea that humans have the right to exploit the earth should not be connected with Judeo-Christian orthodoxy. It was the fruit of an intellectual Enlightenment thinking that opposed the Judeo-Christian faith. Inspired by the Enlightenment, people only wanted to place humanity at the center of this universe without considering God or taking responsibility for anything else.¹⁵ Postmodernism has set itself against this current in our time. It points out that the Enlightenment and modern science push people into a one-sided straitjacket, leading to new forms of unfreedom and submission. Therefore, the search for dealing with creation has not yet ended, even in the philosophy of social culture.

3.1.2 Assignment with a Positive Connotation

How should we translate the Hebrew רדה/*r-d-h* and the Hebrew כבש/*k-v-sh* in Genesis 1:26–28? Traditionally רדה/*r-d-h* is translated as "rule" and כבש/*k-v-sh* as "subdue." The Old Testament scholars Klaus Koch (b. 1926) and Norbert Lohfink (b. 1928) assume that רדה/*r-d-h* is consistent with the Akkadian *redûm*, which has the meaning of "guide" or "lead."¹⁶ One can then think of a shepherd who guides, protects, and accompanies his sheep. God's command to rule over the animals is then not a command of oppression and exploitation. It is maintenance of the salvific order. It calls upon people to act caringly and responsibly towards God's fauna and flora.

As a shepherd, he should give animals access to healthy food and clean water. Koch and Lohfink further state that כבש/*k-v-sh* points out that humans are allowed to make the earth habitable by arranging areas

13. Westermann, *Genesis 1–11*, 159.
14. Hamilton, *Genesis 1–17*, 138.
15. Bouma-Prediger, *For the Beauty*, 67–86.
16. Koch, "Gestaltet die Erde," 223–37; Lohfink, "Macht," 11–28.

for culture and nature. People are free to use the land to build cities, to farm, and to promote nature. As the steward of God, he may bring harmony to the planet and lead the animals with a gentle hand into the area assigned to them.

A challenge for this explanation is the use of כבשׁ/*k-v-sh* in the later conquest of Canaan. The term is then interpreted militarily for subjugating peoples (Num 32:22, 29; Josh 18:1–2). So King David says that God has delivered the former inhabitants of the land to him: "The land is subdued [כבשׁ, *k-v-sh*] before the Lord and his people" (1 Chr 22:18). Elsewhere the term is related to the conquest of the nations around Israel (2 Sam 8:11), the enslavement of men and women (Jer 34:11, 16; Neh 5:5; 2 Chr 28:10), and as a reference to sexual assault (Esth 7:8). Consequently, the term is placed in the context of the exercise of power. Only in Ezekiel 34:4 is this not the case. But also in that text, it refers to the abuse of power by the leaders of Israel. It is therefore difficult to think in Genesis 1:28 of peaceful, arable farming and a pleasant way of dealing with the land. After all, we cannot ignore the other contexts of the word.

In similar contexts, the Hebrew רדה/*r-d-h* can be found. It refers to Solomon's reign "over all the region west of the Euphrates from Tiphsah to Gaza, over all the kings west of the Euphrates" (1 Kgs 4:24; cf. Ps 72:8), to the reign of the King of Babylon (Isa 14:6), of Egypt (Ezek 29:15), of Israel (Isa 14:2) and the expected King (Ps 72:8; 110:2), or of other rulers who overpower their enemies (Neh 9:28; cf. Lev 26:17). It also occurs in the sense of the master supervising his servant (1 Kgs 5:30; 9:23; 2 Chr 8:10), where God's Torah calls the overseer three times to do this from a respectful attitude (Lev 25:43, 46, 53). In all these situations, רדה/*r-d-h* points to rule other peoples. Only in Ezekiel 34, we saw that this is not the case. In a prophetic word, it is about the dealings of the shepherds of Israel with their people. They have "ruled" their sheep (רדה, *r-d-h*) and treated them "with force and harshness" (v. 4). The term is not used anywhere else in the Bible for governing people.

If we also take into account the applications of כבשׁ/*k-v-sh*, we see that each time it concerns situations in which a person gains power over something else. The control over it is taken over or established. It is not shown how that rule is exercised over the nations in the land, the nations around Israel, or the enslaved men and women. The term does not focus on the actual reign but on its initiation. This implies that the task of "subdue" and "dominion" in Genesis 1 should not be used to legitimize violence against the earth and life on it. Nor may it be interpreted as merely a call to care for creation. The massive subjugation and exploitation of nature in bio-industry cannot be traced back to God's command in Genesis 1. The terms only refer to the starting position that humans receive concerning animals. How people exercise their dominion over creation should be viewed from a broader biblical-theological reflection. In this, it becomes visible that creation remains God's property and that humans are merely its delegated rulers.

3.1.3 Representatives of the King

God's commission to rule over animals and subdue the earth has often been related to God's desire to create people in God's image and likeness.[17] Humans are then image-bearers of God and must carry out their task in this creation from God's example. God precedes people in the execution of what this means. This becomes deeply visible in biblical history because God humbles himself, becomes human, and wears a crown of thorns (Phil 2:7).

In ancient times it was customary to consider the king of the land as the image of God. Thus the Egyptian pharaoh was "the corporeal [son of Re] ... the good Lord, the image of Re, the son of Amon."[18] Although only the king was the image-bearer of God in these myths, the Bible applies this to all people: men and women are together image-bearers of God. Genesis democratizes the idea of humans as image-bearers.

However, terms such as "rule" (רדה, *r-d-h*) and "subdue" (כבש, *k-v-sh*) are nowhere in the Bible related to this royal perspective. This makes it a legitimate question whether we can think in this direction. Even in Psalm 8:5, humankind is royally spoken of as "a little lower than God." The psalmist does not use these terms. Instead, he writes that humanity has been given dominion over God's work (מָשַׁל, *māshal*). Being created in God's image is also mentioned in Genesis 1, next to the call to rule creation and to subdue the earth. This calls for a reflection on how God deals with creation.

Presumably, the Bible dissociates itself from the king's perspective mentioned above. In the eyes of the nations, this image is inextricably linked to serving God as a slave. The creation of humans is then entirely at the service of the religious cult from the beginning. Man and woman

---

17. Wright, *Mission*, 427; Murray, *Cosmic Covenant*; Barr, "Man and Nature," 22.
18. Wildberger, "Abbild Gottes," 487.

are made to accurately wear the yoke of their god and serve him through daily hard work. In Genesis 1, the creation of humanity does not stand in a religious context. From the beginning, it is related to the control of animals. Humans are allowed to use the animals in their dealings with the land. They are allowed to use them to pull the plow or to guard the sheep. In this use, there is no aim to abuse the animals because "the righteous know the needs of their animals, but the mercy of the wicked is cruel" (Prov 12:10). That is why there are several times instructions in the Bible that deal with the excellent care of animals. Well-known examples are the statutes of the Sabbath, on which the animals also receive rest (Exod 20:10; 23:12), helping an animal that succumbs under a burden (22:4), and letting a working ox eat from what it encounters (Deut 25:4). In this, one realizes that God is the Owner of all animals: "For every wild animal of the forest is mine, the cattle on a thousand hills. I know all the birds of the air, and all that moves in the field is mine" (Ps 50:10–11). In God's majesty and exaltation, the Creator cares for these creatures. "The eyes of all look to you, and you give them their food in due season" (Ps 145:15). In the same way as God, humans should rule over animals.

The fact that there are mainly animals related to "rule" in Genesis 1:26 indicates that humans can only reign over living things. Plants cannot be ruled in the full sense of the word. The relationship between humans and plants is separately discussed in Genesis 1:29–30. Therefore, the expression "of the earth" in Genesis 1:26 concentrates on the entire animal world.

Later on, these wild animals will be a threat to humans. Although Psalm 104 testifies to how God cares for the lion, this animal is a danger to humans. For example, a lion plague placed the people of Samaria in great distress (2 Kgs 17:25; cf. Exod 23:29). Other animals, such as bears and snakes, could also pose a significant threat. Even a massive plague of insects could cause the harvest to fail and expose humans to the danger of famine. In Job 38–41, we learn that humanity is incapable of controlling all these animals. The animal world contains friends and foes. It is a constant threat that can cause considerable instability in society. Therefore, God's blessing is that the wild animals are banished from the land (Lev 26:6; Ezek 34:25).

If humanity fulfills the task of management in the right way, the forces of chaos on earth will be subdued. Then creation will live in harmony with God. God's plan with this creation will then find its fulfillment. If humanity would reject God's command and break the relationship with

God, it would also be an attack on creation. Creation desires to fulfill God's plan.

The psalmist testifies that God has entrusted the work of his hands to humans. God has "put all things under their feet" (Ps 8:6b). Nevertheless, a person is not allowed to dispose of God's creation with his own hands. Creation is of value in God's eyes. Whoever ignores this fact should realize that God is righteous and comes to the aid of his "defenseless" creation.

For this reason, several times in the Bible, creation is described as a power that turns against infidelity. This is the case with the plagues in Egypt, the temptations in the wilderness, the battle in Canaan, and the events in the book of Revelation. We will deal with these stories in chapter 7.2 and 11.1. Creation then turns against humankind. Another well-known example is the exile of Israel. This took place because the people did not grant the land a year of Sabbath. "All the days that it lay desolate it kept sabbath, to fulfill seventy years," until all the Sabbath years that were not observed were made right (2 Chr 36:21; cf. Lev 26:43).

The prophet Hosea draws the people's attention to the negative consequences of their attitude to creation already in his time. Because of their crimes, "the land mourns, and all who live in it languish; together with the wild animals and the birds of the air, even the fish of the sea are perishing" (Hos 4:3). At the same time, we can point to lesser-known examples, such as the land turning against Adam and Cain because of their transgressions (Gen 3:17; 4:12).

3.2 NAMES TO THE FIRST ANIMALS

3.2.1 In God's Footsteps

A Person for the Earth

A proper application of God's call to manage his creation is expressed in Genesis 2. As God brings order to creation through the Word in Genesis 1, Genesis 2 describes how God brings order in the garden of Eden. We learn that God creates humans as a help to the earth:

> When no plant of the field was yet in the earth and no herb of the field had yet sprung up—for the Lord God had not caused it to rain upon the land, and there was no one to till the ground. (Gen 2:5)

The earth needed a human being. People are required to meet the needs of the land. In the original Hebrew text, this is strongly expressed by the etymological similarities between the words "human" (אָדָם, ādām) and "earth" (אֲדָמָה, ădāmāh). God created the first human from the earth and placed him in the garden of Eden "to till it and keep it" (v. 15). Thus, the first human stands from the beginning in the service of the land that belongs to God. God did not want to leave his garden to fate. He realized that its care is necessary.

So other creatures were not only there to serve humanity. It was the other way around, according to Genesis 2. Like in Genesis 1, we see how humans are part of a greater whole under God's care. In Genesis 2, we read again that God forms all animals:

> So out of the ground the Lord God formed every animal of the field and every bird of the air, and brought them to the man to see what he would call them; and whatever the man called every living creature, that was its name. (Gen 2:19)

In Genesis 1, the animals were formed *before* the creation of humans. In Genesis 2, they are created *after* the creation of Adam. Some thought that God only brought the animals together into one group in Genesis 2.[19] Another possibility is that God only adds a few animals to the animals in the garden. He thus eventually formed "all" animals.[20] A third proposal reads Genesis 2:19 as a remark about the past: after God created all the animals of the earth, God brought them to Adam.[21] We find that choice in some translations:

> Now out of the ground the Lord God *had formed* every beast of the field and every bird of the heavens and brought them to the man to see what he would call them. And whatever the man called every living creature, that was its name. (ESV, cf. NIV)

The animals are made by God from the same earth as Adam and are referred to as "living" like Adam (2:7).

After God has made all these animals, Adam is instructed to give names to the animals. As God mentions different elements in Genesis 1, Adam is allowed to do so in Genesis 2. Giving names is related to God's

---

19. Freedman and Maurice, *Midrash Rabbah: Genesis*, 17.4.
20. Cassuto, *From Adam to Noah*, 129.
21. For this grammatical choice, see: Collins, "Wayyiqtol," 117–40; Cassuto, *From Adam to Noah*, 129.

example. What happens in Genesis 2 is an elaboration of what God means by his command to Adam to manage creation in Genesis 1:28.

Names and Numbers

Giving names is a sign of unique dignity. It testifies to the privilege a person receives. As viceroy, Adam follows his Creator's footsteps and takes it upon himself to manage God's creation responsibly. He may recognize, respect, and express God's creation's colorful nature by giving names to animals. In this way, the special relationship between humans and animals is expressed. In this chapter, as on the sixth day of creation of Genesis 1, humans and animals are related. Humans take care of animals in a particular way, just as God does (cf. Ps 104). Love of God manifests itself in the respect that people take for what belongs to God. Therefore, how a person deals with creation is often understood as a reflection and measure of the relationship humans have with the Creator. The original creation reflected the glory of the Maker. "After the world had been created, man was placed in it as in a theatre, that he, beholding above him and beneath the wonderful works of God," wrote John Calvin (1509–64) in his notes on Genesis.[22]

In later times we learn that humans give to their descendants names that are related to animals. This naming of other creatures shows that providing names is not an abstract, intellectual activity. It is a relational activity. Through relation, it is possible to understand the voice of the other. A relationship without a name means detachment. We see this, for example, in the use of numbers in animal experiments. Using numbers instead of names makes it easier for researchers to distance themselves from the animals they exploit. You don't experiment with Rover, but with CH-377.

It reminds me of the story of a family that had bought two lobsters in the morning for a luxury dinner. Back home, the mother put the animals in a half-full bathtub to stay alive and be prepared for the evening. However, she had forgotten that her children much enjoyed the animals. From dawn onwards, they spent hours watching the two lobsters move. After a few hours, it was time to cook the lobsters. As she went to the bathroom, she wanted to take the lobsters and prepare them for the meal. There, she suddenly encountered considerable resistance from her children. She

---

22. Calvin, *Genesis*, 64.

could put all the lobsters of the world in her cooking pot, but she had to stay away from Charlie and Choppie. Without any awareness, the children had managed to bond with the lobsters by giving them names. As a result, the evening meal went a little differently than planned.

Animals and the Woman

In Genesis 2, Adam does not provide numbers for animals. They get a name and are therefore related to himself. Because of this, Adam will establish that he is alone. When giving names to animals, Adam may have asked himself, "What kind of garden is this?" According to a Jewish tradition, all animals had a partner; they even passed by Adam in pairs to receive their name.[23] Genesis 2 places Adam through this incident in relation to both the animals and his later partner. This relational aspect is so central in Judeo-Christian tradition that the Jewish rabbi Sjlomo Yitzchaki (Rashi, 1040–1105) even dares to refer to an essential tradition of the old rabbi Eleazar. Eleazar writes about the cheerful words, "This, at last is bone of my bones" (Gen 2:23) of Adam, after the creation of the woman, saying this suggests that Adam had a sexual relationship with any beast and animal but remained unsatisfied until he had sexual relationship with Eve.[24]

After having tried sex with all animals, Adam finally found his partner and extinguished his sexual urge. In Jewish tradition, this thought caused the necessary anger. Reproduction with animals was strictly forbidden in God's Torah (Lev 18:23). Consequently, the explanations of Rashi and Eleazer were interpreted as a reference to intellectual or spiritual sex. Adam only scientifically examined the temperament of the animals.[25] In giving names to them, Adam, in any case, determined that "there was not found a helper as his partner" (Gen 2:20). Giving names to the animals caused Adam to discover that he was alone. God's choice to bring the animals to Adam so that he would give them names can then be explained as God's educational choice to teach Adam.

God then brought Adam into a deep swoon and formed the woman. From the body side of Adam, the building material for the woman was taken. The Jewish interpretation of this is that God decorated the woman

---

23. Freedman and Maurice, *Midrash Rabbah: Genesis*, 17.5.
24. Neusner, *B. Yebamot*, 63a.
25. Lawee, "Reception," 52–53, 57.

as a bride with beauty for her husband. When this bride meets the spouse, they marry each other under a dome of precious stones (cf. Ezek 28:13).[26] By giving names to the animals, Adam discovered that he had no wife. The commission that God gives to the first human in the garden ensures a positive development on earth. Animals are named, and what is "not good" is improved.

Thus, Genesis 2 shows what it means that a person rules over God's creation. To this day, there is no parallel with this story in extrabiblical literature. Although there are numerous stories of a great flood on the earth, there is no analogy with giving names to animals by a sort of Adam.

3.2.2 Wild and Field Animals

Two Fronts Opposite Each Other

Adam gives names to all the domestic animals (the cattle), all the birds, and all the animals of the field (Gen 2:19–20). The fish are not mentioned in this situation. This lack of attention is remarkable for those who realize that there were more than fifty names for fish in ancient Egypt.[27] Furthermore, the question is how to imagine the relationship between humans and "every animal of the field." In some translations, "every animal of the field" is given the designation "wild animals" (e.g., NIV, NLT). These are animals that are not domesticated. So, it is about the wild animals of the field, outside the garden. Adam also gives these animals their names (Gen 2:19–20). In what relation do these animals stand with the animals of the garden? What are these "animals of the field" or "wild animals"? Is there a peaceful existence between these "wild animals" and the livestock of the garden? It is possible that the author of Genesis consciously speaks in terms known to us today? With an animal of the field, we think of a lion, and with an animal of the garden, we think of a cow. Can we, therefore, think of a geographical separation between the animals of the garden ("the cattle") and the animals of the field ("wild animals"), or is that a distinction that we only make in our times?

This question is also raised when we read in Genesis 3 that the snake, a wild animal, is more crafty than any other wild animals. There is no mention of domesticated animals here. It concerns the category "wild

---

26. Freedman and Maurice, *Midrash Rabbah: Genesis*, 18:1–3. See also the Targums on this part of the text.

27. Riede, *Im Spiegel der Tiere*, 168n11.

animals" or "animals of the field." This category already exists in Genesis 3:1. If this were not the case, the snake would have been the craftiest of *all* animals: all the wild animals and all the garden animals. That is not the case. The snake is only the king of the jungle. The biblical text consciously emphasizes that it concerns "the wild" or "the field" as a geographical area outside the garden. Because of that geographical indication, there is a parallel with Adam. Adam also came from outside the garden and was subsequently placed in the garden (Gen 2:7–8). In the garden of Eden, Adam received God's commission to cultivate and guard the garden (2:15). An animal from outside the garden questions that commission. The animal who is more crafty than any other wild animal gets into conversation with the humans. In this way, two kingdoms face each other.

The snake is not a terrifying creature. The animal speaks to humans. That's something only God has done so far. The serpent is exceptional in the story of creation because of this speaking. The snake also succeeds in making humans perceive the forbidden fruit differently: "So when the woman saw that the tree was good for food, and that it was a delight to the eyes, and that the tree was to be desired to make one wise" (Gen 3:6a). Thus the tree of knowledge gets the quality of every other tree "that is pleasant to the sight and good for food" (2:9).

Consequently, the snake presents itself as a wild animal with capacities that only humans possess. What happens is abnormal and lets us taste something of the tension between the two worlds. What the snake says sounds severe and religious. The seducer does not say, "I am a flattering monster that wants to take you away from the garden." The petitioner asks a question in which he incorrectly quotes God, adds things, and avoids the trusted name YHWH, which is commonly translated as "Lord" in English Bibles.

Background of the Serpent

Because Genesis 3 presents the seducer as a serpent, an attempt was made to fathom why this animal was chosen. This caused interpreters to relate the serpent (נָחָשׁ, *nāchāsh*) to:

1. Magic (נִחֵשׁ, *nichēsh*), since both words use the same Hebrew letters.
2. The rejuvenating and immortal, since the Semitic word for "serpent" is derived from "life" (חַי, *chaj*) and the skin of a serpent

renews itself regularly. The serpent then faces Eve as the mother of life (Gen 3:20).

3. Negative knowledge, which opposes God. The serpent is "intelligent" (φρόνιμος, *fronimos*) in the Septuagint and Jesus calls upon his disciples to use their experience as actively as serpents (Matt 10:16).

4. Chaos and rebellion, as is visible in the Assyrian language, in the relationship between "snake" (*aiubilu*) and "enemy" (*aibu*). The snake then expresses the rebellion that exists in humanity.

5. Impureness, of which the snake as an animal meets all criteria (cf. Lev 11; Deut 14). It is a wandering, winding, moving animal that is far away from the clean animals.

All these proposals point to the idea that the serpent is more crafty than other wild animals. The serpent appears in Genesis 3 as an "angel of light." It is an insidious evil. Other ideas which the serpent expresses are the slander, the discord, the night, the darkness, the depth, the abyss, the poison, the killing, the penetrating, the hypnotic, the oppressive, the relentless, and the negative sparkling.[28] Nevertheless, Genesis deliberately hides the identity of the power behind the snake. All emphasis is on the speaking of the serpent and not on the exact character of the animal. It is only in the last biblical book that this becomes public: "The great dragon was thrown down, that ancient serpent, who is called the Devil and Satan" (Rev 12:9a). In Genesis 3, all emphasis is on the serpent as animal, the geographical place "of the field," and an indirect rule—"more crafty than any other wild animal."

That the serpent is more crafty (עָרוּם, *'ārûm*) in Genesis 3:1 is a strange fact. It is an ominous concept translated with "naked" (עָרֹם, *'ārm*) in Genesis 2:25, the biblical verse before it. In Hebrew, "naked" and "crafty" come from the same root. However, there is no English word that can replace both meanings.

The wordplay between "naked" and "crafty" recalls other wordplays in Genesis 2–3: Adam (אָדָם, *'ādām*) and the earth (אֲדָמָה, *'ădāmah*), woman (אִשָּׁה, *'isjāh*) and man (אִישׁ, *'ijsh*), Eve (חַוָּה, *chaûāh*) and life (חַי, *chaj*). Later, Eve acknowledges that the serpent is more crafty, when she admits she has been seduced (Gen 3:13). In Jewish tradition, the craftiness of the animal is even more strongly associated with humans' nakedness.

---

28. Charlesworth, *Good and Evil Serpent*; Garrett and Kaiser, *NIV Archaeological Study Bible*, 8.

According to the Jewish teacher Halfon ben Qoria, Adam was absent in the conversation between the serpent and the woman. The reason for this was that Adam had just slept with his wife and fell asleep to rest from this activity. This explains why the serpent is also referred to as "naked." The animal had observed how man and woman had intercourse with each other and developed a passion for the woman, which it then deceived.[29]

That is a nice story, but nowhere do we find a confirmation of this thought in the Bible. Questions such as why the snake could be craftier than other wild animals or more information about what happened outside the garden are left unanswered. By temptation, the serpent is cursed by God, and the "wild animals" or "animals of the field" will turn away from it (Gen 3:14). Humans will also eat from the field's crops because they must leave the garden (3:18). With this, the field has become the place of doom. This is strongly expressed in the Septuagint, Syrian, and Latin translation of Genesis 4. There Cain invites his brother Abel to go to the field. "Cain said to his brother Abel, 'Let us go out to the field.' And when they were in the field, Cain rose against his brother Abel and killed him" (4:8). This gives the field a negative aftertaste from the beginning.

3.2.3 Speaking Animals

A Unique Phenomenon

The negative talking serpent in the garden of Eden recalls the speaking of the donkey at the wandering prophet Balaam. In the Bible, the serpent is the first animal which speaks to humans. The donkey is the last animal who does this (Num 22:22–35).

To this day, the events of the speaking serpent and the speaking donkey seem unique in the ancient Middle East. Nowhere in Mesopotamia do we find a parallel. We hear only about speaking plants and animals in parables (Judg 9:8) and poetic texts (Ps 19:1; Job 38:7, 35). An example is this ancient fable by the Greek poet Aesop (~620–560):

> A long time ago, a mighty lion lived in a distant land. Once, when he was exhausted from hunting and the heat, he went back to his den and fell into a deep sleep. As he slept, a mouse passed by, sunk into her thoughts. She ignored where she was going and ended up in the lion's den. The mouse tripped over the back of a sleeping lion. Suddenly the lion woke up and caught the mouse.

29. Freedman and Maurice, *Midrash Rabbah: Genesis*, 18:6; 19:3.

He was just about to insert his teeth when the mouse begged him for mercy. The mouse promised to reward the lion for his release. The lion roared out, laughing, and left the naive mouse alive. Not much later, it happened that he owed his life to the mouse. The lion was captured by a bunch of hunters and tied to a tree with a rope. The mouse heard him moaning in pain and went straight for it. He gnawed the rope and freed the lion. Then the mouse squeaked, "You had to laugh like that because you could not believe I would do anything in return? From now on, remember that there is gratitude in mice too."[30]

In old fables, however, conversations between people and animals do not take place anywhere else. Remarkably, this is even absent in fable stories. The only exceptions are some ancient Egyptian myths.[31] In later times, some Greek myths are added.[32] However, in both cases, these are texts that call themselves fables. This clearly distinguishes them from the accounts of the talking serpent in Genesis 3 and the speaking donkey in Numbers 22. These biblical texts want to present themselves to us as historical events.

Connectedness in Speech

Because only the serpent and the donkey speak in the Bible, it is fascinating to compare both texts and look for similarities and differences. In both situations, we discover that humans, Eve and Balaam, do not react strangely when these animals speak. Making a chat with a serpent or a donkey is seen as an everyday affair. The animals do not have to answer for their bizarre behavior. Without introduction, they start a conversation with humans. In both events, we learn that they pretend to have a deeper understanding of the relationship between God and humans than Eve or Balaam have. They want their conversation partners to share in that knowledge. Just as the donkey wants to reveal to Balaam something that God has revealed, the serpent seeks to show Eve what God wants to hide. They do this by starting with a question in both cases. The serpent asks, "Did God say, 'You shall not eat from any tree in the garden'?" (Gen

---

30. My translation and paraphrase of Aesop's tale "The Lion and the Mouse."

31. Lichtheim and Loprieno, *Ancient Egyptian Literature*, 211–15; Lichtheim, *Ancient Egyptian Literature*, 156–59.

32. Cf. Homer, *Iliad*, XIX.404–24.

3:1), and the donkey asks, "What have I done to you, that you have struck me these three times?" (Num 22:28).

In the garden, the serpent talks to Eve about the correct interpretation of God's commandment, as if that were the most normal thing in the world. The conversation ultimately leads to Eve turning away from God and taking the fruit of the tree of knowledge. Her eyes are opened after she has done so, and she acknowledges that the animal has deceived her. The serpent's negative goal has been achieved: Adam and Eve have broken God's commandment. This ultimately leads to a cherub with his sword blocking the way to the tree of life (Gen 3:24).

While the snake wants to ruin humanity by going against God's commandment, the donkey with Balaam wants to achieve precisely the opposite. In the story of Balaam, we encounter another heavenly being. An angel of the Lord blocks with his sword the way on which Balaam travels with his donkey (Num 22:23). The donkey recognizes this danger and endures pain and contempt to save his lord's life. His attitude is opposed to that of the seductive serpent. Yet this rescue is not taken in thanks. Balaam becomes more and more confused each time: first, he lands on a field (v. 23), then he is pressed against a wall (v. 25), and finally, the donkey simply lays herself down beneath him (v. 27). The prophet becomes furious and does not see the danger. He hits the donkey with his stick. The lifesaver is beaten by a seer who is seeing blind.

In Numbers 22, we see that God opens the mouth of the donkey. The donkey gets a voice and asks Balaam the question, "What have I done to you, that you have struck me these three times?" (Num 22:28). Balaam reacts numbly. In his anger, he hardly seems to notice that the animal has learned to speak miraculously. Balaam replies as if he is accustomed to arguing with his donkey every day. He bluntly mentions that he would kill the donkey if he had a sword. The animal is treated as a rebellious slave. After this incident, Balaam's eyes are opened, as was also the case with Adam and Eve. Like them, he is now taken out of his euphoria and confronted with what happened. His life seemed to be in great danger (Num 22:31), and the seer saw less than the donkey. However, Balaam changes little in his attitude. There is no apology to the donkey that saved his life. Balaam continues his path to king Balak to curse the people of Israel. He doesn't care about the incident and thinks he will remain autonomous over his mouth. Eventually, it will turn out that this is not true. It turns out to be more comfortable for the donkey to pronounce the correct words than for the seer Balaam.

As the resistance of the donkey to the angel of the Lord grows, the donkey first moves out to the meadow (Num 22:23), then pushes itself against the wall (v. 25), and then lies down on the ground (v. 27). Balaam must acknowledge with tears in his eyes that the blessing over Israel also grows in his statements. In the beginning, he speaks of a great people (23:10), then of a people with majesty (v. 24), of a people similar to the gardens of Eden (24:5–6), and of people from which a star rises (v. 17).

Then Balaam concludes with three spells in which a curse resounds that should stop Israel. But this curse becomes a blessing. It even leads to Balak cursing the prophet (Num 24:10). Balaam's three spells remind us of the talking of the donkey and the striking of the animal three times. As God instructed Balaam, the prophet will only say what God want him to say. The donkey and Balaam are obedient instruments in God's hand. Balaam must acknowledge that Israel is a nation blessed by God, to which Balaam or Balak cannot change anything.

Significance for the History of Salvation

Let's juxtapose both stories of the speaking animals in broader salvation history: Through the choice of Adam and Eve to listen to the serpent, enmity has finally come between the serpent and humans and between humans themselves (Gen 3:14–19). Adam and Eve must leave the garden where they walked with God and end up as exiles in the area outside the garden. There they look hopefully forward to the moment when God wants to walk again with people on earth.

In Balaam's story, we see a movement in the other direction. The people of Israel have been released from the slave house of Egypt and are now returning to the land that God promised to the ancestors. It is a movement from exile to the home where God promises to walk (Lev 26:12). That is the land where the people should have no fear for wild animals: "I will remove dangerous animals from the land" (Lev 26:6b). The Bible does not mention that people will speak to the animals in these coming days, as happens in the animations of Walt Disney. It will be a time in which humans and animals will live in complete harmony. This will be like before the disobedience of humanity. Only death has not yet been lifted in the promise of Leviticus 26:3–12. Presumably, mortality was also not yet present in Genesis 1–2. However, that is still a question. Did death also occur in the animal kingdom before Genesis 3?

4

Death in Original Creation

4.1 GOD'S CREATION AND ANIMAL SUFFERING

4.1.1 The Awareness of Pain and Sadness

Have you ever woken up at night by the noise that animals make when they are involved in a death battle? Whoever experiences this hears animal cry, the sound of bones breaking and of flesh being torn off. Nature is full of atrocities. Various documentaries testify toward this cruelty. One animal is defeated and devoured by another. For example, the redbacked shrike pricks the beetles that he catches alive on a thorn bush to keep them fresh as long as possible. The lion, who discovers that a lioness has cubs, first kills the cubs and then mates with the lioness. Amongst insects, some spiders and grasshoppers eat their partner after the act of love. Cats play with mice before they kill them, and polar bear mothers do not hesitate to devour their youth when starving.

    This reminds me of the well-known example of the English biologist Charles Darwin (1809–82) about the larvae of the parasitic wasp. The parasitic wasp brings these larvae into the body of a caterpillar. The larvae feed themselves with the inside of the body from the caterpillar, which is still alive. They leave the vital organs intact until all the other meat is almost consumed. For those who observe this from nearby, it is a terrible misfortune. The thought that animals kill each other for survival is horrific.[1] Charles Darwin wrote to the botanist Joseph Hooker, "What

---

1. Darwin, *Correspondence Vol. 8*, 224.

a book a devil's chaplain might write on the clumsy, wasteful, blundering low and cruel works of nature."[2] The universe that suckled us is a monster, a robot programmed to kill. The entire animal kingdom is a kingdom of pain, nature red in tooth and claw.

Why are certain animals meat eaters (carnivores) and other animals plant eaters (herbivores)? An animal like the tiger is characterized by eating the meat of other animals. This world in which animals attack and digest other animals does not relate easily to the Jewish-Christian testimony of a good God who created this world. After all, the Christian faith confesses that the love of God is so great that the Son of God died for this creation. The cross of Jesus Christ, the Son of God, is the central message of love in the gospel. Jesus "emptied himself, taking the form of a slave, being born in human likeness. And being found in human form, he humbled himself and became obedient to the point of death—even death on a cross" (Phil 2:7–8). That proclamation of self-sacrifice is at odds with the self-preservation in the animal kingdom. Why would an all-good and all-powerful God create such an inherently violent and painful, dark nature?

For the Canadian evangelist Charles Templeton (1915–2001) this was a reason for saying farewell to God. Templeton was a cofounder of *Youth for Christ* (YfC), who held numerous evangelistic campaigns worldwide together with Billy Graham (1918–2018). But after it all he wrote,

> The grim and inescapable reality is that all life is predicated on death. Every carnivorous creature must kill and devour another creature. It has no option. How could a loving and omnipotent God create such horrors? . . . Surely, it would not be beyond the competence of an omniscient deity to create an animal world that could be sustained and perpetuated without suffering and death.[3]

In the past, several attempts have been made to deal with the tension between the proclamation of a good Creator and the atrocities in creation. Some chose the Cartesian idea that animals experience no feelings or pain.[4] The behavior of a parasitic wasp is then only perceived as terrible for humans. It is nothing more than a projection of human emotions. Can this be true?

---

2. Darwin, *Correspondence Vol. 6*, 178.

3. Templeton, *Farewell to God*, 197–99.

4. Trethowan, *Essay in Christian Philosophy*, 41, 92; Raven and Needham, *Creator Spirit*, 120.

In recent decades, scientific research on evolutionary biology, cognitive ethology, and social neuroscience yielded much evidence showing that animals could suffer and experience emotional and physical pain. The available data on this research proves that anyone who claims that animals have no emotions and feel no pain is wrong. In the summer of 2005, an example of animal emotions was exposed to us in the brilliant movie *The March of the Penguins*. This movie shows the emotional life and suffering of penguins. It became visible how intensely penguins took care of their eggs and their nestlings in dangerous conditions.

This kind of data already led years ago to the rise of the neo-Cartesian approach that animals could feel pain, but their self-awareness was too low to know what suffering was.[5] For example, scientists discovered that crabs and fish experience empirical pain. But still, it remains unclear whether they also have a form of reflective suffering.[6] Can they feel abandoned, rejected, or betrayed by other animals? Do animals suffer when something happens to their offspring or "friends"? A dog can temporarily respond to the howling of another dog, but stops when the howling is over. A dog does not continue howling when another dog was tackled hard by his owner a week before. There is no awareness of suffering found in this. Another question is to what extent mosquitoes, lice, flies, and rats can experience pain. Mosquitoes have minuscule brains. They have no neural structures that are needed to experience emotion. These are biological themes of considerable discussion.

At the same time, researchers realize that the level of self-awareness for experiencing suffering does not have to be high. Neurological studies indicate different similarities between humans and mammals.[7] From these observations, we can assume a relationship between what we recognize as pain and what animals feel as pain.

4.1.2 God's Ethical Choice for Evil

Another solution for the above-signaled tension is to state that animals experience pain, but this does not conflict our faith in a good Creator. The suffering in the animal kingdom is not of moral importance. The

---

5. Blocher, "Theology of the Fall," 168. Cf. Dougherty, *Problem of Animal Pain*.

6. Elwood and Appel, "Pain Experience," 1243–47; Sneddon, "Evidence for Pain," 153–62.

7. Morley, *God in the Shadows*, 153–58.

French systematic theologian Henri Blocher (b. 1937) gives an argumentation similar to this:

> In the case of the donkey devoured by the lion, the term "evil" is questionable: we confuse it with evil only in terms of an anthropomorphic projection onto the victim and of an imaginary identification.[8]

The question that arises is whether this "evil" can easily be separated from the "evil" humans experience as the consequences of sin like Blocher wants to state. In any case, it is a weak conclusion to note from this philosophical reflection on "evil" that animals could not suffer and that "there is no evil, properly speaking, except for humans."[9]

The idea is often stated that what humanity perceives as animal suffering is created by God as good and positive. Animals that die give nutrients and space to other animals. Wild animals ensure that domestic animals stay together in groups and collectively graze area by area. Because they stay in groups, plants in other areas can recover. Besides, wild animals ensure that domestic animals do not strip the land due to increased population. If these animals would strip the land, that could have a significant impact on other animals.

However, for many, this view is difficult to accept. Confronted with suffering, death, and pain in the animal kingdom, they do not feel called to praise God's glory as Creator. This was the complaint of the English theologian and philosopher Austin Farrar (1904–68). He saw the struggle of death in the animal kingdom as a reason to see the enormous vitality and force of God's greatness.[10] However, in such a death struggle, most people feel a cry for God's justice and redemption in their hearts. Suppose the character of God is characterized by love, grace, and peace. In that case, it is not easy to see the struggle, cruelty, and death in the animal kingdom as free of tension. They agree with the testimony of the ancient Elihu, "Therefore, hear me, you who have sense, far be it from God that he should do wickedness, and from the Almighty that he should do wrong" (Job 34:10).

---

8. Blocher, *Evil and the Cross*, 33.
9. Blocher, *Evil and the Cross*, 33.
10. Farrer, *Love Almighty*, 53.

Suffering a Higher Purpose

Another proposal views the suffering in the animal kingdom as a conscious creation of God. The creation is a "fallen creation." In love and grace, God created the world to achieve a higher divine purpose. The church father Augustine of Hippo (354–430) followed this approach in imitation of the Greek philosopher Plotinus (204–270 BC). According to Augustine, people often do not recognize how admirable

> fire, frost, wild beasts, and so forth . . . are in their own places, how excellent in their own natures, how beautifully adjusted to the rest of creation, and how much grace they contribute to the universe by their own contributions as to a commonwealth.[11]

Earlier, he wrote,

> The same account which is given of monstrous births in individual cases can be given of monstrous races. For God, the Creator of all knows where and when each thing ought to be or to have been created because he sees the similarities and diversities which can contribute to the beauty of the whole.[12]

The dark horrors in creation were necessary to make the excellent and beautiful more visible. They serve as contrasts to other fascinating aspects on earth, contributing to its beauty as a whole. So, suffering in the animal kingdom reveals evil. Humans can make a voluntary choice against evil and choose well. Suffering is an instrument that guarantees the freedom of life. Without an evil death or a capricious war, no one would know what life is and what peace is. It is like a valuable pearl placed on a dark cloth as contrast to show its beauty.

Closely linked to Augustine's proposal is the idea that animal suffering has a higher purpose of revealing God's character. The dying and suffering animals would show that God chooses the way of pain and death in salvation history. Jesus Christ is the Lamb who gave his life and was slain for this world. Animal suffering refers to the exalted Lamb in creation.[13]

Nevertheless, all these proposals meet resistance. In the end, no matter how beautiful the illustration of the dark cloth and the pearl sounds, it would also mean that God needs evil to achieve good. So, God chooses

---

11. Augustine of Hippo, *City of God*, XI.22.1.

12. Augustine of Hippo, *City of God*, XVI.8.

13. Murphy and Ellis, *Moral Nature*, 118–22, 174–78; Rolston, "Does Nature Need," 205–29.

to form animal suffering from the beginning for the sake of theological-aesthetic interests. However, in many cases, animal suffering is entirely pointless. The American writer Mark Twain (1835–1910) makes this very clear in his reflection of Noah's ark.

> The microbes were by far the most important part of the Ark's cargo, and the part the Creator was most anxious about and most infatuated with. They had to have good nourishment and pleasant accommodations. There were typhoid germs, and cholera germs, and hydrophobia germs, and lockjaw germs, and consumption germs, and black-plague germs, and some hundreds of other aristocrats, especially precious creations, golden bearers of God's love to man, blessed gifts of the infatuated Father to his children.[14]

Let's question: What is the use of a deer caught up in a forest fire, severely injured and burned, and fighting for its life for several days, without anyone taking notice of it? Whoever observes the suffering in nature realizes that theological-aesthetic goals are challenging to fit in with the God who is revealed in Jesus Christ. If this approach is right, animals have no value in themselves and can be tortured if it benefits others. This proposal cannot be combined with the Christian testimony of a loving and gracious Creator who, through Jesus Christ, wanted "to reconcile to himself all things, whether on earth or in heaven, by making peace through the blood of his cross" (Col 1:20). If God is directly responsible for the suffering of animals, it would be a testimony of a sadistic and limited deity who is incapable of achieving something useful without having evil serve as a foundation. It would be similar to parents who let their children go through a brutal, gruesome process of suffering and pain to give them a "better" upbringing by which the child can discover what peace and love is. When animal suffering is the work of a loving God, what would the result of a hateful devil look like?

This proposal puts God's nature as a perfect and good Creator under pressure. When we attribute animals' suffering to God's plan in creation, we call good what is evil. In biblical revelation, God did not create evil. Only the dark doom, which comes as a judgment over the wicked, is typified by the prophets as an evil caused by God (Isa 45:7; Amos 3:6). Because of this, the prophets protect the people against false images of God. They call their listeners to avoid other gods and turn themselves

---

14. Twain, *Letters from the Earth*, 30–31.

to God to prevent evil. The mischief of wickedness is only reversible by turning to the good God of whom the Bible testifies.

God Gives Predators Their Prey

The proposal that God did not create or want animal suffering is challenged by poetic texts that praise God's dealings with predators. The psalmists praise God's greatness, saying, "The young lions roar for their prey, seeking their food from God" (Ps 104:21). Recognizing that God "gives to the animals their food, and to the young ravens when they cry" (147:9), God asks Job, "Can you hunt the prey for the lion, or satisfy the appetite of the young lions, when they crouch in their dens, or lie in wait in their covert? Who provides for the raven its prey, when its young ones cry to God, and wander about for lack of food?" (Job 38:39–41). Besides, God feels responsible for the vulture, whose young ones slurp up blood (39:30).

These verses are in the context of God's provision. God cares for all animals, just as God cares for all people, good and evil. Still, that does not mean that God is the Creator of corrupt activities of animals and humans. The Bible only praises the greatness of God in dealing with creation. It honors the works of God's provision for creation. Even after Genesis 3, God deals with everything in wisdom. The poet of Psalm 104 is impressed by the number of creatures and the width of the sea (v. 24–26). Verse 27 relates this large number to God's providence. Nowhere in Psalm 104 or Job 38–40 will we find the idea that God is the Creator of the atrocities in nature. The lack of this reference makes it challenging to accept the statement that "for Genesis, Job, and the psalmist, animal death is thus likely part of God's good creation from the beginning."[15] The context of Job 38–39 and Psalms 104 and 147 is a setting of God's providence wherein the wild animals also get their place. Therefore, it is unjust to kill wild animals because they do not fit in creation. God takes care of them.

Jesus quoted the previous texts of the raven when he speaks about God's provision: "Consider the ravens: they neither sow nor reap, they have neither storehouse nor barn, and yet God feeds them. Of how much more value are you than the birds!" (Luke 12:24). These words indicate that God takes care of all animals. They do not answer the question of

---

15. Faro, "Question of Evil," 209.

whether God created these animals as predators. They only testify that God continues to care for these animals with the same love as for humans, even though many of these animals are meat eaters. God did not abandon animals and humans after Genesis 3. God "makes his sun rise on the evil and on the good, and sends rain on the righteous and on the unrighteous" (Matt 5:45). So, God is not the Creator or Architect of evil and chaos in this world. God is the One who takes care of this creation. God's character as Creator is in accord with God's nature as Savior. If evil is God's companion at the beginning of creation, it would be absurd to assume this companion is counteracted as God's adversary at the completion of creation. This would mean that the original friend changes too quickly into an enemy. However, nowhere is evil a "friend of God." In the biblical witness of creation and completion, evil is always opposed to God as an enemy.

4.2 SUFFERING AS AN INTRUDER

4.2.1 Genesis 3 and Suffering

Orthodox Jewish-Christian doctrine often chose to separate God and evil from each other and believe in an amazing original creation. That means that animal suffering did not belong to the design or plan of God. "God did not make death, and he does not delight in the death of the living," we read in the Jewish Wisdom of Solomon (1:13). Through the redemptive work of Christ, we discover that every suffering, every corruption, and every horror, goes against God's intention for this creation. Evil is not a humble servant in God's purpose. It is an enemy power that resists that goal.

This explains why redemption is related to the entire cosmos. Christ is "the Lamb of God who takes away the sin of the world [κόσμος, kosmos]!" (John 1:29). Sin is not only limited to humanity. It penetrates every corner of creation.

When and why did animal suffering arise? In Christian doctrine, there are different views on this question. The ancient idea that suffering is a consequence of human disobedience is well known. Humans lost their place in the garden by accepting the testimony of the serpent in Genesis 3. After this act of rebellion, the word is spoken, "cursed is the ground because of you" (Gen 3:17). As a result, evil was given the keys to corrupt creation. We find that thought in the Jewish work 4 Ezra 4:11–12:

> For I made the world for their sake, and when Adam transgressed my statutes, what had been made was judged. And so the entrances of this world were made narrow and sorrowful and toilsome; they are few and evil, full of dangers and involved in great hardships.

Another old Jewish source is the Life of Adam and Eve 10:1—11:3:

> Then Seth and Eve went towards paradise, and Eve saw her son, and a wild beast assailing him, and Eve wept and said, "Woe is me; if I come to the day of the resurrection, all those who have sinned will curse me saying: 'Eve hath not kept the commandment of God.'" And she spoke to the beast, "You wicked beast, do you not fear to fight with the image of God? How was your mouth opened? How were your teeth made strong? How did you not call to mind your subjection? For long ago, you were made subject to the image of God." Then the beast cried out and said, "It is not our concern, Eve, your greed and your wailing, but your own; for it is on your account that the rule of the beasts hath arisen. How was your mouth opened to eat of the tree concerning which God commanded you not to eat? For this reason, our nature also has been transformed."

According to these sources, all evil and death in the animal kingdom originated in human disobedience. Often, Christian tradition viewed this as a punishment from God. However, the difficulty is that the Bible never describes animal suffering as God's punishment. Instead of *punishment*, it is would be the *result* of what humans did. Humans had responsibility for all of creation, and because of that, it got drawn into the consequences of disobedience. Animals now had to suffer as a result of human missteps.

4.2.2 Death to All through One Human

A statement that is often related to this theological idea is found in Romans 5:12, "Therefore, just as sin came into the world through one man, and death came through sin, and so death spread to all because all men sinned." Through the sin of "one man," suffering and death came into the animal kingdom. The disadvantage of this idea is that the apostle Paul focuses on humanity in the context of this biblical text. He clarifies that by Adam's disobedience, death is a fact in the life of "all people": all died through one man's trespass (v. 15). Opposite to this is the justification that comes through Christ, the last Adam, to "the many" or "all people"

(vv. 19, 21). In this context, the apostle does not extend this to the animal kingdom. That would also be strange because animals are never called "justified by Christ."

Thus, from a biblical-exegetical viewpoint, it is incorrect to use Romans 5:12 as "proof text" for the proposal that animals died at Genesis 3. The theme of creation is not in the text of Romans 5. It will be brought up by Paul three chapters later. In Romans 8:20–21, he writes, "For the creation was subjected to futility, not of its own will but by the will of the one who subjected it, in hope that the creation itself will be set free from its bondage to decay and will obtain the freedom of the glory of the children of God." By this "futility" and "bondage to decay" interpreters thought of the suffering in the animal kingdom.[16] The disobedience of Adam then led to a cosmic fall to which all of creation got drawn. The difficulty here is that Romans 8 does not speak about "Adam." There is only a "him" who subjected creation. This observation makes us alert to look deeper at the thought that Adam was the cause of animal suffering.

4.2.3 Animal Suffering in Genesis 1–2 and Genesis 6

In Genesis 3 we only hear about the curse of the arable land. We do not encounter the thought of a cosmic fall that affected the animal kingdom and many other things (cf. Gen 5:29). We only discover that the field will be more difficult to cultivate. Thorns and thistles will grow there (3:17–18; cf. 4:12). God also judges the serpent. In Genesis, it is only the disobedience of the serpent, which the writer connects with the curse over the animals: "Cursed are you among all animals and among all wild creatures" (Gen 3:14a). Animals will abandon the serpent; his descendants are in enmity with the woman's offspring; he will crawl on his belly and eat dust. The craftiest of the wild animals becomes the loneliest of all animals. The serpent who tempted humans to eat now himself will eat dust. The serpent is degraded to a vacuum cleaner hose. Genesis 3 stays silent about the chaos in distant galaxies, the arrival of earthquakes and natural disasters, the emergence of the second law of thermodynamics, or animal suffering.

The suffering that other animals nowadays endure seems, in many cases, more significant than the curse of the serpent. The serpent can still defend itself against wild animals, but the domestic cattle cannot. These

---

16. Cf. Chang, *Knechtschaft*.

observations made room in Judeo-Christian doctrine for other proposals on the origin of animal suffering. One suggestion was to connect the cause of all evil and misery with the situation of Genesis 6. There we read about violations between human daughters and "sons of God" (6:1–4). This causes the earth to be full of evil in Noah's days (6:5), and therefore evil impacted all facets on earth.

Another choice was to place the animal suffering in an earlier time than Genesis 3. The reasons for this are the military interpreted terms God uses in Genesis 1–2. Humans are commanded to "subdue" the earth (Gen 1:28) and "keep" or "guard" the garden of Eden (2:15). These terms are later used to subdue other nations (Num 32:22, 29; Josh 18:1–2; 2 Sam 8:11; 1 Chr 22:18) and to enslave men and women (2 Kgs 28:10; Neh 5:5; Jer 34:11, 16). It is therefore difficult to think in Genesis 1–2 of a time of quiet arable farming or some idyllic way of dealing with the land. This idea is close to contemporary scientific approaches that evil was already there before human existed.

It appears in Genesis 3 that through the serpent, evil is already on the watch to assert its influence on the earth. God's garden has to be guarded against the invader, and the area outside the garden is subjected according to God's desires. These kinds of statements raise the suspicion that hostile powers are already present in creation. If Revelation 12:9 states that Satan used the serpent in Genesis 3, then that also raises the question of *when* Satan chose evil. In Jewish-Christian tradition, it is not easy to assume that God created Satan maliciously. Therefore, the idea is that somewhere between Genesis 1:1 and Genesis 3:1, Satan's disobedience took place.[17] However, Genesis is again silent about such resistance of Satan towards God. Therefore, the questions that concern us here are mainly accessible from a systematic-theological reflection driven by a broader biblical-theological perspective.[18]

The fascinating aspect of the proposal that animal suffering already took place before Genesis 3 is that it closely follows the theory mentioned above concerning Genesis 6. In both events, a resistance of the heavenly powers towards God is involved. The "sons of God" who populate the

---

17. Boyd, *Satan*, 247–48, 293–318; Jenson, *Systematic Theology*, 151; Lloyd, "Are Animals Fallen?," 158–60; Creegan, *Animal Suffering*, 148. From a critical view see Williams, *Ideas of the Fall*, 495.

18. See detailed: Dougherty, *Problem of Animal Pain*; Creegan, *Animal Suffering*; Murray, *Nature Red*; Southgate, *Groaning of Creation*. From an evolutionary perspective, see Johnson, *Ask the Beasts*.

world with giants through human daughters are, according to many, also angelic powers (see 2 Pet 2:4; Jude 1:6).[19] Lacking any introduction, Genesis mentions these "sons of God," revealing that there is not only light shining on earth from heaven. The power of darkness also wants to establish its works on earth and "sowed weeds among the wheat" (Matt 13:25). God's testimony of the event in Genesis 6 is that "the wickedness of humankind was great in the earth, and that every inclination of the thoughts of their hearts was only evil continually" (Gen 6:5). To the hostile heavenly powers behind this, attention is only briefly paid at the beginning of Genesis. Terms such as "have dominion" (1:28), "guard" (2:15), "more crafty than any other wild animal" (3:1), and "sin is lurking at the door" (4:7) arouse our curiosity. Even in Genesis 6, the identity of evil does not come fully into the picture. All attention focuses on the relationship between God and this creation. It is, therefore, necessary to investigate the biblical testimony of the first chapters of Genesis.

4.3 THE TREE OF LIFE AND CARNIVORES

4.3.1 Mortal Humans on a Battlefield

Two Trees in the Garden

From Genesis 1:2, several terms in the biblical text indicate that evil is lurking. God's choice to place humans in a demarcated garden in the land of Eden ("lovely") with the assignment to "guard," "preserve," and "subdue" the earth (Gen 1:28; 2:15) already indicates this. Sometimes scholars also interpret the expression תֹהוּ וָבֹהוּ/*tohû wābohû* (Gen 1:2) as a chaotic state, because it is elsewhere only used in the context of judgment (Isa 34:11; Jer 4:23).[20]

However, because there is no indication of judgment in Gen 1, the expression implies only that the earth is an unfruitful and uninhabited land, barren and empty (cf. Gen 2:4b–7).[21] In Genesis 1, we find no indication of a fight between gods, as we do in the Babylonian creation stories *Enuma Elish*. Creation is only the function of the sovereign God, resulting

---

19. Cf. 1 En. 6–19, 21, 86–88; Jub. 4:15, 22; 5:1; LXX-A reads *angellos*. See detailed: Mathews, *Genesis 1–11:26*, 324–32.

20. Sailhamer, *Genesis Unbound*, 37–45, 99–108; Collins, *Genesis 1–4*, 42–43.

21. See also Tsumura, *Earth*, 41–43.

in an orderly and reasonable world. By the power of God's word and Spirit, everything comes into being, is subdued, and is put in perspective.

Humans are placed in a garden surrounded by land that can become a battlefield for them. So, the world can become a place of struggle between the powers of evil and goodness. From the beginning, the phrase "it was very good" (Gen 1:31) does not denote that there is no imperfection in creation. Genesis 2 reveals that by eating from the "tree of the knowledge," humans can acquire knowledge of evil besides good. However, before that happens, the reader is informed that what God made was good. No crime was laid upon the world by God's hand.

This idea fits in with the Jewish-Christian orthodox statement that evil forces already existed before Genesis 3 and 6. In Genesis, "good" has priority over "bad," and evil is a consequence of disobedience. God enables humans in the garden to bring blessing to the whole of creation by controlling and subduing the evil powers beyond it.

In the garden, the tree of life and the tree of knowledge of good and evil are gifts from God. It is possible that through the tree of knowledge, humans could distinguish right and wrong, like the king-judge Solomon did (1 Kgs 3:9).[22] However, how this would work is not revealed in Genesis. We only read that man is not allowed to *eat* from the tree of knowledge. Humans do not have to taste good and evil to know about it. They should choose life, so that they and their children may live. This is comparable to many of us who fortunately never experienced a murder to realize that murder is a terrible evil.

Next to the tree of knowledge is the tree of life. Because of this tree, humans do not have to fear death. This is the tree from which humans can eat and life can be tasted. By eating the "fruit of life," humanity knows eternal life. Without this tree, humans do not live forever (Gen 3:22). Scholars conclude from this data that God created humans mortally.[23] For eternal life, humans were dependent on the tree of life. This could imply that animals, who like humans were formed from the earth's dust, were also created mortally. The difference between humans and animals in the garden was that humans had access to the tree of life.

This theological idea can be supported by biology. If animals at the beginning of Genesis would have been immortal and multiplied themselves at the same rate as today, this would have led to significant disasters.

---

22. Beale, *New Testament*, 65–73.

23. Faro, "Question of Evil," 208; Waltke, *Old Testament Theology*, 257; Fretheim, *God and World*, 77; Barr, *Garden of Eden*, 4.

Some insects and small animals reproduce so rapidly that they would have covered the whole earth at the end of the creation week. This would have resulted in all plants' total consumption found on earth, which would have unbalanced the entire relationship between plants and animals.

A way out of these observations forms the theory that the circumstances of the multiplication of animals and plants in the original creation were different from today. If insects and small animals multiply slowly, and plants multiply fast, this would be different. The mayfly or up-winged flies would then only receive their final names after Genesis 3.

God's Mission to Human Beings

Apart from these considerations, Genesis 1–3 shows that humans and animals were created mortally by God. So, when God says to Adam that he dies on the day he eats from the tree of knowledge, humanity already realizes what death is from what can be seen in the animal kingdom. Despite the above-mentioned militaristic terms that indicate a battlefield, this situation of Genesis 1–2 is seen as "good." In Genesis 1–2, all emphasis is therefore placed on human responsibility towards God and creation. The people of God receive the blessing of multiplication together with the animals. Thus, God is on the side of life. In the garden, humans have the advantage that they are protected and can eat from the tree of life. God plans that humans will ultimately overpower evil and show therein God's image. That plan becomes a reality through the human *par excellence*: Jesus Christ. Christ is the image of the invisible God and the last Adam who accomplishes everything.

Instead of staying in God's presence and accepting God's plan on earth, humans decide to believe the words of the serpent. They choose to submit themselves to its religious thoughts to know good and evil, and as a result take away access to the tree of life (Gen 3:22–23). What humans reap through that disobedience is death because the road to the tree of life is blocked (cf. Rom 5:12; 1 Cor 15:21). From that moment, they are caught under the rule of the ruler of death (Heb 2:14). God's command of begetting children and inhabiting and subjecting the earth is now being strengthened. The woman will suffer at birth (Gen 3:16), and the man will suffer in his dealings with the earth (3:17). Only Jesus Christ reverses this existence. Christ completes God's plan and offers salvation to humans. Whoever connects with Christ conquers and gains access to the tree of life (Rev 2:7; 22:2).

From these brief reflections, we can conclude that animals have not necessarily been created immortal. In the biblical revelation we find no reason for this. Speaking about the tree of life to give humans eternal life argues for the opposite. There is no mention of a tree of life for animals. But when animals could die at the beginning of Genesis does that also mean that there was already a battle among them? This is an issue we now want to address.

4.3.2 The Origin of Meat Eaters

Evil entered creation before Genesis 3. From a paleontologist's perspective, suffering and violence permeated the world millions of years before humans existed. From this recognition, some suggested that the punishment for human disobedience was retroactively applied to creation.[24] Animals were punished millions of years ago based on humans' disobedience, which was yet to come. However, this kind of explanation reflects a very bizarre form of justice. It cannot be reconciled with biblical revelation.

Even if we grant the assumption that the Genesis narrative is a myth, we must consider it inspired and make some sense out of its depiction. When we confess that animal suffering was still there before humans' disobedience, a parallel becomes visible with the gospel of Christ. Like Christ is up against the forces of evil to realize God's plan with creation, the first humans have to go up against the forces of evil to realize God's plan with creation. In both events, there is room for a redemptive function. So, we must be careful projecting future promises of animal peace in texts such as Isaiah 11 and Isaiah 65 back into the biblical creation story of Genesis 1–2. This also becomes visible for those who compare the descriptions of the new heaven and the new earth in Revelation 21–22 with the original creation in Genesis 1–2. Darkness, night, and sea, which we know from Genesis 1, can no longer be found in the descriptions of the new creation of Revelation. The future means no return to the beginning. From this perspective, we have to be careful to conclude that it was the same at the beginning as at the end. The garden of Eden is not yet the new earth. There are parallels but also contrasts between the initial state and the end state. Humanity is from the beginning the instrument through

---

24. Without references mentioned in Boyd, *Satan*, 255n33.

which God gives salvation to all creation. That the animal kingdom can also become a plaything of the powers of evil is shown by the incident of Jesus and the pigs in the land of the Gadarenes (Matt 8:28–31).

The British writer C. S. Lewis (1898–1963) asks if humans, during their first coming in this world, did have to accomplish a saving mission in the animal kingdom:

> It may have been one of man's functions to restore peace to the animal kingdom, and if he had not joined the enemy he might have succeeded in doing so to an extent now hardly imaginable.[25]

That we can hardly imagine the result, like Lewis mentions, is entirely accurate. The digestive systems of meat eaters differ considerably from those of herbivores. Whoever deals with the question of how strong animals have changed due to human disobedience should not be limited to just teeth. Many meat eaters' physique and instinct are so complicated that it is hard to deny that an intelligent Designer is responsible. The lion is characterized by an accurate hunting instinct, immense muscle strength, and a digestive system that ideally consumes raw meat.

Another example is the venom of the snake, consisting of very complex chemical reactions. It can effectively paralyze the other's nervous system. Many other animals can be added to this list. They are too complicated to be seen as the "deformation" of a reasonable creature in the beginning. After all, that would be the same as a classic car "deforming" into an airplane. Therefore, many orthodox Jews and Christians will not accept that these intelligent designs are attributed to evil forces.

These complicated animals seem to be made in this way from the beginning. Otherwise, evil would be as mighty and exalted as God. It is unacceptable for Jews and Christians that such complicated and dangerous animals would arise without God's intervention. The Bible doesn't state anywhere that evil made all these dangerous animals. Only God is called the Creator of life. Therefore, the chemist Jonathan Sarfati (b. 1964) says that in Genesis 1, God designed all animals already as meat eaters and/or herbivores, but the meat eaters only really ate meat after Genesis 3:

> God foreknew the Fall, so He programmed creatures with the information for design features for attack and defence that they would need in a cursed world. This information was "switched on" at the Fall.[26]

---

25. Lewis, *Problem of Pain*, 140.
26. Sarfati, *Refuting Evolution*, 90.

The difficulty with this idea is that meat eaters then needed different digestion and physique to function optimally. Would God have created them multifunctional with positive or negative development possibilities?

Another option is that God made the gruesome and wild animals after Genesis 3. Then again, we must assume that God is the Creator of horrific animals. However, Genesis only witnesses one moment when God made all creatures.

4.3.3 Descent from Harmony to Suffering

From Herbivores to Carnivores

In Genesis, we read that God gives humans the food of "every plant yielding seed . . . and every tree with seed in its fruit" (Gen 1:29), and to all the animals of the earth and in the sky "every green plant for food" (v. 30). So, humans are not instructed to consume the meat of fish, birds, or terrestrial animals. An interesting exception to this interpretation comes from the French theologian and reformer John Calvin (1509–64). He summarizes Genesis 1:29–30 as a piece of advice and sees few problems when humans consume the meat of animals from the beginning.[27] However, most biblical scholars accept God's food ordinances in Genesis 1:29–30 as normative. The life of another should not be ended to feed someone else. We'll come back to that in chapter 13, on vegetarianism.

This pattern of harmony in the animal kingdom appears several times in the Bible. In Genesis 2 we see that God brings all animals to Adam to give names to them. There is no mention of any suppression of wild animals or predators. Later, the animals arrive at Noah's ark without any struggle:

> Of clean animals, and of animals that are not clean, and of birds, and of everything that creeps on the ground, two and two, male and female, went into the ark with Noah, as God had commanded Noah. (Gen 7:8–9)

Also this time we do not get the impression that Noah needs to protect the animals from each other. Only in Genesis 9:3, we hear for the first time that God allows humans to consume animals. Therefore, the food instructions in Genesis 1:29–30 suggest that the animals in Genesis 1–2 were not yet in conflict with each other, but this tendency was possible.

---

27. Calvin, *Genesis*, 99–100.

In the beginning, there was harmony between the creatures in God's original creation. All were considered one big family and ate vegetarian food. Just as humanity had the choice to eat from the tree of knowledge and turn against God's commandment, animals also had the option to turn against God. God gave all living creatures freedom. This becomes visible in Genesis 3 when the serpent has its questions about God. The serpent is the superior of the "animals of the field" or the "wild animals" (Gen 3:1, cf. chapter 3.2.2). Then things go wrong. Instead of extending God's blessing to the whole creation and subjecting the field, humans follow the serpent and subject themselves to this more subtle animal of wild creatures.

At the same time, God's goodness becomes visible to humans. God promises that evil will ultimately be overcome. The new heaven and the new earth which God has in mind for creation will not be lost. Humanity will be placed in a plan of salvation that will culminate in this final, glorious future condition. That is the moment when God's plan is accomplished. The situation in Genesis 1–2 is, therefore, seen as a good start. However, it is not the "Edenic paradise" we often want it to be. According to the church father Irenaeus of Lyon (~134–202), God has designed a creation in which humans will develop and freely show God's character on earth. Like young children or young Christians, they start with milk and grow (cf. 1 Cor 3:2):

> Man, a created and organized being, is rendered after the image and the likeness of the uncreated God—the Father planning everything well and giving his commands, the Son carrying these into execution and performing the work of creating, and the Spirit nourishing and increasing [what is made]. Still, man makes progress day by day and ascends towards the perfect, approximating the uncreated One. For the Uncreated, that is God, is perfect. Now it was necessary that man should in the first instance be created, and having been created, should receive growth; and having received growth, should be strengthened; and having been strengthened, should abound; and having abounded, should recover [from the disease of sin]; and having recovered, should be glorified; and being glorified, should see his Lord.[28]

The development of free will and human personality is a product of challenge and response. So, God is not a puppet master of humans

---

28. Irenaeus of Lyon, *Adversus Haereses*, IV.38.3.

or creation. With the act of creation and in history, God chooses to be dependent on creaturely conditions for the manifestation of the Son. This choice for freedom makes it possible to develop moral characters and virtues like courage, patience, and compassion. So, the actualization and fulfillment of human perfection are located not in the beginning but in the end. The temporal orientation is not towards the past but towards the future. The first original creation in its state of goodness should not be idealized. Never in the Bible is this the case. God does not romanticize it, and neither should we.

The English philosopher and theologian John Hick (1922–2012) writes in imitation of this idea that there would also have been a conscious distance between God and creation in the beginning.[29] However, this assumption is not necessary. Humans' choice to eat from the "tree of the knowledge" is sufficient to create openness for disorder and create a distance between humans and God. So, in the beginning, there is peace between nonhuman and human creatures who choose freely. This means that there are also antithetical potentials in nature. Water which refreshes and quenches thirst can also be drowning or breathable. A medicine that relieves suffering can cause crippling psychological addiction. The sun, which gives light and life, can parch fields and bring famine.

Freedom to Choose

In the beginning, animal suffering and human suffering are not found on earth. The only exception is that animals die, and humans can eat from the tree of life. However, these mortal humans and mortal animals do not kill each other. It is only in Genesis 9:2 that God states that animals get awe and fear of people.

These considerations lead to the conclusion that decay in the animal kingdom has been a gradual event. This moves from the disobedience of the serpent and the humans in Genesis 3 to the corruption of all earth in Genesis 6. In the hands of good humans, nature receives a blessing. In the grip of evil humans, it becomes a dark death weapon. In Genesis 1–3, it appears that the power of evil and death is asserted to the lives of humans through the serpent. This reveals that evil forces can influence humans and all creatures and make them hostile to God's purpose.

---

29. Hick, *Evil*. See also for Moltmann's idea of the *zimzum*: Hausoul, "Evaluation," 137–59.

This theological claim of evil powers is also found in Christian theology, which states that no explanation can be satisfactory unless it includes some appeal to such powers.[30] From this perspective, the famous American systematic theologian Gregory Boyd (b. 1957) writes,

> Jesus never attributed genetic mutations, deformities, blindness, deafness, leprosy, blood diseases, fevers, falling towers, barren trees, life-threatening storms, or death itself to God's providence or to "natural" features of his Father's creation. He consistently identifies them as evidence of the reign of the kingdom of darkness here on earth, a kingdom that his whole ministry was intended to destroy.[31]

These sinister forces, which are mentioned by Jesus and the apostles, are also present in the Old Testament.[32] They influence the free will of the serpent, which controls the free will of humans, and makes nature a war zone. God keeps the serpent accountable for that act. The animal has freely chosen for evil, just as humans decided to do. This responsibility of animals is also affirmed elsewhere in the Bible (e.g., Gen 9:5; Exod 21:28–29). Nowhere does it say that an animal is "ignorant."

From Genesis 3 onwards, animal and human sufferings on earth are increasing. Anyone who reflects on the suffering in the animal world discovers that humans also cause a large part of this suffering. In their brutality, people choose to mistreat or neglect animals. People don't want to know anything more about a protective and guarding role like God gave humanity in Genesis 2:15. Although humans can be a healing presence in this corrupt world and teach animals good things, also violence is also taught. Dogs are beaten and kicked, cats are left to their fate, unwanted animals are released into the wild, and livestock are herded for more significant economic gain. Difficulties arise in the animal world due to environmental pollution and the misuse of the earth's resources. Entire forests are wiped away from the globe without attention being paid

---

30. Cf. Boyd, *Satan*, 284; Kelly, "Problem of Evil," 29–42; Levenson, *Creation*. For discussion and confrontation, see Swinburne, *Existence of God*, 202–21; Mundia, *Existence of the Devil*, 384–93.

31. Boyd, *Satan*, 292.

32. See Luke 4:6; John 12:31; 14:30; 16:11; Acts 26:18; 2 Cor 4:4; Eph 2:2; 1 Pet 5:8; 1 John 5:19; Rev 12:9. These insights of the NT writers could be developed from the OT warfare of the Leviathan and Rahab against God (Job 9:13; 26:12–13; 41:1–34; Ps 74:14; 89:9–10; Isa 27:1), and the raging waters of chaos, whose defiance threatened creation (Job 7:12; 38:6–11; Ps 74:10–17; 104:7–9; Prov 8:27–29).

to the habitats of numerous animals in them. God's task to humans to manage their creation is trampled underfoot in all of this. Especially for those who know themselves to be addressed by the God of the Bible, the challenge is to reflect God's good nature in dealing with animals in this fallen creation.

From the very beginning, creation looks forward to the moment when evil is subdued within it. Therefore, at the beginning of the last biblical book, the praise of "every creature in heaven and on earth and under the earth and in the sea, and all that is in them," sounds, "To the one seated on the throne and to the Lamb be blessing and honor and glory and might forever and ever!" (Rev 5:13). This biblical testimony shows that God is the Creator and Redeemer, who does not forsake the work of his hands and completes his plan with creation. The statement "it is good" will then prove to be truly good through the redeeming work of Christ. It will be able to banish the powers of death, suffering, pain, and sorrow from creation. Therefore, the central question of the biblical writers is not when evil came into creation. Their focus is on how humans can bring life's blessing to earth in the light of God.

5

Humans and Animals

5.1 ANIMAL SKINS FOR THE FIRST HUMANS

5.1.1 A Pessimistic and Optimistic Approach

Animal Skins as a Sign of Death

A FIRST BIBLICAL MENTION, which may indicate that an animal is dying, can be found at the end of Genesis 3. After the first people received the official names Adam and Eve, God made clothes for them out of skins: "The Lord God made garments of skins for man and for his wife, and clothed them" (Gen 3:21). From where did these skins come?

Often interpreters assume that God specially slaughtered animals to provide Adam and Eve with these sheets.[1] But that is not the only explanation we find in Judeo-Christian history. According to a Jewish interpretation, God made the clothes out of snakeskin:

> God, the Lord, prepared for Adam and his wife honorable clothes
> from the skin of the serpent, which he had shed from him.[2]

This also fits the explanation that the clothes for Adam and Eve were made of the skin of the great sea monster Leviathan, which we already

---

1. Keil and Delitzsch, *Pentateuch*, 106.
2. Bar Nafha and Buber, *Midrash Tehillim*, Ps 92:1.

mentioned in chapter 2. Jewish literature praises this animal as a creature of great glory (cf. Job 41:17).³

Another explanation is that they were goatskins. The presence of goatskins on the tabernacle as a top layer would remind us of this (Exod 26:7). Those who see the sheets as a reference to the messianic salvation prefer to think of lambskins. After all, the Messiah "was oppressed, and he was afflicted, yet he did not open his mouth; like a lamb that is led to the slaughter, and like a sheep that before its shearers is silent, so he did not open his mouth" (Isa 53:7).

God had to kill animals in all these cases to provide humans with clothes. For some, this killing went way too far. They could not imagine that God would do such a thing. According to them, God created animal skins out of nothing. But this explanation is not apparent since there is no mention of "creating" (בָּרָא, bārā') animal skins, but of "making" (עָשָׂה, 'āshāh). Animals had to die to "make" sheets. These animal skins had to remind Adam and Eve of the profound consequences of their choice for disobedience. Because of their transgression, death took hold of humanity, and great mischief came to earth.

Augustine of Hippo (354–430) and Adamantius Origenes (~184–253) thought that the animal skins symbolically referred to mortality. Mortality had become an unavoidable part of humankind after disobedience. This testimony was later adopted by many.⁴ At the same time, it was emphasized that Christ would replace these animal skins in the future. In the completion, white clothes would replace the animal skins. Those white clothes referred to the eternal light. Christians were traditionally called to be baptized in white garments.⁵ Augustine then added the call to come to the baptismal service in goatskins or sheepskins, in memory of Genesis 3 and humanity's sinful brokenness.⁶

God's Priestly Garments

Another interpretation did not primarily relate the clothes of the first people to brokenness. It opted for a more positive understanding and stated that the clothes that Adam and Eve received were the same as those

---

3. Neusner, *B. Baba Batra*, 74b.
4. Calvin, *Genesis*, I.182.
5. Jerome, *Letters and Select Works*, 64.19.
6. Augustine of Hippo, *Sermons*, 216.10; Augustine of Hippo, *City of God*, XV.20.4.

worn by the high priest in Israel. The American biblical scholar Gregory Beale (b. 1949) mentions the Jewish view that the first people received the high priestly clothes that Satan lost in his rebellion against God.[7] That thought is connected with the obscure words in Ezekiel:

> You were in Eden, the garden of God; every precious stone was your covering, carnelian, chrysolite, and moonstone, beryl, onyx, and jasper, sapphire, turquoise, and emerald; and worked in gold were your settings and your engravings. On the day that you were created they were prepared. With an anointed cherub as guardian I placed you; you were on the holy mountain of God; you walked among the stones of fire. (Ezek 28:13–14)

The gemstones that Ezekiel mentions are very similar to the gems on the breastplate of the high priest. Interpreters see in these words an indication that Satan used to have a high priestly function. After his fall, Satan lost these clothes and they were given to Adam and Eve.

In this explanation, the focus is not on the "sheets" or "skin." The clothes only indicate that they are natural clothes that the first people receive. The emphasis is on the priestly glory with which God clothes the first people. The Jewish book of Jubilees also discusses this idea of priesthood and mentions a sacrificial service by Adam:

> God made them clothes from sheets of skin and clothed them with them. Then he sent them out of the garden of Eden. On the day when Adam was sent out of the garden, he offered a fragrant sacrifice, incense, galbanum, embalming resin and spices in the morning, at the rising of the sun. (Jub. 3:26–27)

These descriptions are reminiscent of the incense that Moses placed in the meeting tent before the covenant text, where God met him (Exod 30:34–36).

5.1.2 Nudity or Clothes?

Priesthood in the Garden

Why did Adam and Eve receive these priestly clothes only after their disobedience? From various elements in the story of creation, it can

---

7. Beale, "Colossians," 867.

be concluded that the garden of Eden was the prototype of God's later temples on earth.[8] There are the following parallels to consider:

1. God walks in Eden and wants to live in the temple (Gen 3:8; Exod 25:8).
2. People should guard both the garden and the temple (Gen 2:15; Num 3:7–8; 8:25–26).
3. Cherubs preserve the inaccessible garden and the virtually inaccessible ark of the covenant (Gen 3:24; Exod 25:18–20).
4. The shape of the tree of the holy lampstand evokes associations with the tree of life (Gen 2:9; Exod 25:31–40).
5. The garden entrance and the tabernacle entrance are in the east (Gen 3:24; Exod 27:9–16).
6. Images of plants and flowers in the temple remind us of the garden (Gen 2:8–9; 1 Kgs 6:18, 29, 32, 35; 7:18–20).
7. A river rises in Eden and in the temple that the prophets describe (Gen 2:10; Ezek 47:1–12; Zech 14:8–9).

It is plausible to conceive the garden as a prototype of God's future cosmic temple from these biblical lines. That future cosmic temple would have been realized when humanity had subdued the earth. So, the garden was the place of honor where humans served as the first priest in God's presence.

Nakedness

After God placed Adam in the garden and ordered him to cultivate and guard the garden, all the animals were brought to him to give them names. In this process, Adam acknowledges that he is alone. God then makes the woman out of the side of man. After man's song of praise to his wife, we learn that the first man and woman are naked: "And the man and his wife were both naked, and were not ashamed" (Gen 2:25).

Although people are not ashamed of one another, the Bible nowhere values nudity as positive (cf. Gen 9:22–23; Lev 18:6–10; 20:17–19). With uncovered parts of shame a human may not appear before God (Exod

---

8. Hausoul, *New Heaven*, 172–73; Beale, *New Testament*, 617–20; Beale, *Temple*, 66–80, 182–83; Kline, *Kingdom*, 31–32, 54–56; Wenham, *Genesis 1–15*, 61. For a critical reflection see Block, "Eden," 1–30.

20:26; cf. 28:42–43). This is also the attitude people take toward God after they have eaten from the tree of knowledge. Adam and Eve realize that it is not suitable for a person to appear naked before God. Thus, they are neither cold nor uncomfortable with each other (Gen 3:8). Adam says to God, "I heard the sound of you in the garden, and I was afraid, because I was naked; and I hid myself" (v. 10). The presence of God is the reason for covering up. Humans realize that they are not allowed to appear uncovered before God. Insight has been gained between what is right and what is wrong.

From this background, it is unclear whether God wanted human nudity to last *forever*, from Genesis 2:25 onwards. Genesis 2:25 is the only verse in Genesis 2–3 that describes the condition of humans and reveals something that will later be interpreted differently. Just as Genesis 2:4–6 is an introduction to God's choice to create human beings, Genesis 2:25 may be an introduction to God's decision to give clothes to humans. Readers may already be beginning to wonder about clothing when they look at God's instructions around food in the passage in between (Gen 2:7–24). Is the care for clothing not also related to the care for food (2:9, 16–17)?

In Jewish tradition, this tension is resolved by assuming that the first people wore clothes. Their clothes were luminous, consisted of light, or were made of various gemstones from Eden. After banishment from the garden, they had to leave it, and the clothing of light (אוֹר, 'ôr) was replaced by the clothing of sheets (עוֹר, 'ôr).[9] A disadvantage of this tradition is that the story of creation nowhere mentions that the first people wore clothes. Are there other solutions to being naked?

The Relationship between Genesis 2 and 3

Although many intuitively assume a period of time between Genesis 2 and 3, the text presents itself as continued story. It is not easy to read Genesis 2 and 3 as this constant moment in time. We feel it would be too much if giving all the animals names, the creation of the woman, and the disobedience and consequences in Genesis 3 took place right after each other. Then the first people would have experienced an intense first moment. Very intense I would say.

---

9. Freedman and Maurice, *Midrash Rabbah: Genesis*, 20.12; Hyrkanos, *Pirkê de Rabbi Eliezer*, 14.20.

Humans and Animals

In Jewish tradition, we find the idea that Genesis 2 and 3 happened on the same day. It is even claimed that the first day of humanity consisted of twelve hours. According to this Jewish tradition, the following events occurred in these twelve hours:

a. 1st Hour: Collection of earth dust.

b. 2nd Hour: Kneading from earth to person.

c. 3rd Hour: Kneading of limbs.

d. 4th Hour: Donating the spirit of life to the person.

e. 5th Hour: Human being stands upright.

f. 6th Hour: Human gives names to animals.

g. 7th Hour: Woman is made of man.

h. 8th Hour: Man has fellowship with his wife and receives twins: Cain and his sister.

i. 9th Hour: Man is ordered not to eat from the tree of knowledge.

j. 10th Hour: Man eats from the tree of knowledge.

k. 11th Hour: God addresses humans on their disobedience.

l. 12th Hour: Humans are banished from the garden.[10]

Christian theologians also stated that Eve was created at the sixth hour of the sixth day and sinned immediately. Therefore, God expelled them from paradise at the seventh hour.[11] Of course these times were chosen as parallel to Christ's death on the cross and the darkness from six to nine o'clock (Matt 27:45–51).

Although we can ask really serious questions about this detailed legendary timetable, we discover that it is no problem for Jewish tradition to link Genesis 2 and 3 temporally. That is our point. There is no time difference in the text of Genesis 2–3. It would also be obscure whether there would be time between creating the man and the woman (Gen 2:1–24) and giving proper names to each other (3:17–21). That would be a strange thing to happen.

Besides, speaking of the "nudity" (עָרֹם, *'ārom*) of the humans in Genesis 2:25 and the more "crafty" (עָרוּם, *'ārûm*) serpent in Genesis 3:1

---

10. Neusner, *B. Yebamot*, 62a. Cf. Neusner, "T. Sanhedrin," 38b; Hyrkanos, *Pirkê de Rabbi Eliezer*, 11; Kara, *Yalkut Shimoni*, Gn49.

11. Cf. Le Goff, *Medieval Civilization*, 176.

creates a smooth transition. It is underpinned by equality in theme and place. So, we agree with the observation of the famous German Old Testament scholar Claus Westermann:

> The expulsion from the garden presumes logically a period during which the man and the woman sojourned in the garden. However, the narrator's intention is not to describe two successive phases or situations, but to present an event which caused the present state of human reality to be what it is.[12]

The snake doesn't appear on stage "after a long time." Evil does not want to waste time and breaks in after God has made the woman. From this perspective, the serpent interrupts the process in which God exemplarily intends to provide food, intimacy, and clothing for humans (cf. Exod 21:10). The garments would then be received by humans as the next step. Between the demand for intimacy with a fellow human being and the yet-to-be-delivered need for clothing, the snake penetrates the story. As God recognized in Genesis 2 that it was not right for a human to remain alone, biblical readers can acknowledge that it is also not right to appear naked before God.

After the human disobedience God does not allow himself to be confused in this process towards humans. He does not allow himself to be taken away from his intentions. Although people have made clothes for themselves out of fig leaves to cover their shame, God realizes they are insufficient. He makes new clothes for the man and woman out of skins.

5.1.3 Clothes Make the New Self

Suppose the clothes that Adam and Eve received are a positive reference to priestly service. In that case, we realize that human disobedience does not undo God's desires with creation. The commandment to humanity in Genesis 1:28 will continue, even after the incident in Genesis 3 (cf. Gen 9:1). There is a remarkable parallel with Genesis 1:26 ("Let us make humankind in our image, according to our likeness") and the divine plural in Genesis 3:22, "See, the man has become like one of us, knowing good and evil." In Genesis 1, according to God's likeness, humans are positively connected with the glory to manage the earth. In Genesis 3, according to God's likeness, humans are negatively associated with knowing good and

---

12. Westermann, *Genesis 1–11*, 235.

evil. After this event God accepts humanity and continues his commission. God clothes man and woman.

According to a Jewish explanation of Genesis, Adam and Eve's clothes depicted all land animals and birds. They remind them of God's command to rule over these animals. These clothes were passed on to the descendants. They ended up in the hands of Methuselah and Noah. Ham stole Noah's clothes and gave them to his son Cush, who hid them for years and then gave them to Nimrod. Nimrod wore these clothes and declared himself "mighty hunter" over the animal world (Gen 10:9). However, Nimrod was defeated by Esau, who took the clothes for himself. These were the most precious clothes of Esau that Jacob put on when he deceived his father Isaac (27:15).[13]

Although this legend does not contain any factual material, it points to the importance of Adam and Eve's clothes and their relationship to the mission of creation (Gen 1:28). The new garments are within a priestly focus concerning life in the ultimate victory. That victory is what God promised in Genesis 3:15. Despite all evil, God will complete creation. There will be a creation in which evil is banished, and God feels at home. The last Adam will realize this new creation. He calls his followers to lay off "the old self with its practices" and to attract "the new self" (Col 3:9–10).

At an early age, Christians associated the change of costume in Colossians 3 with the change of outfit in Genesis 3. They realized that both texts foresaw the function that the righteous would receive as eternal priests in the future garden city: "The throne of God and of the Lamb will be in it, and his servants will worship him" (Rev 22:3b). These future blessings are even more understandable when we realize that in ancient times the reception of a new garment was related to the reception of a new social position, as happened to the patriarch Joseph (cf. Gen 41:42). That's how Paul writes:

> As many of you as were baptized into Christ have clothed yourselves with Christ. . . . And if you belong to Christ, then you are Abraham's offspring, heirs according to the promise. (Gal 3:27, 29)

In this verse, being clothed stands with being a social heir. From this biblical revelation, the clothes in Genesis 3 offer more than protection against the cold. The clothes make Adam and Eve heirs of future

---

13. Zlotowitz, *Bereishis 1:1—28:9*, 136n1.

creation. They refer to the future when they will be clothed with Jesus Christ, which characterizes the righteous. Therefore, on the last page of the Bible, we read, "Blessed are those who wash their robes, so that they will have the right to the tree of life and may enter the city by the gates" (Rev 22:14).[14]

5.2 HUMANS USE ANIMALS

5.2.1 Animals and Earlier Life

Domestic Animals as Prosperity

In ancient times, living focused firmly on agriculture. A large part of the population was dependent for its livelihood on its own arable and livestock farming. Domesticated animals were seen as a part of family life with humans under one roof. This created a great connection between people and animals. Both ate from the same land and drank from the same well. The cow, the sheep, the goat, the chicken,[15] and the donkey were friends to humans. They helped in daily work. Animals offered milk or eggs as food to humans and provided raw materials such as manure, wool, skin, hair, and bone. In Israel, poor farmers had at least one ox for work on the land. In exchange for that favor of the animal, people took responsible care of it.

Those who wanted the domesticated animals to multiply had to provide more food. Often, however, the land yield was too low to meet the desire for high fertility. From that background, donating an animal as a sacrifice to God had a high cost for a less prosperous family. For those who were wealthier, it was easier. Fewer cattle meant then less food. Abraham, Lot, Isaac, Jacob, Jethro, Job, and Nabal were economically prosperous people. Abraham possessed sheep, goats, oxen, donkeys, and camels (Gen 12:16; cf. 20:14; 24:35). Lot owned sheep, goats, and oxen (13:5). "The land could not support both of them living together; for their possessions were so great that they could not live together" (v. 6). Isaac "had possessions

---

14. Instead of the common "who wash their clothes," about fifteen Greek manuscripts read "who do his commandments." Because this last reading was chosen for the production of the *Textus Receptus* (1516), we can still find it in translations which rely on it. Interpreters agree that the common variant is correct.

15. Although there are no chickens mentioned in the Bible, we know from ancient Israeli iconographic images (Iron Age II) that they occurred in Israel. In 1 Kings 4:23 the ESV mentions young chickens ("fowl"). Also the cat is missing in the Bible.

of flocks and herds, and a great household, so that the Philistines envied him" (26:14). Jacob's property "grew exceedingly rich, and had large flocks, and male and female servants, and camels and donkeys" (30:43; cf. 32:6). Jethro, the Midianite priest and father-in-law of Moses, owned several sheep and goats (Exod 2:16; 3:1). Job "had seven thousand sheep, three thousand camels, five hundred yoke of oxen, five hundred donkeys, and very many servants; so that this man was the greatest of all the people of the east" (Job 1:3). Nabal "was very rich; he had three thousand sheep and a thousand goats" (1 Sam 25:2). In the eyes of their contemporaries, all these men had succeeded in building up a fertile herd of cattle, which could be maintained from a blessed land yield.

Especially in times of crop failures, the herd could shrink considerably. There was then a danger that the wealth would be taken entirely out of a person's hands. This imminent danger made people reluctant to slaughter their animals. The meat was usually eaten only on essential occasions or at specific ceremonies, such as weddings or sacrificial celebrations. Those who ate meat every day were seen as rich people who could party daily. He could afford to isolate animals from the herd and fatten them up. King Solomon was thus able to present a festive treat on the table every day:

> Solomon sent word to Hiram, saying, "You know that my father David could not build a house for the name of the Lord his God because of the warfare with which his enemies surrounded him, until the Lord put them under the soles of his feet." (1 Kgs 5:2–3)

The prophet Amos later points out that this prosperity is also present on a small scale among the leaders of Israel, "who lie on beds of ivory, and lounge on their couches, and eat lambs from the flock" (Amos 6:4). Solomon and many Israelites realized that this great prosperity was an undeserved blessing from God. "Solomon offered as sacrifices of wellbeing to the Lord twenty-two thousand oxen and one hundred twenty thousand sheep. So the king and all the people of Israel dedicated the house of the Lord" (1 Kgs 8:63). That this kind of sacrifice cost the Israelites something is clear from the above background. Giving an ox to God was the same as providing a car to God (and I know there is still a huge difference between giving God an American Tesla or a German BMW). But anyway, you didn't do that quickly out of automatism. It is therefore impressive that Nehemiah, in a time of poverty, gave the population a rich feast every day:

> Moreover there were at my table one hundred fifty people, Jews and officials, besides those who came to us from the nations around us. Now that which was prepared for one day was one ox and six choice sheep; also fowls were prepared for me, and every ten days skins of wine in abundance. (Neh 5:17–18a)

Animals were precious. Therefore, anyone who mistreated his animals could be compared to a fool who sawed off the branch on which he sat. He caused himself and his family considerable damage. Whoever was wise gave his animal enough to drink, food, and rest. He did not rush it too much and was alert that it did not get hurt. You were just as good with your animals as today's man is towards his car (anyway: BMW or Tesla)—those who weren't were robbing themselves. We find a reasonably familiar saying in Proverbs: "The righteous know the needs of their animals, but the mercy of the wicked is cruel" (Prov 12:10). However, the above background clarifies why there are relatively few other biblical rules concerning animals' treatment.

Wild Animals

Nowadays, we see animals mainly as temporary instruments that provide us with food or entertainment. As support in our daily work, animals have become almost redundant in our culture. An exception to this is the dog that guards our house when we are absent. If you are resourceful, you will discover more possibilities in which animals support daily work. In my garden, for example, five fish swim in a large, deep, transparent water tank. They get enough to eat through the rainwater and clean the water of algae. This, in turn, ensures that our three chickens can drink clean water directly from this water basin. I also make grateful use of two guinea pigs in my beautiful Flemish garden. They walk freely around and help me mow the grass in the morning and evening. Since 2016, my lawnmower has stayed in the barn. In my residential area, however, it remains the fact that most of the animals are on the plate.

Opposite the domesticated animals in the Bible are the wild animals, which were a threat to humans and their households. They were dangerous competitors and were found in all sorts of species because of the varied climate. These included dangerous bears, roaring lions, poisonous snakes, and many other wild animals, which easily appeared in peripheral areas to make their victims there. This led to frequent hunting in the Middle East. The Assyrians were mostly known for this, as the endless reliefs about lion hunting in the British Museum of London show. Assyrian gamekeepers even had expensive lions imported from Africa because they were more aggressive than lions in the Middle East. The Old Testament nowhere speaks extensively about hunting. However, we do learn that Solomon offered "deer, gazelles, roebucks" on the table daily (1 Kgs 4:23). There must have been a lot of hunting to satisfy this kind of daily menu.

In addition to the danger of the large wild animals, there was the danger of the small wild animals. Grasshoppers could destroy an entire crop and eat a land bare. Famine and other calamities threatened humans and animals. Both shared the same fate. For example, Joel mentions that not only the land dwellers but also the cattle suffered terribly from a plague of locusts that devastated the land harvest and a great drought that followed:

> Is not the food cut off before our eyes, joy and gladness from the house of our God? The seed shrivels under the clods, the storehouses are desolate; the granaries are ruined because the grain has failed. How the animals groan! The herds of cattle wander about because there is no pasture for them; even the flocks of sheep are dazed. To you, O Lord, I cry. For fire has devoured the pastures of the wilderness, and flames have burned all the trees of the field. Even the wild animals cry to you because the watercourses are dried up, and fire has devoured the pastures of the wilderness. (Joel 1:16–20)

In these poetic words, it becomes clear that the people and the animals, yes, even the wild animals of the field, cried out in the hope that God was feeding them.

5.2.2 Animals and the Old Rulers

In ancient times, rulers liked to show how significant their impact on earth was. The kings of Mesopotamia built extensive royal gardens and large parks. In them, they offered to the public numerous plant and animal species that they had gloriously collected.

The Assyrian prince Tiglath-Pileser (r. 1114–1076 BC) built an animal park where specific animals and valuable trees could be found. His later successor, Ashurnasirpal II (r. 883–859 BC), did the same near the Assyrian town of Nimrud. To provide the animals in this area with sufficient drinking water, he built an impressive water supply. Numerous reliefs by the Assyrian king Sargon II (r. 721–725 BC) are also known; depicting various trees and animals in the parks he built. His successor, Sennacherib (r. 704–681 BC), chose to create several gardens near the town of Nineveh.[16]

Another famous example are the legendary hanging gardens of Babylon, which are counted among the world's seven classic wonders. These gardens are said to have been built by King Nebuchadnezzar II (r. 605–562 BC).[17] Various trees, shrubs, and flowers were planted on the walls built by Nebuchadnezzar. They would serve to cheer up his depressed wife, Amytes. Amytes came from the natural regions outside cultural Babylon and was often homesick for her former surroundings.

Such animal and tree parks remained present in later cultures. After the Babylonians, it were the Persians, who dedicated themselves to their construction. For all these rulers, the permanent gardens testified to their greatness. They convinced people that the king had enough power and insight to keep the land fertile. If he could take care of so many unique plants and animals, he could take care of his people. At the same time, these gardens and parks also served for hunting. In the fifth century BC, the Persians built complete game parks in which they imitated the natural habitat of the animals. In these parks, wild boars and other wild animals were released to hunt. When the king wanted to serve his guests a dinner with delicious meat dishes, he and his guests in the wildlife park chose and shot the meat pieces for this purpose. Whoever was able to overpower the wild animals showed that he was brave. With such qualities present in their king, people had nothing to fear. A disadvantage, however, was that the animals were given too little time to conceive. It didn't take too long until they were extinct and the area was neglected as a silent moment of glory.

Also, in spectacles, the kings liked to show off the animals they had subdued. An example is the Egyptian king Ptolemy II Philadelphus (309–246 BC). He organized a fabulous spectacle in the Egyptian town of Alexandria in the year 274 BC: a festive procession organized in honor of his father, Ptolemy I Soter (367–283 BC), and the Greek god of wine and joy, Dionysus. Numerous inhabitants of his empire received

---

16. Gleason, "Gardens," 383–85.
17. Wiseman, "Mesopotamian Gardens," 137–44.

an opportunity to enjoy the parade's exceptional animals' great splendor. Twenty-six elephants led the way. They were followed by different kinds of goats, antelopes, ostriches, wild donkeys, and camels. The camels carried precious spices with them. After these animals followed the hunters; they took part in the parade with gilded hunting skewers and accompanied Indian dogs. Behind the hunters were men with rods from which live peacocks, pheasants, and other birds hung. This group was followed by fat oxen, a big white bear, fourteen leopards, sixteen panthers, several lynxes, a giraffe, a rhino, and twenty-four lions.[18]

5.2.3 Animals in the later Roman Empire and Europe

Demonstrating Power by Animals

The Romans adopted the idea that the power of the ruler was expressed through victory over animals. It happened that the amazement at the parades quickly gave way to sensationalism. In 167 BC, the Romans devised condemnation to death by beasts (*damnatio ad bestias*). Dismembered soldiers were publicly torn apart by lions. After all, it was written in the Jewish books that God used wild animals to punish humans (Lev 26:22; Deut 32:24).

Many felt that animal fighting should also be part of popular entertainment. For many Romans, these spectacular shows were a small positive point of light in their existence. The rulers could use them to increase their popularity. Animals were forced to fight each other in bullrings and were killed for entertainment. Rulers of the wilderness, such as elephants, lions, and tigers, were hunted and shot in the large stadium *Circus Maximus* in Rome. Yet, not everyone in the Senate was happy with this mass slaughter. Was it because they saw with pain in their hearts how bad it would be for the environment if they continued like this? At night did they lie awake in bed with tears rolling down their cheeks because of the great suffering they inflicted on the animals? Of course not! Their anger had little to do with ecology or animal welfare. The debate was all about the money. Were such shows a benefit for their politico-economically position? Because of the trade of animals, the inhabitants of Carthage could earn a lot of money and get to the economic and military top. The

---

18. Athenaeus of Naucratis, *Deipnosophists*, V.22–32.

debates about this were quickly ended because of the favor of the people. Everything had to indicate that Roman power knew no limits.

In 61 BC, the consul Lucius Domitius Ahenobarbus had a hundred bears killed by his hunters just in order to exalt himself. In 58 BC, the Roman politician Marcus Aemilius Scaurus had the idea to release and shoot a hundred leopards, panthers, and lions in an arena. On this occasion, a hippopotamus and five crocodiles were for the first time in Roman history shown to the public. In 55 BC, Gnaeus Pompey Magnus (106–48 BC) offered a gigantic spectacle. During gladiatorial fights, twenty elephants, six hundred lions, four hundred and ten leopards, one lynx, and numerous monkeys were killed. Until the opening of the Coliseum in AD 80, no one would dare surpass this number. Even the famous general and politician Julius Caesar (~100–44 BC) and the first emperor Caesar Augustus (63 BC–AD 14) would not do so. Julius Caesar turned up his shows with many elephants, four hundred lions, some Thessalian bulls, and one giraffe. Emperor Augustus killed three thousand five hundred wild animals, including lions, leopards, bears, and crocodiles. Emperor Caligula (AD 12–41) held a show with four hundred bears and four hundred African wild animals, and emperor Nero (AD 37–68) had four hundred bears and three hundred lions killed in one day—and then they call animals "beasts."

Large Increase

The later emperor Titus (r. AD 79–81) did not hesitate to organize a spectacle show of no less than a hundred days during the inauguration in the Coliseum (AD 80). In this show, more than nine thousand domestic and wild animals were slaughtered. This included fights between cranes and between elephants. Both women and men acted as animal fighters and lost their lives. In the following years, these numbers would only increase. Emperor Trajan (AD 53–117) brought eleven thousand animals into the arena "for entertainment" in AD 110. Emperor Gordian I (157–238) organized a luxury hunt for his friends around AD 235. During this hunt, two hundred deers, thirty wild horses, one hundred wild sheep, ten moose, one hundred bulls, three hundred ostriches, thirty wild donkeys, one hundred fifty bears, two hundred geese, and two hundred pale red deer were killed in the arena.

Spectators often sat in rows for days watching the victories of humans over the wild animals. Slaughtering the animals before the eyes of the people proved that the Romans had subdued the animal world. Wild animals such as the lion, the leopard, the tiger, and the elephant frightened many people. This was mostly the case with the elephant due to its unfamiliarity, size, and weight. They were gladly captured by the rulers, carried away in triumphal marches, or deployed in the arena. Everyone had to acknowledge how incredible imperial power was.

Simultaneously, this attitude provided an opportunity for hunters, animal traders, and transporters to build up a growing industry. They made large profits because the demand for animals was high and the supply small. Because the animals had to be taken further and further afield, many found work in this industry. Those who lived on the edge of the empire, where wild animals were still abundant, were often pleased that the Romans brought these wild animals to Rome. It was these animals that had made their lives miserable and destroyed many a field. Mostly lions were often a plague on the edge of the empire.

The animals in these remote areas had to be caught and transported by land and sea to their destination. This took time and energy. According to the price-edict (AD 301) of Emperor Diocletian (AD 244–311) a lion cost 125,000 to 150,000 denarius, a lioness 100,000 to 125,000 denarius, a leopard 70,000 denarius, a bear 20,000 to 25,000 denarius, an ostrich 5,000 denarius, a wild boar 4,000 to 6,000, a deer 2,000 to 3,000 and a wild donkey 5,000 denarius. In the New Testament, a denarius is mentioned as the daily wage for an ordinary worker (Matt 20:2). It was only in the third century that economic challenges would cause this type of show to diminish.

Taming and Love of Animals

Many shows also revealed how well humans could tame nature. Tigers and lions were taught to hunt rabbits and deliver them alive to the guards. An inhabitant of Carthage managed to let a lion walk next to him quietly during the walk. A Syrian got a lion so far that it humbly began to wallow over the ground in front of him. In Alexandria, monkeys walked around reading letters and playing the flute or a harp.[19]

---

19. Cf. Pliny the Elder, *Naturalis Historia*, 8.56–58.

Emperor Caligula (r. AD 37–41) had a great love for his horse Incitatus. One day before the race, his soldiers guarded the horse's stable so that it could enjoy absolute silence and was not startled from sleep. This stable was made of marble, the manger of ivory, and the carpets of purple. Also, beautiful pearl necklaces hung around the horse. It had its servants and even household goods to serve guests, who took part in a banquet on behalf of the horse. Caligula loved this horse so much that he regularly invited it for dinner. The horse was then given grains of barley in a golden manger. Caligula was so fond of the animal that, according to some, he even wanted to appoint it consul.

This successful and loving relationship between humans and animals would continue for a long time. After the decline of the Roman Empire, the hunt for wild animals continued. The hunting of small and large game grew so strongly that laws were enacted in the thirteenth century to better protect wild animals. Disturbances in nature caused enormous insect and rat infestations. By law, it was decreed that hunting was only allowed during specific times.

Free Pass for Assault

From the seventeenth century onwards, the great emphasis on human freedom grew in the West. Humanity had to rid itself of all kinds of power structures. Fate had to be taken into one's own hands by free and enlightened people. God called us to subdue the earth under our feet. From the fifteenth century onward, many European countries thought mainly of subjugating other "less civilized" countries. They were made "Christian" in the name of the faith and changed into European colonies. As we saw in chapter 3.1, this free thinking was the basis for the abuse of God's command to rule over the earth and the exploitation and harming of animals.

From then on, there were few wild animals in Western Europe. They were threatened in their existence by hunting, poaching, and local exploitation. Purchases of firearms for the common people, for example, caused the number of birds in Europe to fall sharply. In popular magazines, hunters triumphantly published the number of birds they shot. Whoever achieved the highest number was considered "hero of the day." In this way, the French king Louis XVI August (1754–93) managed to shoot no less than 572 birds within eight hours—a insane highscore.

This happened not only in Europe, but also in America. American bison, which populate the prairies of North America, almost disappeared from the face of the earth in 1884. Hunters built sophisticated bison-hunting trains from which they could shoot at the herds. The rise of the steam locomotive made people realize that all animals would make way for modern industrialization. Animals were no longer necessary for city dwellers. The steam locomotive was more interesting for traveling.

After the steam locomotive, the engine made shorter transport distances possible. The work in agriculture did not require animals any longer. Smaller animals were given a new purpose. They were adopted as pets and had to provide a cozy atmosphere in the house. Another destination was scientific experiments with small animals. Other animals were for consumption only. People researched how to make the environment, reproduction, and nutrition of the animals economically optimal to produce a good profit. The bio-industry shamelessly exploited animals and saw them merely as an economic commodity. The animal was subject to the purse of humans. It was mass-bred to function for consumption. The testimonies about these events still reach us through media.

Nevertheless, people started protesting against the exploitation of animals. Associations for the protection of animals arose. They point out to society that in the past, religions often did not positively influence animals. This applies to both Western and Eastern religions. The East, like the West, was not spared by the impacts of Enlightenment thinking and industrial rise. Both restricted the living space of the animals. In India the Ganges is critically polluted because many use the river to dump their dirty sewage, untreated industrial chemicals, and incomplete cremations. According to the World Health Organization (WHO), the river is a death hazard for the many young children exposed to the water.[20] China suffers from enormous environmental pollution, which far exceeds all previous infections in industrialized countries.

Such problems can also be found in ancient times. Polytheists in ancient Mesopotamia worshiped the earth as a goddess. But these peoples were also known for their aggressive agricultural practices, exuberant animal hunting, and devastating acts against nature during wars.[21]

It is therefore impossible to declare only one country or one religion guilty of environmental problems. Humans have a terrible tendency to

---

20. Hartl, "Environment."
21. Richter, "Environmental Law," 342.

exploit the natural environment for themselves. Today, no religion or culture can be found that succeeds excellently in its dealings with nature. However, the current growing awareness of environmental problems does ensure that human responsibility for nature comes to the fore. We realize that nature is not there to satisfy our inner hunger for materialism—those who attack nature attack themselves. We rediscover how important it is to find a healthy attitude when dealing with nature. An example of this is God's dealings with humans and animals at the announcement of the great flood. There we discover how God decides to make a covenant not only with humans, but also with animals. Doing so, God appears to be the Creator and Savior of both nonhuman creatures and human creatures.

6

God's Covenants with Animals

6.1 GOD'S SORROW OVER EVIL

6.1.1 Destruction on Earth for Humans and Animals

Violent People

THE STORY OF NOAH's ark is well known. Most of us have been familiar with it since we were young. Noah receives God's commission to build an ark because there will be a great flood over the earth. Animals and humans are allowed to enter the ark to secure themselves against the flood.

Before Genesis describes how the animals get to Noah's ark, it mentions the "sons of God" having sex with the daughters on earth, producing "giants" (*nephilim*) on earth (6:1-4). These "sons of God" and "giants" stand between the positive indication that Enoch walked with God (5:22-24) and that Noah found grace in God's eyes (6:8). Traditionally, the "sons of God" and "giants" have been viewed negatively. Because the "sons of God" (בְּנֵי־הָאֱלֹהִים, *bənê ha'ĕlohîm*) in the biblical book of Job (1:6; 2:1; 38:7) and the Psalms (29:1; 89:7) refers to heavenly powers, interpreters thought of demonic forces.[1] Jude 1:6-7 would then point to these events after the example of Cain and the story of Sodom and Gomorrah:

---

1. Cf. 1 En. 6-19, 21, 86-88; Jub. 4:15, 22; 5:1. The Alexandrian text of the Septuagint translates "sons of God" also with "angels" in Genesis 6:1-4.

> And the angels who did not stay within their own position of authority, but left their proper dwelling ... [and] indulged in sexual immorality and pursued unnatural desire.

Another explanation is that the "sons of God" are positive and point to Seth's God-fearing descendants. They make bad marriages with the godless daughters of Cain. Because "sons of God" refer elsewhere to heavenly powers and the term "giants" has a negative meaning, we prefer the first explanation. Cosmic powers then hope to establish their empire on earth and let their descendants, the giants, control the land. These giants have traditionally been related to the later Enakites, Emites, Zamzumites, Refaites, and Zuzites.[2] They are seen as "heroes that were of old, warriors of renown" (6:4). The Hebrew description of the giants is militaristic.[3] This explains the translations "warriors" and "heroes" (NRSV, NIV; cf. Gen 10:8–9).

Although "heroes" sounds promising and positive, God's testimony is weighty: "The Lord saw that the wickedness of humankind was great in the earth, and that every inclination of the thoughts of their heart was only evil continually" (6:5). What is happening on earth touches God in the depths of his heart. Nothing goes in the direction that God has in mind for creation. The "very good" in Genesis 1:31 has turned into a "very bad" in Genesis 6:5. For this reason, God decides to exterminate people, land animals, and birds. The decay that began in Genesis 3 and 4 reaches a bottom in Genesis 6. But also, God's grace has a new peak at this event. Noah finds grace in the eyes of God in these circumstances (6:8). God sends a flood of water over the earth to cleanse it and remove the effects of evil. Even after that flood, people will remain corrupt and sinful (8:21). But a new beginning will be made by the flood.

All Creatures Are Corrupt

After Genesis 6:5, the evil of the earth is mentioned again in Genesis 6:11–12. These verses clarify that corruption is not limited to humans. The land animals and birds are also drawn into evil. Although the change

---

2. Anakim ("long neck," Num 13:21–33; Deut 2:10–11, 21; 9:2; Josh 11:21–22; 14:12, 15; 15:14; Judg 1:20; Amos 2:9), Emim ("terrorist," Gen 14:5; Deut 2:10), Zamzummim ("conspirators," Deut 2:20), Rephaim ("giants," Gen 14:5; Num 13:33; Deut 2:11, 20; 3:11, 13; Josh 12:4; 13:12; 15:8; 17:15; 18:16; 2 Sam 21:16, 18; 1 Chr 20:4, 6, 8), and Zuzim ("predatory creature," Gen 14:5).

3. Keil and Delitzsch, *Pentateuch*, 108–9.

of water was certainly not easy for some fish, we know that many fish can survive in salt and fresh water.[4] Plant seed can also keep for an extended time in saltwater and adhere to floating parts. At the same time, we realize that many aquatic animals were exposed to tremendous water turbulence and died. Evidence of this are the many fossils from that time. Everything is sucked into ruin, just as humans and animals were sucked into moral bankruptcy before the flood.

Consequently, the term "corruption" (שחת, sh-ch-t) occurs seven times in Genesis 6–9 (6:11–13, 17; 9:11, 15). This expresses God's dissatisfaction with the situation on earth. For this reason, God does not act arbitrarily if he wants to destroy all people and animals on earth. His judgment is in line with what his creatures are doing. The destruction that "all creatures" seek will come upon them in full force.

The term "all flesh" or "all creatures" (כָּל־בָּשָׂר, kŏl-bāshār) in Genesis 6:12 is essential. Traditionally, we tend to think only of humans when using this term. Yet this term refers to humans *and* animals both linguistically and in the context of Genesis 6–9.[5] Specifically, it concerns all land animals, all birds, and all people. Thus, Noah must gather "all flesh" into the ark (6:13, 19; 7:15–16) because God wants to exterminate "all flesh" (6:17; 7:12). So, "all flesh died that moved on the earth, birds, domestic animals, wild animals, all swarming creatures that swarm on the earth, and all human beings" (7:21). Hence, in Genesis 9, God calls humans and beasts into account (v. 5) and makes a covenant with both (v. 8–17).

More accurately, the Hebrew expression כָּל־בָּשָׂר/kŏl-bāsjār should be translated "all flesh." This indicates that we are talking about people, land animals, and birds. The aquatic animals are excluded. Only once in the Bible are they referred to as "flesh" (בָּשָׂר, bāshār). This is the case in Leviticus 11:11, where it concerns aquatic animals that have no fins and scales and thus can easily be classified as "not fish." Outside of this text, the Bible maintains the old classification of our current menus where we still distinguish between fish and meat dishes. Anyone who speaks of "meat" refers to cattle, game, and poultry. Those who talk about fish refer to aquatic animals. So the water catastrophe only affects those who participate in destruction. These are the people, the land animals, and the birds. The aquatic animals are left out. Noah has no place for them in the

---

4. Charron, "Escape to Sterility," 22.

5. Fretheim, *God and World*, 80–81; Stipp, "Alles Fleisch," 173; Harland, *Value of Human Life*, 100; Hamilton, *Genesis 1–17*, 279; Sarna, *Genesis*, 51; Wenham, *Genesis 1–15*, 171.

ark. So, as in Genesis 1–3, the forces of evil have once again managed to make their mark on the land. The earth is depraved.

Humans and a large part of animals were deprived before the arrival of the flood. That animals have a will for evil and are called to account by God is not new in Genesis. In Genesis 3, the serpent was the first animal to be called to account by God. This animal succeeded in sowing evil on earth. We realized from Christian traditions that evil powers could be hidden behind this (chapter 4.2). In Genesis 6, the same could happen. There are heavenly powers and military powers on earth (6:1–4), after which God calls the earth "only evil continually" (6:5). It then turns out that animals and people are ruining both their lives and the planet. This contradicts God's command to humanity to positively militarize the earth so that the creation reflects God's divine nature (Gen 1:28).

Identity of Injustice

What exactly was this destruction among land animals and birds? The biblical text remains ambiguous. There is only an earth "filled with violence" (6:11, 13). Jewish tradition says that animals participated in this injustice by mating with other species:

> This teaches that [the men of the generation of the flood] made a hybrid match between a domesticated beast and a wild animal, a wild animal and a domesticated beast, and every sort of beast with man and man with every sort of beast.[6]

This Jewish source also mentions that animals chose to have sexual intercourse with humans before the flood.[7] Then the animals did the same evil as the heavenly powers, the "sons of God." They "saw that they were fair; and they took wives for themselves of all that they chose" (Gen 6:2), "pursued unnatural lust" (Jude 1:7). Sexual perversion was not new. It appeared shortly after the death of Abel, when Lamech praised himself in a hymn for his violence and profligate sex (4:19, 23–24).

Another possibility is to think of a reckless relationship with each other. In God's covenant with people and animals after the flood (Gen 9), God nowhere speaks of sex. God speaks extensively about food, and there are sanctions for eating animal blood and shedding human blood

---

6. Neusner, *B. Sanhedrin*, 108a. Cf. Freedman and Maurice, *Midrash Rabbah: Genesis*, 28.8; Buber, *Midrash Tanhuma*, §12–15.

7. Neusner, *B. Sanhedrin*, 54b.

(9:2–6). This may indicate that the destruction of animals and humans was rather that they attacked, killed, and ate each other.[8] After the disobedience in Genesis 3, the decay and impact of evil became more significant on earth. Evil was growing. Adam, Eve, and Cain could still leave the garden area (3:23; 4:12, 16). In Genesis 6, leaving an area is no longer possible. The whole earth is full of violence. Evil has subdued the land and multiplied in every corner (6:5, 11–12).

This background may explain the distinction between "pure" and "not pure" animals in Genesis 7. It is striking that many "not pure" animals appear later in biblical texts (Lev 11; Deut 14). Exceptions include the camel, donkey, hare, and horse (Lev 11:4, 6). All pure animals of the biblical food laws are, in any case, herbivores.[9] People are protected to eat blood through these food laws because, after the flood, it sounds, "You shall not eat flesh with its life, that is, its blood" (Gen 9:4; cf. Lev 17:14).

6.1.2 God Offers Deliverance in an Ark

Animals Aboard

Noah builds an ark for nonhuman and human animals. Numerous children's bibles present this ark as a small half walnut with all kinds of animals on deck. Noah is depicted as an older man with a white beard holding the captain's wheel or waiting, looking out of a nostalgic window in the belly of the walnut. The biblical description of the story is entirely different. Because in general the story is well known, Christian proclamation is often challenged to investigate it more deeply.

In Genesis, there is an accurate description of what Noah's ark should look like. It was a boat of 300 x 50 x 30 el, or ~150 x 25 x 15 m, taking into account the different el-lengths of antiquity (45–52 cm). As a result, the ark was almost as long as one and a half football pitches and had a capacity for five hundred and thirty single-car garages. In this ark, there had to be room for a large number of animals and humans. Noah had to bring at least one male and one female of each animal group on board. On the cleansed earth, new species would arise from that group, as happened in Genesis 1.

---

8. Cf. Stipp, "Dominium Terrae," 64; Lawee, "Sins of the Fauna," 74.

9. For more information on these food laws see Houston, "What Was the Meaning?"; Fletcher-Watts, *Study of Deuteronomic*; Kornfeld, "Unreinen Tiere."

How much space in Noah's ark would these animals occupy? Today, an exact calculation is impossible. Nevertheless, we can give a global analysis. Let's look at the current number of animal species and consider that many of them can live in water. We arrive at the following overview:

Land animals	Aquatic animals
Mammals (3,700 x 2 pieces = 7,400)	Fishes (incl. cyclostomata, 20,600)
Birds (8,600 x 14 pieces = 120,400)	Tunicates (1,700)
Reptiles (6,300 x 2 pieces = 12,600)	Echinoderm (e.g., sea urchin, 6,000)
Amphibians (2,500 x 2 pieces = 5,000)	Scyphozoa (e.g., jellyfish, 9,000)
Worms (32,000)	Sponge (5,000)
Arthropods (insects, 1,000,000)	Unicellular organism (27,000)
	Mollusca (e.g., mussels, 130,000)

The column of land animals also includes species that live in the water. For example, the whale and the dolphin are both mammals, and shrimps and crabs are considered arthropods. Only land animals and birds that do not survive in the water go aboard the ark. This concerns a total of 145,400 species (7,400 mammals + 120,400 birds + 12,600 reptiles + 5,000 amphibians). Likely, not all males and females of the 32,000 worms and 1,000,000 arthropods will be included. They can easily survive outside the ark. A huge part of all animals does not have to go onboard. The number that does is small.

Basis Types

The 145,400 animal species mentioned above can still be biologically traced back to basic types (N) from a common ancestor. However, many of the basic types that once lived are already extinct (N†). Let's assume that this is twice as much as the basic types we know today (e.g., N† = 2 x N). That is a very pessimistic assumption.[10] In the table below, this has

10. Lehmann, *Paläontologisches Wörterbuch*, 41, 217; Larwood, *Extinction and*

been collated based on current data from the biological reduction to the basic types (N). It takes the number of species from the previous table, indicates the total number of basic types ΣN (= N + N†), and considers the number of animal species Noah has to bring.

Category	Types	N (basic type)	N†	ΣN	m/v/clean	Σark
Mammals	3,700	185 (1:20)	370	555	2 (unclean)	1,110
Birds	8,600	172 (1:50)	344	516	14 (clean)	7,224
Reptiles	6,300	210 (1:30)	420	630	2	1,260
Amphibians	2,500	83 (1:30)	166	249	2	498
		Total				10,092

This calculation leads to a total of 10,092 animals in the ark (total Σark). They would reproduce on the cleansed earth after the flood and recreate the variation, as in Genesis 1. How much space was needed to take all these animals on board?

Space in the Ark

As mentioned earlier, the ark had a size of 300 x 150 x 50 el (Gen 6:15). If we calculate with the smallest el size of 45cm, it gives a dimension of 135 x 22½ x 13½ m. This provides a total volume of about 41,000 m³. The ark has three floors of 135 x 22½ m² (Gen 6:16). That gives a total loading volume of about 9,000 m². If we imagine this visually, it concerns a capacity of approximately 550 cargo wagons or an area of 280 cargo wagons. Each cargo wagon can accommodate 130 sheep (36,400 sheep in no less than 280 cargo wagons). How is this division within the ark feasible? If we calculate from the average surface area an animal needs, we arrive at the overview below. The first two columns are taken from the previous table. The number of m³ per animal is taken from biological schemes.

Survival.

Category	Σark	≈ m³/animal	Σm³ in ark
Mammals	1,110	3	3,330
Birds	7,224	0.25	1,806
Reptiles	1,260	0.5	630
Amphibians	498	0.5	249
		Total	6,015

This means that mammals need an average of 3,300 m³ of space in the ark. For the amphibians, this is much less; it is even less than 10 percent of this amount: 249 m³. To get all animals into the ark, an average volume of 6,015 m³ is needed. There is plenty of room for that because the ark had a capacity of 41,000 m³. So less than 15 percent is occupied by animals. All other space (85 percent) can be used for other purposes. According to researchers, a quarter (25 percent) of the area was needed for food and drink. This means that less than half of the ark (60 percent) has not yet been filled. It should be borne in mind that we have chosen the most unfavorable situations each time in the calculations described here. We also overlooked the possibility that Noah took the smaller, younger animals rather than the larger, older ones into consideration, which again would give more room for other things in the ark. All that space provided plenty of room for people. However, they did not board. It remained at eight people and an enormous number of animals. Other people rejected the testimony of God.

6.1.3 The Raven and the Second Adam

The Spirit and the New Beginning

One hundred and fifty days after the eruption of the floods, the ark on Mount Ararat comes to a standstill (Gen 8:4). This happens because God sends a "wind" over the earth so that the water sinks (8:1). This "wind" (רוּחַ, *rûach*) reminds us of the story of creation in Genesis 1, where the "spirit" (רוּחַ, *rûach*) floats over the water (1:2). In Hebrew, "wind" and "spirit" are the same word. This parallel between Noah's water and the water in the story of creation is reinforced by the verb "passing" (עָבַר, *'āvar*), which in the Hebrew grammatical *pi'el* form (the active intensive verb form) only occurs in: (1) the creation in Genesis 1:2; (2) the happening in Genesis 8:1; and (3) the description of God's care as an eagle in Deuteronomy 32:11.

Thus, the ark comes to rest five months after the beginning of the flood (7:11). That is the same day on which Israel later celebrates the feast of firstfruits (Lev 23:9–14), the day the manna in the land ends (Josh 5:12), and the day Christ as firstborn rises from the dead (three days after Passover).

All these events testify to a new beginning. After forty days, Noah opens the ark's window and lets out a raven that flies back and forth until the earth is dry. This event is exceptional for those who realize that Noah subsequently three times sends a pigeon out of the ark. The pigeon is well-known to return to its transmitter. Noah can easily find out if the water on the bottom of the earth has diminished. But why did Noah first choose a raven?

The Raven of Noah

The Jewish interpreter Philo of Alexandria (~20 BC–AD 50) described the raven as a sign of evil and the dove as a sign of virtue. The raven flew back and forth above the ark because there were enough carcasses in the water for this wild, unclean black bird of prey. The restful, pure pigeon did not need this atmosphere of death and returned to the ark. So Noah made a mistake out of his biological incompetence. His experiment failed as a result.[11] But is this really the case? Did Noah correct himself by using a pigeon after the raven?

An answer to the raven's usefulness is the statement that this bird "went to and fro until the waters were dried up from the earth" (Gen 8:7). So the bird of prey continues to fly out and coming back. It does so even after Noah has sent out his first pigeon. Noah then takes this pigeon back (8:9), but doesn't do that with the raven. The raven's flight suggests that it does not feed on the remains of the carcasses, as Philo of Alexandria and others imagine. Whether such corpses will remain after hundred and fifty

---

11. Philo of Alexandria, "Genesis," II:35–39. Cf. Sarna, *Genesis*, 57–58; Keil and Delitzsch, *Pentateuch*, 148–49; Wenham, *Genesis 1–15*, 185–86; Cassuto, *Genesis: Part Two*, 107–10.

days of flooding, with all kinds of other creatures being able to use them as food, is doubtful. Flying back rather indicates that the ark is where the raven finds food.

The English theologian Walter Moberly (1952) relates the flying of the raven to the "wind" that floats over the mass of water (Gen 1:2; 8:1). This image is imitated by Noah in the flight out and back of the raven.[12] It reminds God and Noah that dry land must emerge from the mass of water, as it did on the third day of creation (1:9–10). The pigeon is then used to check whether the dry land emerges. So, Noah's choice to send out the raven is the expression of active faith. Noah trusts that God is faithful and that the water gives way to the dry land for a second time. Simultaneously, the flying back and forth of the raven gives Noah the reassurance that the earth's soil is not littered with carcasses.[13] All memories of the former destruction on earth have been erased by the flood. A new beginning can be made, as was the case in Genesis 1.

Adam and Noah

Reflecting on these parallels between Genesis 1 and Genesis 8, it is also possible to look at various similarities between Adam and Noah. Just as Adam has been encouraged to take responsibility towards the animals and give them names, Noah gets the commission to build an ark. Both men are given God's task to take care of the land animals and birds that come to them. With Adam, this happens before evil spreads everywhere; with Noah, this occurs after corruption has spread around.

After the flood, God chooses to bless Noah: "God blessed Noah and his sons, and said to them, 'Be fruitful and multiply, and fill the earth'" (Gen 9:1). This blessing is substantially the same as the blessing that Adam and Eve received (1:28). God places Noah and his descendants in the line of the blessing of Adam and Eve. Both families are the beginning of a new generation and give a fresh start to life on earth. Noah is a second Adam, departing on the cleansed earth from the same grace that the first Adam began on the original earth. The great flood of water does not nullify God's desire for this creation.

In the covenant of God with Noah, food is at the center. This is also the case with the first human being. With Noah, there is a ban on

---

12. Moberly, "Why Did Noah," 352–53.
13. Keiter, "Noah and the Dove," 263.

eating—"You shall not eat flesh with its life, that is, its blood" (Gen 9:4)—as it sounded to Adam—"You may freely eat of every tree of the garden; but of the tree of the knowledge of good and evil you shall not eat, for in the day that you eat of it you shall die" (2:16–17). Life and death are dealt with in these eating commandments. Humans choose for or against life by what they eat.

Adam and Noah ultimately choose the disobedience that brings a curse on their offspring. With Adam, this happens because he eats from the tree of knowledge. This causes creation to be cursed and turn against him, his wife, and all descendants. With Noah, it happens because he drinks too much of his vineyard. He gets drunk and undresses, is seen by his son Ham, and curses his grandson, "Cursed be Canaan; lowest of slaves shall he be to his brothers" (9:25).

In both cases, these two men are naked. In Adam's case, this is due to ignorance about dealing with nudity in front of God. When he becomes aware of this, he covers himself with fig leaves (3:7, 10). With Noah, it is because of his drunkenness. He lays down naked in his tent. When his sons realize this, they hide his nakedness with a garment (9:22–25).

At the same time, there is also a word of hope in both events. In the curse that God pronounces on the serpent, the promise of victory over evil is heard: "I will put enmity between you and the woman, and between your offspring and hers; he will strike your head, and you will strike his heel" (3:15). In the curse Noah utters on his grandson, there is the wish to connect the offspring with God: "Blessed by the Lord my God be Shem; and let Canaan be his slave. May God make space for Japheth, and let him live in the tents of Shem; and let Canaan be his slave" (9:26–27).

6.2 GOD'S COVENANT WITH ANIMALS AND HUMANS

6.2.1 God's Blessings for Noah and his Sons

Ban on Eating

No matter what happened on earth before the great flood, all this does not cause God to give up his relationship with humans. After the great flood, God chooses to continue with humanity and animals. God desires love and faithfulness and gives his fundamental "yes" to creation. Just as God blessed Adam and Eve as the first people, he blesses Noah and his sons on the newly cleansed world.

God announces that harmony between nonhuman and human animals will be drastically disturbed after the flood. There will be "fear and dread." This is a language of war that later sounds between Israel and Canaan (Deut 11:25). The contrast with the garden of Eden has become even more significant than it was before the flood. There is no longer any harmony, as there was in Eden and when the ark was being prepared (Gen 2:19–20; 6:18–20). There are awe and fear "on every animal of the earth, and on every bird of the air, on everything that creeps on the ground, and on all the fish of the sea" (9:2). The only category that is missing is "tame animals." Because humans are allowed to eat animals, "fear and dread" will arise in the animal kingdom (9:3).

This is the first time in the Bible that God allows humanity to consume animals. Interpreters disagree as to whether God allowed humans to do so even after Genesis 3. The reflections in chapter 6.1 lead in the direction that God did not allow this. Animals eating humans, humans eating animals, and animals eating each other was one of the possible causes of the flood. The character on earth then becomes more grim and bloody after the disobedience in Genesis 3. When God allows humans to consume animals, God seems to give in to this world's brokenness.[14] It is a consequence of what happened to humans and animals before the flood. Therefore, God cannot be seen as the primary creator of this statement. It is the result of humans, land animals, and birds, who chose to chase after the destruction in Genesis 6. According to the Jewish book 1 Enoch, the "sons of God" were also guilty of drinking and eating blood:

> In the days when the sons of humans multiplied, they had beautiful handsome daughters. The sentinels, the sons of heaven, looked at them with longing and said to one another, "Come, let us choose for ourselves women from among the daughters of man and bear children." . . . [After their marriage to the daughters], they worked for the sons of human beings. Still, they could not provide for themselves. The giants [who were born from this] killed and devoured the sons of humans. They also sinned against the birds, the land animals, the crawling animals, and the fish. They ate their flesh and drank their blood. (1 En. 6:1; 7:1–3)

We find the same thought in the Jewish book of Jubilees: "You must not live like those who ate blood" (7:27). The violence between people, land animals, and birds before the flood explains why God speaks immediately

---

14. Otto, *Theologische Ethik*, 229–30.

of animal food and blood eating after the flood. His words are a reaction to the previous abuses and serve to curb the resulting destruction.

God does that by commanding humanity not to eat blood. God, the Creator, is the source of life and has every right to blood. The blood bears witness to life, which only belongs to God as Source of Life. Killing an animal to eat it should not be taken lightly. That is why people are forbidden to eat blood after the flood. This commandment will be repeated in the Mosaic Torah (Exod 20:13; Lev 3:17; 7:26–27; 17:10; 19:26; Deut 12:16–24; 1 Sam 14:32–34) and the New Testament (Acts 15:20). This commandment cannot be found in extrabiblical literature. That makes it unique.[15] The "blood" (דָּם, *dām*) is linguistically excluded. Only "all flesh" (כָּל־בָּשָׂר, *kŏl-bāsjār*) has blood of life (Lev 17:14). Nowhere in the Bible is it said that fish have blood of life. Therefore, the Jewish tradition permitted eating the blood of fish.[16]

God's Retribution

God's agreement limits the mutual evil that arose between humans and animals before the flood. In the future, the depravity in Genesis 6:11–13 must be avoided. All creatures bear the responsibility not to degenerate again into acts of violence. Humans must realize that they are each other's sister and brother. They must avoid the sin of Cain in Genesis 4. Cain murdered his brother Abel and then asked God innocently, "Am I my brother's keeper?" (Gen 4:9). The relationship with Genesis 4 is expressed in Genesis 9 through the use of "brother" (אָח, *'āch*). This expression can only be previously found in Genesis 4:8–11.

God also demands retribution from all animals for their life. The fact that animals are given the same responsibility as humans is strange today. In ancient times, however, this was normal.[17] Exodus 21:28–32 pronounces the verdict on a cow that kills a human, and Leviticus 20:15–16 states that in the case of bestiality, human *and* animal must be killed.

So, in the covenant of Genesis 9 there is a new directive: whoever kills a human must be killed. The basis for this is the testimony of Genesis 1:26. Humans are made in the image of God (Gen 9:6). Because this dedication did not exist before, God chose differently with Cain. Cain

---

15. Milgrom, "Blood," 1115.
16. Bischoff, *Das Blut*, 19, 22.
17. Fensham, "Liability of Animals," 85–90.

had to leave the area where the murder took place and wandered across the earth, knowing that the land had turned against him. However, God protected Cain from blood vengeance (Gen 4:10–12, 15). But a human could abuse God's judgment as a license to kill a fellow human being. He could think that God was protecting the murderer, just as he did with Cain. Such abuse seems to be present when Lamech says, "I have killed a man for wounding me, a young man for striking me. If Cain is avenged sevenfold, truly Lamech seventy-sevenfold" (4:23b–24). Because violence prevailed before the flood, God had to intervene and curb the lust for murder. Nowhere in the Bible is the death penalty for murderers so extensively discussed as in Genesis 9. This provision instructs people to bring a murderer to justice. God and humanity are responsible to stop evil (9:5–6). In the elaboration of this, it concerns a death penalty by the government, which has to be alert for time, place, and circumstance to avoid executing an unintentional killer (Exod 21:13; 22:1–2; Num 35:6–34; Deut 19:1–13) and has to use two witnesses for a verdict (19:15).

God's Choice for Life

Sometimes people explain that God's statements in Genesis 9:1–7 hold back humans from randomly slaughtering and eating animals. This is an abuse of the biblical text. It does not do justice to the context. In Genesis 9, God decides to limit evil in these matters. What is central is not the killing of animals, but the choice of life. These statements are framed by God's blessing to humanity to be fruitful, become numerous, and spread on earth (9:1, 7). The commission for humans on the cleansed earth is an extension of the commission to the first humans at the beginning of creation (Gen 1:28). It is about the choice for the life God gives.

The origins of destruction, evil, and death lie in this choice. Humans can decide to follow and trust God in this. Because Adam and Eve did not guard the court, evil gained access to the garden, and because they questioned God, death became a reality in their lives. Genesis 4–6 shows how people's choices can lead to evil, gaining the upper hand on earth and leaving its horrible effects in this cosmos.

Through the choices of Cain and Lamech, evil struck the families (4:1–23). In all those depths, God remained faithfully and lovingly present in the lives of humans. Thus, Genesis 4 begins with Eve, who calls upon "the help of the Lord" (v. 1) and ends with humans in the time of Enosh who began "to invoke the name of the Lord" (v. 26). Between these two positive expressions, we learn in the story of Cain how God cares for the first killer. While Cain does not know what it means to guard his brother against evil, God knows how to protect Cain from evil (4:15).

But it is not only families that are characterized by evil. In Genesis 6, God concludes with a feeling of deep sorrow that the whole earth is depraved and full of injustice. Such universal statements about evil and depravity are not found at the end of Genesis 3, as is often claimed. The so-called "fall" should therefore not be limited to Genesis 3. Also, Genesis 4–6 belong there, although a word like "fall" does not appear anywhere in those chapters. While God saw in Genesis 1:31 that "it was very good," he acknowledges in Genesis 6 that "all flesh," both humans and animals, are characterized by a depraved walk of life (v. 12). God wants to limit this again. The testimony about this in Genesis 6–9 reveals God's goodness and grace. Great attention is paid to God's choice for creation. God wants to make all elements of depravity disappear from the earth's soil (6:7). That is why God chooses the ark as a way out to bring humans and animals together again and let them survive the flood together (6:8, 18–19). However, humans and animals remain as depraved as before. This is why God chooses to avoid any flood as a judgment of evil (8:21). After the flood, God restructures his dealings with depravity. Of course, God's judgment will remain, but it will be carried out within limits set. Sin and evil thus seem to keep their freedom. Yet, God has always promised to stop both. This already shows how God is going along the path of suffering that characterizes creation. Therefore, cross and resurrection are on the horizon of God's choices around the flood in Noah's days.

6.2.2 God's Covenant with Creatures

God's Choice for Humans and Animals

In Genesis 9, God makes a covenant of peace with creation. This covenant will be essential for all other biblical covenants. The Old Testament scholar Terence Fretheim (1936–2020) sees the covenant in Genesis 9 as an umbrella under which all other biblical covenants have a place.[18] Both humans and animals are involved in this alliance: "I am establishing my

---

18. Fretheim, *God and World*, 87.

covenant with you and your descendants after you, and with every living creature that is with you, the birds, the domestic animals, and every animal of the earth" (Gen 9:9–10). After all, the animal world was also characterized by depravity.

God chooses for humanity once again. Whatever happens on earth does not cause God to give up his relationship with humankind. He decides to continue and make a covenant with humans and animals. In this, God repeats that he will not again judge the earth by a flood (Gen 9:11; cf. 8:22). God chooses for love and faithfulness in creation and gives a fundamental "yes" to earth and creatures. The book of Isaiah later reminds the Israelites, who are in captivity, of this covenant (Isa 54:6–10). Then, again, the goal is to assure the people that destruction and judgment do not lie in God's heart. God will make a covenant of peace that will be as firm as the covenant with Noah. This covenant of peace is also mentioned by the prophet Ezekiel (34:25–31; 37:26). There it is connected with the call to multiply (Gen 9:1, 7; Ezek 37:26). However, the struggle between humans and animals remains in this covenant. Other biblical texts point to this end of the struggle (Isa 11:6–9; 65:25; Hos 2:18).

In the meantime, humans cause themselves a great deal of harm and suffering. That suffering does not happen because of God. It is not the way creation is meant to function. God chooses not to hit the earth with a flood. No matter how great the pain is in God's eyes, it touches him, even more when he has to hit people and animals with disasters.

The Rainbow

The rainbow serves as a covenant sign between God and creatures. God places his "bow" (קֶשֶׁת, qesjet) in the clouds. This choice for a rainbow is nowhere found in other flood stories. The Hebrew קֶשֶׁת/qesjet refers to a mathematically curved line, such as a battle bow (cf. Deut 32:42; Hab 3:9–11; Zech 9:14). Some saw the image of such a warbow in the rainbow. This bow is with its convex side facing upwards and not downwards. The warbow then shot its arrows into the air and no longer into the earth.

Others saw a parallel in the Babylonian deluge story. There the Babylonian god Marduk hung his bow from the stars after his victory over Tiamat. From this background, the rainbow was a hallmark of peace and reconciliation. The rainbow reassures people. There is no longer any threat to fear from heaven.[19] Besides this, the rainbow is also connected to God's love and grace. In the first chapter of the prophet Ezekiel, the rainbow is related to the firmament (Ezek 1:26–28). This is reminiscent of the firmament in Genesis 1, which separates the "water above" from the "water below." So, the rainbow symbolically expresses that God guarantees creation that the "water above" no longer descends on the earth. The bow supports the forces of heaven and surrounds the earth, despite the depravity present on earth.

Twice God emphasizes in the covenant that the rainbow is a reminder for the Omniscient (Gen 9:15–16). Suppose this rainbow is a new phenomenon, first introduced in Genesis 9. In that case, it means that rain had never fallen from the sky before that time. The rainbow would otherwise have appeared in the sky before. In Genesis 2, there is no rain yet. The land there is humidified by a vapor (v. 5–6). The rainbow is then an entirely new phenomenon that God uses as a sign of the covenant. Noah and his fellow human beings would be the first people to observe this beautiful, colorful arch. If Noah saw dark clouds hanging over him, he would be allowed to hold on to God's promise. He was allowed to know that there would be no more flooding over the earth and only had to take his umbrella outside with him.

6.2.3 The Promise of God's Covenant

Years after the events in Noah's life, the prophet Hosea talks about a future covenant in line with Noah's covenant. This happens in the turbulent years around 731–33 BC. That is when the Assyrian prince Tiglath-Pileser III (r. 745–727 BC) in Israel caused destruction and devastation. As a result, the damage caused to the people and the impact of the country's wild animals was considerable. At that time, God said,

> I will make for you a covenant on that day with the wild animals,
> the birds of the air, and the creeping things of the ground; and
> I will abolish the bow, the sword, and war from the land; and I
> will make you lie down in safety. (Hos 2:18)

This testifies to a future renewal of creation, already mentioned by Moses:

---

19. Zenger, *Gottes Bogen*, 125; Brueggemann, *Genesis*, 84; Cassuto, *Genesis: Part Two*, 136.

> I will grant peace in the land, and you shall lie down, and no one shall make you afraid; I will remove dangerous animals from the land, and no sword shall go through your land. (Lev 26:6; cf. 26:45; Deut 4:31)

On the day of renewal, God makes a covenant reminiscent of the eternal covenant with Noah and the animals (Gen 9:8–17). Contrary to the covenant with Noah, God is herein no covenant partner. It is a covenant for Israel and the animals. In contrast, Noah's covenant was a covenant of God with human and nonhuman animals (Gen 9:9–10). God's goal with this, just as in Noah's covenant, is to bring peace on earth. This happens because God restores his relationship with humans and the relationship between humans and nature.

The animals which Hosea mentioned destroyed in his time the fields and vineyards as a judgment of God: "I will lay waste her vines and her fig trees.... I will make them a forest, and the wild animals shall devour them" (Hos 2:12). They are wild animals, birds of prey, crawling animals, and insects attacking agriculture.

God promises that these animals in the future will live in harmony with humans. This also applies to birds of prey and poisonous reptiles. God will ensure that they no longer attack Israel. Ezekiel takes up this subject and extends it to the wilderness and forests:

> I will make with them a covenant of peace and banish wild animals from the land, so that they may live in the wild and sleep in the woods securely. (Ezek 34:25)

In this way, God reveals himself permanently through the prophets as a God of love:

> Because the Lord your God is a merciful God, he will neither abandon you nor destroy you; he will not forget the covenant with your ancestors that he swore to them. (Deut 4:31)

When the Assyrians dominated Israel, this must have been an excellent prospect. It is a prospect that also applies to creation. After all, what is happening in Israel is significant for the whole of creation. God aims to give peace and tranquility to the work of his hands. In the future, people and animals will enjoy this fully. This includes enjoying a good harvest, as the prophet Hosea later announces (Hos 2:23–25). These are the blessings which creation awaits (Rom 8:20–21).

Noah's covenant is thus a basis for God's later plans for creation. It reveals where God will take this creation. These principles are included in the events between Noah's time and the completion of creation. Therefore, in the next chapter, we will go into more detail about this particular time.

7

God Stands Up for Animals

IN SALVATION HISTORY GOD cares for animals. Some core texts from the Torah that often pass in the review of this are the Sabbath day, which also includes animals (Exod 20:8–11), the handling of the stubborn ox (Exod 21:28–31), the handling of the animals of fellow humans (Exod 23:4–5; Deut 22:1–4), the goat that may not be boiled in the mother's milk (Exod 23:19), the handling of the bird's nest (Deut 22:6–7), the uneven yoke (Deut 22:10), and the muzzles of the animals (Deut 25:4). It is possible to categorize these seven entries according to the values they emphasize for animals. In this chapter we would like to dwell briefly on two settings that give rest to the animal (the Sabbath day, the muzzles, chapter 7.1.1), two settings that indicate respect for the parents (the bird's nest, the buck in the mother's milk, chapter 7.1.2), two restraints that protect animals from abuse (animals of neighbors, the unequal yoke, chapter 7.1.3), and restraints that demand animal rights (the stubborn ox, sex with animals, and touching the mountain, chapter 7.2.1).

7.1 REST, RESPECT, AND PROTECTION FOR ANIMALS

7.1.1 God gives Rest and Food to Animals

The Sabbath

The Ten Commandments, which Moses receives on Mount Sinai, also pay attention to animals. This happens in the commandment that receives the most attention—the so-called commandment of the Sabbath:

> Remember the sabbath day, and keep it holy. Six days you shall labor and do all your work. But the seventh day is a sabbath to the Lord your God; you shall not do any work—you, your son or your daughter, your male or female slave, your livestock, or the alien resident in your towns. For in six days the Lord made heaven and earth, the sea, and all that is in them, but rested the seventh day; therefore the Lord blessed the sabbath day and consecrated it. (Exod 20:8–11)

The commandment of the Sabbath touches all in the household. It applies to employers and employees, Jews and strangers, people and animals, and serves the welfare of all. It is a moment that causes the daily rhythm of humans and animals to stop and provides peace.

The mention of the animals at this insertion is unique in antiquity. This is not always noticed in the Judeo-Christian proclamation of the Sabbath. It testifies to the welfare that God gives to animals. Thus, the Sabbath marks a red line through a workaholic culture that has plagued humanity several times in history. Based on the seven days of creation, humans are entitled to know that God chooses breaks in time. Humans apply this to the animals for which they are responsible.

Failure to Muzzle the Bovine Animal

The animal must not be overworked or abused. Because of the Sabbath, "your ox and your donkey may have relief" (Exod 23:12). For this reason, it is not permitted to hire the animal on the Sabbath for work by non-Jews. Even if the animal accidentally ends up in a difficult situation on the Sabbath, humans should choose to interrupt their rest and help the animal (cf. Mat 12:11; Luke 14:5). Consequently, the protection of the animal is above the Sabbath rest. This attitude towards animals is entirely different from that seen in European history (see chapter 5.2).

There are several other statutes mentioned about human and animal welfare in the Torah. In Deuteronomy 25:4, it states, "You shall not muzzle an ox while it is treading out the grain." After grain harvest in ancient times, people spread the cut culms on the threshing floor. An ox then loosened the grains from the ears by crushing the culms into straw with its hooves. In this work, the ox was allowed to eat freely from what was lying on the threshing floor.

This commandment is not self-evident. A cow can eat daily two to three kilos of food. That is not attractive in a world with high economic interests. The cow then eats too much. The family or the trader would have to miss out on that quantity. However, God commands people in this not to obstruct the animal. It is allowed to enjoy the produce that God gives through the land. This commandment is a formidable challenge in today's society, where a battle is raging around the food industry, which mainly pursues its economic interests and has little regard for the animal's welfare. Thus, the Bible confronts humanity with a God who interferes in our attitude to life and determines how humans grants animals their rest and food.

Care for Animals in the Jewish Tradition

This positive, caring attitude towards animals continues in Jewish tradition:

> Why did God reveal himself to Moses when he was grazing the herds? God liked the loving care that Moses had for the sheep. One day, when Moses was grazing the sheep in the steppe, a sheep lost the group. Moses was looking for the sheep and discovered that it was walking to a pond. So, he thought, you are thirsty, and I didn't notice? He took the lamb on his shoulders and carried it to the water. Then God said, "He who loves the animals entrusted to him is worthy to become the leader of my people."[1]

In rabbinic tradition, we find such statements not only about Moses. We also find them in reflections on David and other righteous people.[2] It holds true in Sirach: "If you own cattle, handle them well" (Sir 7:22). In the Testament of Zebulun, it reads:

---

1. Freedman and Maurice, *Midrash Rabbah: Exodus*, §2.
2. E.g., Schwartz, "Tsa'ar Ba'alei Chayim," 65; Bleich, "Judaism and Animal Experimentation," 69–71.

> My children, I call upon you to follow the Lord's statutes. Show mercy to your fellowmen and also have compassion for the irrational animals. For, for the sake of these things, God blessed me. (T. Zeb. 5:1–2)

Based on the text "he will give grass in your fields for your livestock, and you will eat your fill" (Deut 11:15), Jewish tradition even states that people cannot eat until their animals received food.[3]

In this way, God takes care of people and animals. During the Sabbath year, which comes every seven years, people have to leave the land fallow. They may enjoy a year of complete peace. What grows on the ground in that year is for everyone, including the domesticated animals and the wild animals (Lev 25:1–7). The advantage of leaving the land fallow for arable farming has been pointed out several times.[4] Antiquity contained numerous examples of agricultural practices that turned fertile land into a wilderness through mismanagement. Israel received God's revelation on how they should deal with the land at its best. In that the character of God was expressed. People acknowledged that they were dependent on God and that the land was of God (Lev 25:23).[5] Israel represented this by bringing the tithes and firstfruits of the land (and of animals). By following this, people chose a different path from societies around them. They chose the path of well-being for all, living in peace, and opposing themselves to a purely economic system of living.

7.1.2 God Calls for Respect for Parents

Dealing with the Mother Bird

Commitments for animals concerning respect for their parents are less well known. Often, when hearing these texts, the reader does not understand the exact meaning or background. In Deuteronomy 22:6–7, we find instructions on how to deal with the mother bird and her offspring:

> If you come on a bird's nest, in any tree or on the ground, with fledglings or eggs, with the mother sitting on the fledglings or on the eggs, you shall not take the mother with the young. Let

---

3. Neusner, *B. Gittin*, 62a.
4. Wirzba, *Paradise of God*; Hildenbrand, *Structure and Theology*, 261–62; Hütterman, *Ecological Message*.
5. Hausoul, "Land."

the mother go, taking only the young for yourself, in order that it may go well with you and you may live long.

One possible explanation for this requirement is the protection of the bird population concerned. This instruction is then related to the safety of the flora during war (Deut 20:19–20).[6] In rabbinic tradition, it was assumed that these instructions also applied to other animals. It was necessary to prevent the extermination of two successive generations.[7]

Many find it strange that the old mother bird is left behind. The young bird that is taken away often has a longer life ahead of it than its mother. It can also reproduce just as well as the mother. However, the basis for the choice of the mother can be found in the last words, "that it may go well with you and you may live long." These words remind us of God's instruction to humans that there must be respect for parents.

> Honor your father and your mother, as the Lord your God commanded you, so that your days may be long and that it may go well with you in the land that the Lord your God is giving you. (Deut 5:16)

Parents must be honored as givers of life, not only in their dealings with fellow humans but also in their dealings with animals. Therefore, God's instructions in dealing with the mother bird find their basis in the Ten Commandments.

The Buck and the Breast Milk

One of the most enigmatic statements about animals in the Torah can be recalled in this context. This is the statement that the buck should not be boiled in the mother's milk. This commandment is mentioned three times. Twice it is in the context of the firstfruits of the field—"The choicest of the first fruits of your ground you shall bring into the house of the Lord your God" (Exod 23:19; 34:26)—and once in the context of the food dedication:

> You shall not eat anything that dies of itself; you may give it to aliens residing in your towns for them to eat, or you may sell it

---

6. Hütterman, *Am Anfang*, 110–13; Christensen, *Deuteronomy*, 500; Tigay, *Deuteronomy*, 201.

7. Schochet, *Animal Life*, 151.

> to a foreigner. For you are a people holy to the Lord your God. You shall not boil a kid in its mother's milk. (Deut 14:21)

This instruction ensures that there is a strict separation between milk and meat products in Judaism. Anyone in Israel will seldom experience milk and meat products offered simultaneously. Eating a cheeseburger is a taboo for many Jews. In Jewish Mishnah, we read:

> No meat may be cooked in milk (in order not to violate the law against the cooking of a young in his mother's milk [Exod 23:19; 34:26; Deut 14:21]), with the exception of the meat of fish and locusts. No meat may be placed on the table together with cheese, with the exception of the meat of fish and locusts. . . . A person may put meat and cheese in the same robe, provided that they do not touch each other. . . . If a drop of milk falls on a piece of meat that is boiling in a cauldron and is enough to give the piece a flavor, this piece may not be eaten. If someone is stirring in that cauldron and the milk in the cauldron gives the other one a taste, it should not be eaten.[8]

What is the basis for this curious commandment? Is it an expression of insensitivity when a buck is boiled in its mother's milk? Is it because the buck typically drinks the mother's milk to grow? Then it would be an animal-friendly attitude or moral sensitivity.[9] Often the rejection of an old cultic fertility ritual has been considered. Ugaritic texts recommend boiling a buck in milk.[10] The problem with this is that there is no evidence of such a practice. Even Ugaritic texts only mention boiling a buck in milk. That is not what God is referring to in these instructions. He specifically mentions the boiling of the buck in *mother's milk*.

The South African Old Testament scholar Casper J. Labuschagne (1929–2019) relates this commandment to the ban on eating blood. In the regulations for it, there is mention of blood (Exod 23:18; 34:27). Because mother's milk sometimes contains blood, this may not be consumed.[11] The challenge here is that the consumption of breast milk is usually permitted. The commandment focuses on the combination between the buck and the milk of the mother. The buck, for example, can be

---

8. Neusner, "M. Hullin," 8.1–3.
9. Jacob, *Second Book of the Bible*; Dalman, *Arbeit und Sitte*, 100.
10. Gordon, *Ugarit Handbook*, 174.
11. Labuschagne, "'You Shall Not Boil,'" 6–17.

boiled in his aunt's milk. There is also no question of eating blood in the context. That is why this explanation is not apparent.

The proposal that this commandment opposes the bringing together of the life-giving mother's milk and the dead young animal also lacks completeness.[12] The commandment would then apply more widely and to any combination of meat and milk. The emphasis on the mother would make it easier to think about respect for the mother. The mother is the cupbearer of life, and that life is dishonored when her cub is cooked in her milk. This puts the mother's milk on the same level as the milk of other animals. God forbids this because it goes against the value of respect for the parents (Deut 5:16).[13]

7.1.3 God Gives Protection to Animals

Animals of our Fellow Humans

Several times, we find instructions in the Torah to protect the weaker ones. This is not just about protecting the weak. The protection of the animal does not escape God either. In Exodus 23:4–5, it speaks about the relationship with our neighbor and animals:

> When you come upon your enemy's ox or donkey going astray, you shall bring it back. When you see the donkey of one who hates you lying under its burden and you would hold back from setting it free, you must help to set it free.

This part of the text is mainly about the tendency of injustice to one's fellow human beings. This can happen by ignoring the truth and allowing oneself to be bribed by others (Exod 23:1–2, 7–9), pulling one's arms in front of one's neighbor, or harming one's neighbor in court (v. 3, 6). However, God points out in this text that this can also happen by harming the animals of one's neighbor. The people are not allowed to steal the animals of an enemy or abuse animals from someone "who hates you." Animals are not allowed to become victims of human discord. This restricts the hostility towards a fellow human being. The animal that collapses under a burden must be helped. God does not allow hatred of others to cause animals to suffer. Deuteronomy 22:1–4 repeats this core value.

---

12. Carmichael, "Separating Life and Death," 1–7.

13. Knauf, "Zur Herkunft und Sozialgeschichte Israels," 153–69; Keel, *Böcklein*, 44–45; Haran, "Seething a Kid," 23–35.

Plowing with Animals

A few verses later, in Deuteronomy 22:9–11, there are forbidden combinations. It mentions the sowing of a vineyard with different kinds of seeds (v. 9), the prohibition of plowing together with a cow and a donkey (v. 10), and the prohibition of wearing clothes made of two types of fabric (v. 11). From our subject matter, the ban on plowing is relevant: "You shall not plow with an ox and a donkey yoked together" (Deut 22:10).

This commandment was not a superfluous luxury. In history it was often the case that someone had only one ox and one donkey. The person could then come up with the idea of having his plow pulled by these animals. However, this was forbidden by God. There are too many differences between an ox and a donkey. They ensure that both animals are unnecessarily burdened during plowing. If they work together in one furrow, the unequal yoke they form is tantamount to animal cruelty.

For this reason, God states that only animals of the same species should be used in plowing, with the same gait and different corresponding behavior patterns. The Babylonian Talmud shows that the ox and the donkey are exemplary to illustrate this. The Babylonian Talmud notes ironically that plowing with a goat and a fish simultaneously is not permitted either.[14] Unnecessary discomfort that causes pain to an animal is sufficient reason for God to include this precept in his instructions to Israel. In the past, this has been pointed out by various animal lovers calling for a radical return to God's values. These values testify to a choice for the life of humans and animals. They show that animals have rights. Protecting animals is a God-given commitment. Therefore, wisdom says that "the righteous know the needs of their animals, but the mercy of the wicked is cruel" (Prov 12:10).

7.2 CONNECTIVITY BETWEEN HUMANS AND ANIMALS

7.2.1 Judgment about Animals and Humans in the Torah

In chapters 3 and 6, we discovered that the Bible testifies that an animal that causes mischief must be judged. God appeals to both humans and animals for their actions. This is the case with the spilling of blood. The community is then responsible for responding to this (Deut 21:1–9). God

---

14. Neusner, *B. Sanhedrin*, 59b.

demands the blood of those who shed innocent blood. This is stipulated in the covenant God made with humans and animals (Gen 9:5–6).

> When an ox gores a man or a woman to death, the ox shall be stoned, and its flesh shall not be eaten; but the owner of the ox shall not be liable. If the ox has been accustomed to gore in the past, and its owner been warned but has not restrained it, and it kills a man or a woman, the ox shall be stoned, and its owner also shall be put to death. If a ransom is imposed on the owner, then the owner shall pay whatever is imposed for the redemption of the victim's life. If it gores a boy or a girl, the owner shall be dealt with according to this same rule. (Exod 21:28–31)

In Babylonian and Sumerian laws, we find similar texts. Still, they do not choose the death of the animal. The owner is held responsible for the death of the others and compensates for the injustice.[15] In the Bible, there is no compensation if an animal gores a human in such a way that he or she dies. The animal is responsible and not the owner (Exod 21:28). It must be stoned to death. An exception to this is if the owner knows about the animal's repulsive behavior. In that case, not only the animal but also the owner must be killed. Negligence that leads to someone's death is punished with death. The life of one's fellow human being is of great value to God.

Two other texts are in line with this: animals and humans must not touch Mount Sinai (Exod 19:13; 34:3), and animals must be killed if they are used in sex with humans (Lev 20:15–16). These requirements are not easy. Both demonstrate a strong connection between humans and animals. We prefer to take a closer look at this connection from the events in Egypt and Nineveh.

7.2.2 Animals in Egypt

Cosmic Judgments

The Egyptian pharaoh is opposed to treating animals positively. Through pharaoh's rebellion against God, he puts all people and animals of Egypt in danger. Pharaoh's choice to execute the Israelites through hard labor (Exod 1:11) and mercilessly slaughter their male infants (v. 16) meets divine resistance. God calls upon pharaoh to grant freedom to his people.

---

15. Hammurabi, *Code of Hammurabi*, §250–52; Eshnunna, *Laws of Eshnunna*, §54–57.

God Stands Up for Animals

The reaction is that pharaoh raises his fist to God and oppresses the people even more. This causes pharaoh to proclaim the judgment of God. All people and animals under his rule will suffer because of pharaoh's stubbornness. As a result, the whole of creation is set in motion. Frogs (8:1–2), mosquitoes (v. 12), flies (v. 17–18), and locusts (v. 4) will attack pharaoh and his people because they are holding God's people in captivity.

In four plagues over Egypt, animals are affected. Fish die when the Nile turns to blood (Exod 7:18, 21). Cattle, horses, donkeys, camels, cattle, sheep, and goats of Egyptians are affected by pestilence (9:3, 10). The animals of the Israelites are protected from this (9:4). The firstborn animals in Egypt die along with the firstborn sons. The animals of the Israelites and other nations are protected when, during the Passover, blood is smeared on their doorposts (11:5–7; 12:7, 12–13).

In this way, pharaoh is destroying his nation. His management of Egypt will be as disorderly as the humans' management of creation just before the great flood in Genesis 6–8. Also in that time, animals shared in the judgment. However, God offers protection to animals associated with Israel, as it was in Noah's ark. This background of good management and mismanagement plays a part in later events. Through rebellion against God, people will bring their animals under judgment (Josh 6:21; 7:24; 1 Sam 15:3; 22:19).

> Thus, the plagues are not an arbitrarily chosen divine response to Pharaoh's sins, as if the vehicle could just as well have been foreign armies or an internal revolution. The consequences are cosmic because the sins are anticreational.[16]

The Plagues and the Gods

In the plagues of Egypt the animals are often associated with Egyptian gods. Exodus 12:12 ("on all the gods of Egypt I will execute judgments") refers to this. This is also mentioned in the Jewish book Wisdom of Solomon:

> In return for their foolish and wicked thoughts, which led them astray to worship irrational serpents and worthless animals, you sent upon them a multitude of irrational creatures to punish them, so that they might learn that one is punished by the very things by which one sins. (Wis 11:15–16)

---

16. Fretheim, "Plagues as Ecological Signs," 395. Cf. Enns, *Exodus*, 213, 230.

Thus the plague of frogs humiliates the resurrection god Heqet, who is shaped like a frog. The plague of cattle humiliates the mother goddess Hathor, who has the shape of a cow, and the fertility god Apis, who has the form of a bull. The plague of locusts humiliates Serapis, the locust protector, and Min, the fertility god, before harvest. No clear parallels are found for the plague of mosquitoes and flies. Later the plagues over Egypt are presented as an anti-creation story (Ps 105:28–38). Pharaoh turns not only against God but against creation.

It is possible that the so-called Cannibal Hymn, in the pyramid of Unas of the ancient Egyptian kingdom (2300 BC), refers back to this situation. In this hymn, we learn of a battle between the gods, of deep darkness coming over the land, of the rebirth of the sun after this darkness, and great chaos in the whole of creation. A sentence from this hymn reads, "It is the king who judges, on him whose name is hidden on the day of the murder of the firstborn."[17] It is possible to think of the event in Exodus 11–12. The one "whose name is hidden" reminds us of God's revelation to Moses (Exod 3:13–14). Elsewhere in the hymn, we hear, "The sky is cloudy, the stars are darkened, the plane of the sky shakes, the bones of the gods on earth tremble." It is also possible that this refers to Egypt's plagues. Pharaoh, the merciless killer of male infants and oppressor of God's firstborn, has to taste for himself what it means to lose a firstborn (Exod 11:5).

For those who realize that pharaoh killed all male babies of the Israelites, God's choice to let only the firstborn die in Egypt is a merciful judgment. Everyone in the land has the opportunity to escape this judgment by putting blood on the doorposts. Their firstborn are then positively consecrated to God. This commandment does not only apply to people but also to animals (Exod 13:2, 11–15). Just as humans and animals are judged together, they will be blessed together. A beautiful example of this can be found in the book of Jonah.

7.2.3 Animals in Nineveh

In contrast to the texts that see animals as fellow victims in the judgment of evil regimes, we find biblical testimonies about animals as fellow companions in salvation. A well-known example of this can be found

---

17. Cf. Sweeney, *Pyramid Age*, 124.

in the book of Jonah. At the end of this prophetic work, God asks Jonah whether the animals in the city should not be taken into account:

> And should I not be concerned about Nineveh, that great city, in which there are more than a hundred and twenty thousand persons who do not know their right hand from their left, and also many animals? (Jonah 4:11)

God names the animals at the end of this statement. They are as important to him as the innocent people in the city, who do not know the difference between left and right.

It is striking that there are several similarities between the events in the book of Jonah and the great flood in Genesis 6–9. In both circumstances, we learn that God's heart is touched. In Genesis 6–9, it is the result of a negative situation: "And the Lord was sorry [נחם, *n-ch-m*] that he had made humankind on the earth, and it grieved him to his heart" (Gen 6:6). In Jonah, it happens because of a favorable situation: "When God saw what they did, how they turned from their evil way, God changed his mind [נחם, *n-ch-m*] about the calamity that he had said he would bring upon them; and he did not do it" (Jonah 3:10). Furthermore, each time it is an event connected with forty days. While the forty days of rain in Genesis are associated with destruction (Gen 7:4, 12, 17; 8:6), the forty days in Jonah are connected with recovery and postponement (Jonah 3:4). In both events God sends a wind over the earth (Gen 8:1; Jonah 1:4; 4:8), there is a boat on which God's messengers travel, and there is dry land on which God's messengers make a new start (Gen 8:14; Jonah 2:10).

What is important is that both events involve animals that are actively engaged. Before the flood, animals come to Noah (Gen 7:2, 9). In the time of Jonah, we hear that animals in Nineveh are fasting. "Human beings and animals shall be covered with sackcloth, and they shall cry mightily to God" (Jonah 3:8a) is the king's command. In Genesis, God remembers animals and people (Gen 8:1). In Jonah, God has compassion for animals and people (Jonah 4:11). Besides, it can be pointed out that the name Jonah means "dove." Just as the dove seeks a home in Noah's story, Jonah is characterized by his disobedience in pursuing his own safe home instead of going to Nineveh (Gen 7:4; Jonah 3:4).

Jonah is the only prophet in the Bible called to go to a foreign people and proclaim God's message. He is also the prophet who feels most uncomfortable. In Jewish tradition, there is the legend of the French rabbi Shlomo Yitzchaki (Rashi, 1040–1105) that Jonah was so easygoing that he also enjoyed life in the big fish. According to this legend, this fish was a male fish, which gave Jonah in the belly enough room. Therefore, God made the fish spit out Jonah and called a female fish to swallow him. In this second fish, it was less pleasant for Jonah. There were several embryos present that bothered Jonah. Because of that pressure, Jonah started praying. According to Shlomo Yitzchaki, this explains why the story of Jonah speaks of a fish in the masculine form which swallows the prophet and a fish in the feminine form in which Jonah prays (Jonah 2:1–2).[18]

It is clear from the book of Jonah that God's grace applies to people *and* animals. Like the flood and the plagues over Egypt, there is a deep connection between people and animals. But, unlike pharaoh, Nineveh chooses to turn to God and save her animals. God has a heart for creatures. This attitude is reflected in prophetic statements that speak of God's peace for humans and animals in the future.

18. Ben Jitschaki (Rashi), *Complete Tanach*.

8

God's Peace for Animals

8.1 GOD'S RENEWAL FOR ANIMALS

8.1.1 Wolf Finds Shelter with Lamb

THE PROPHET ISAIAH SPEAKS of a wonderful promise for creation:

> The wolf shall live with the lamb, the leopard shall lie down with the kid, the calf and the lion and the fatling together, and a little child shall lead them. The cow and the bear shall graze, their young shall lie down together; and the lion shall eat straw like the ox. The nursing child shall play over the hole of the asp, and the weaned child shall put its hand on the adder's den. They will not hurt or destroy on all my holy mountain; for the earth will be full of the knowledge of the Lord as the waters cover the sea. (Isa 11:6–9)

In the days of the Messiah, the most helpless and innocent animals will deal with animals that we now categorize as violent. The wolf "seeks shelter" (גור, *g-w-r*) near the lamb, as the alien does to the local residents. Animals we know to be dangerous are then cared for by a small boy.

While monarchs like the Assyrian king Assurbanipal (669–627 BC) had to eradicate large lion pests in the past (chapter 5.2), this will no longer be necessary for the future. The lion will then change in character. He will become a lion as God wants him to be. Just like the ox he will eat "chop" or "cattle feed" (תֶּבֶן, *teven*) as his main course.

In the kingdom of the Messiah, children can play by the lair of a viper and by the even more dangerous basilisk or horned king's adder. Anyone who sees a child near such violent animals today wants to take it immediately away. Under the regency of the Messiah, a child will not be in danger. There is no place for suffering and death in his presence. Through the influence of God's Spirit, the Messiah changes creation. This is what the prophet Isaiah speaks about in the preceding verses:

> A shoot shall come out from the stump of Jesse, and a branch shall grow out of his roots. The spirit of the Lord shall rest on him. . . . Righteousness shall be the belt around his waist, and faithfulness the belt around his loins. (Isa 11:1–2a, 5)

No human or animal will cause any more evil or destruction on God's holy mountain. That area, which in Isaiah's days was still full of injustice, is then full of justice. Mount Zion will be the starting point of peace for creation.

8.1.2 Image and Reality

Symbolic Interpretation

For many, it is inconceivable for a lion to eat animal feed. Biologically, this signifies a significant change for the lion. Is such a changed lion still recognizable as a lion? Therefore, interpreters see these descriptions of Isaiah 11 as mythical imagery. In Jewish tradition, this is done by the famous rabbi Maimonides or Rambam (Rabbi Moshe ben Maimon, 1138–1204). Maimonides thought that the prophet's symbolic description was that peoples would no longer bother Israel in the end. Nevertheless, if we compare Isaiah 11 with ancient myths, there is no parallel with these descriptions.[1]

Others chose to explain the words of Isaiah spiritually. The animals are then symbolic representations towards something else. Opinions differ as to what precisely that "something" is. The American Old Testament scholar John Oswalt (b. 1940) consciously does not want to detail the individual animals in the biblical text of Isaiah. He restricts himself to giving a symbolic explanation of the total. He only explains that in

---

1. For detail: Eliade, *Cosmos and History*.

the days of the Messiah, the fears of uncertainty, danger, and evil will disappear.[2]

An often-heard explanation within the symbolic view is that the animals in Isaiah 11 refer to humans.[3] A parallel for this is Psalm 22, where the psalmist describes himself as a worm (v. 7) and compares his enemies with wild animals and dogs (v. 13–14, 17, 21–22). A comparison of a human enemy with a lion can also be found in Psalm 7:2–3, 57:5, and 58:7. Also, Isaiah 50:17 describes Israel as a herd driven apart by lions. The lions refer in that text to the Babylonian and Assyrian powers that attack Israel (cf. Jer 51:34). In Ezekiel 32:2, the pharaoh of Egypt is the lion of the nations. The prophet also uses this image to describe the wild animals in Isaiah 11 (Isa 5:29; cf. Jer 2:15; 4:7). But just as in Isaiah 11, there is no indication that these wild animals are nations.

This calls for caution in the symbolic interpretation. Often the strong animals are symbols for the leaders and the upper class, and the tame animals indicate the weak in society. The Korean theologian Kyung-Chul Park (b. 1962) tries to substantiate this with texts from the ancient Near East in which peace among animals is a motive to recognize the leaders of the nation as good rulers.[4] A direct connection with the leaders of the country is also present in the biblical text because the animal peace in Isaiah 11:6–9 immediately follows the government of the Messiah in Isaiah 11:1–5.

Isaiah and Animals

Still, it remains impossible to receive certainty from Isaiah 11 as to whether the prophet wants his listeners to interpret these descriptions of animal fear symbolically as references to people, as in Isaiah 59:11: "We all growl like bears; like doves we moan mournfully. We wait for justice, but there is none; for salvation, but it is far from us."

In the book of Isaiah, there is often attention for animals. People throw their idols to rats and bats (2:20). Babylon is populated as a judgment by wild animals, such as desert animals, owls, ostriches, goats, hyenas, and jackals (13:21–22). In the cities of Aroer, near Damascus, grazing cattle dwell as judgment (17:2). In Nubia, wild animals and vultures come

---

2. Oswalt, *Isaiah 1–39*, 283.
3. E.g., Webb, *Message of Isaiah*, 190.
4. Park, *Gerechtigkeit Israels*, 351.

to judge the land (18:6). In Babylon, desert animals dwell (23:13). Israel's fortified city is occupied by grazing calves (27:10). For the prophet, Egypt is the domain of wild animals, such as the lioness, lion, snake, and cobra (30:6). As punishment, Israel becomes a haven for untamed animals, such as wild donkeys, and at the same time a grazing ground for the tamed cattle (32:14). Edom is overpowered by wild animals such as dwarf owls, porcupines, ravens, and long-eared owls (34:11), jackals, ostriches (v. 13), hyenas, billy goats (v. 14), and the arrow snake (v. 15). God will soon free Israel from jackals (35:7), lions, predators, wild animals (v. 9). During that liberation, the wild animals, jackals, and ostriches honor God (43:20). Israel is raided by field and forest animals (56:9).

In these prophetic statements, the prophet shows that Israel and the nations fail to be good rulers over God's creation (cf. Isa 3:1–7).[5] The famous explorer Christopher Columbus (1451–1506) also had to establish this. After the discovery of America, he wrote,

> God made me the messenger of the new heaven and the new earth, of which he spoke in the Apocalypse by St. John, after having spoken of it by the mouth of Isaiah, and he showed me the spot where to find it.[6]

Sometime later, Columbus would find that he had not yet found the place where Isaiah 11 is a reality. The untamed animals of the field, of which the serpent was the most cunning, still manage to seize the habitat that God gives to humans (cf. Gen 1:28; 2:15). Cities that humans were allowed to build and populate from God's hand are then judged by the wild animals, as happened in Genesis 3. Opposed to this is the reign of the Messiah, where people and animals live in peace with each other. What no people on earth can achieve will be brought by the Messiah.

From these biblical-theological observations, we let the primary physical explanation, which comes to the fore in Isaiah 11, include the symbolic explanation. Both are not mutually exclusive if we consider the testimony of Genesis 1–3, which is of significance for biblical revelation both physically and spiritually. That the prophet wants to let more shine through than physical animal peace can also be deduced from the seven animals he lists in verse 6 and in verses 7–8.

---

5. Wenkel, "Wild Beasts," 253–59; Mouw, *When the Kings Come*, 4, 35.
6. Froom, *Prophetic Faith*, II.171.

Liberation of All Creation

When it comes to the physical explanation of this passage, we are reminded that the Messiah frees the whole creation from the curse and blesses it richly (Rom 8:19–22). When he appears, there is no more mutual enmity between humans and animals:

> No lion shall be there, nor shall any ravenous beast come up on it; they shall not be found there, but the redeemed shall walk there. (Isa 35:9)

> "The wolf and the lamb shall feed together, the lion shall eat straw like the ox; but the serpent—its food shall be dust! They shall not hurt or destroy on all my holy mountain," says the Lord. (Isa 65:25)

> I will make with them a covenant of peace and banish wild animals from the land, so that they may live in the wild and sleep in the woods securely. (Ezek 34:25)

These expectations are described in the Jewish-Hellenistic *Sibylline Oracles*:

> Young women were joyful and bearable in joy. The Creator of heaven and earth gave you joy in eternity. In your midst, he will dwell. You will have an immortal light. Wolves and lambs will eat grass together on the mountains. Panthers will graze together with a buck. Bears will be together with wandering calves. The carnivorous lion will eat straw from the feeding trough as an ox does, and a little boy will lead him around with a leash. God will tame the wild animals of the earth. Infants shall sleep with dragons and serpents, and nothing shall befall them, for God's hand shall be upon them. (III.788–95)[7]

The Hellenistic Jewish philosopher Philo of Alexandria (20 BC–AD 50) wrote,

> Then it seems to me that bears, and lions, and leopards, and those beasts which are found only in India, elephants, and tigers, and all other animals whose courage and strength are invincible, will change from their solitary and unsociable habits, and adopt a more gregarious life, and, by a gradual imitation of those animals which live in troops, will become softened and accustomed to the sight of men, being no longer in a constant state of

---

7. My own translation from Dutch.

excitement and fury against him, but rather feeling awe of him as their ruler and natural master, and will behave with proper respect to him; and some of them, with exceeding greatness of tameness and affection for their master, like Maltese dogs, will even fawn upon them and wag their tails with a cheerful motion. Then the species of scorpions, and serpents, and other reptiles will keep their venom inoperative. The Egyptian river will produce those animals, which are at present carnivorous and which feed on man, called crocodiles and hippopotami, in a tame and gentle condition. The sea too will produce numerous kinds of animals, among all of which the virtuous man will be sacred and unhurt since God honors virtue and has given it immunity from all designs against it as a proper reward.[8]

These testimonies are in line with the prophetic expectation that the Messiah will realize an unprecedented animal peace on earth in the future. As in heaven, it will be on earth. A little boy will take care of a young lion. That is a promise that may find its foundation already in the statement of God to Israel. People will no longer find wild animals in their midst by obedience (Lev 26:6). This happens because wild animals turn into domesticated animals.

Animals were dragged into ruin by the first Adam, but the last Adam will redeem these animals. In the kingdom ruled by the Messiah, animals will live in peace. In the prophecy of Isaiah 11, this animal peace is poetically described.

The Eternal Judgment of the Serpent

The first pair of animals (wolf and lamb) and the fifth pair of animals (lion and cow) from Isaiah 11 return in Isaiah 65:25:

> "The wolf and the lamb shall feed together, the lion shall eat straw like the ox; but the serpent—its food shall be dust! They shall not hurt or destroy on all my holy mountain," says the Lord.

This text accompanies the announcement of the new heaven and the new earth (Isa 65:17–25). Wolf and lamb, which generally cannot be placed together, interact and eat food together. This meal stands radically against the idolatrous meal in Isaiah 65:13. There is no more evil and injustice on the holy mountain of God (cf. Isa 11:9, 11). All animals feed

---

8. Philo of Alexandria, "Rewards and Punishments," 89–90.

on vegetable products. Thus the lion, like the ox, eats hay. This theme of eating is also related to the serpent. In the future, it will not eat plants but dust. This judgment echoes the description of Genesis 3:14 by using the same word for serpent (נָחָשׁ, *nāchāsh*). The serpent that seduced humankind eats dust forever. The prophet Micah already used the serpent's behavior as an image for the nations that had resisted God (Mic 7:16–17).

This judgment of the serpent will continue in the new creation. The curse on the serpent will not be lifted. While every creature, wolf and lamb, lion and cow, is freed from the curse, the seducer has no part in the redemption. From these changes and similarities in the animal kingdom, the prophet shows that the new creation does not only ultimately encompass human society but brings blessing to the whole cosmos. Isaiah 65:25 and Isaiah 65:17 are thus thematically connected in the prophetic part of Isaiah 65:17–25 because they both mention the climax of cosmic renewal. Concerning the salvation and blessings of God's people are the salvation and benefits of animals. The designation of "new heavens and the new earth" (Isa 65:17) may imply that there will be renewed people and renewed animals in the new creation. We will come back to this in chapter 12.

8.1.3 Humans and Animals in Peace

Isaiah 11 and 65 describe the blessings of safety and beauty that the Messiah will bring to earth. He is the exquisite king. Through his courage and deeds, he gives a tremendous blessing to the planet and brings fertility and peace to the land. Thanks to his goodness, the land bears rich fruit, and flora and fauna bow before him. Everyone can hear through this reign of the Messiah that peace is becoming reality, and wild animals will no longer disturb humanity. What no human succeeded in doing will happen: human animals and nonhuman animals will live in peace with each other. These are not cheap, romantic descriptions in the book of Isaiah. What the prophet writes clashes also in his time with the harsh reality of life. The prophet does not live in a dreamy Disneyland. Around Isaiah, it is still a jungle of chaos, in which animals tear each other apart and in which lions and snakes threaten human beings. Isaiah sees in his time that the lamb is attacked by the wolf, the ox by the lion or the bear, and the infant by the viper.

Because the lamb and the cow belong to the domestic animals, the prophecy of Isaiah 11 and 65 is limited to the relationship between wild animals and human households. From God's Torah, it is realized that it is not God's intention that wild animals attack human homes. With the coming of the Messiah, there will be a blessed, peaceful harmony between humans and animals—that is, unharmed life for humanity. Artists such as the American Edward Hicks (1780–1849) and the Jew Fritz Eichenberg (1901–90) excellently depicted this harmony in their individual works of art, and the English poet Alexander Pope (1688–1744) and American poet William Meredith (1919–2007) cast it in an elegant form. Each of them shows the great blessing that the earth receives when the Messiah rules. There will be a new beginning and an end to death and suffering. Everyone may realize that then the weakest creatures will know safety. This will lead to the glorification of God (Isa 12:1–6).

From a scientific perspective, this expectation seems challenging. If the lion changes so much that it eats shredded wheat, will the lion then not disappear because of this change of anatomy? The same questions arise with the idea that animals lived in peace with each other at the beginning of creation (see chapter 4). Our knowledge from biology and astrophysics does not lead us to hope for a future world where violence and death are forever gone. It is only by faith that we realize from biblical testimonies that death and violence do not belong to God. In that case, it is possible to believe that God will renew and positively change this world. If God chooses to redeem the world and make it conform his image, all evil elements must give way. So, God's character is a wake-up call to reflect on the future of creation.[9]

Because Isaiah 11 and 65 speak of harmony between animals and humans, we realize that the relationship between creatures is more significant than is often thought. The peace of the Messiah also manifests itself in this: "His authority shall grow continually, and there shall be endless peace for the throne of David and his kingdom" (Isa 9:7a). Just as human disobedience to God brought decay into the lives of other creatures, the obedience of the Messiah brings blessing into the lives of creatures. The Prince of Peace chooses to rule the earth from God's character and make the glory of the Creator everywhere visible. He conquers evil that is still overgrowing the earth today. Because of this he is the Person par excellence who fulfills God's desire for humans to subdue the earth. Then

---

9. E.g., Hausoul, "Theology and Cosmology."

creation fulfills the dream that God always had. This is more than a return to the garden of Eden. Eden was only the starting point of God's plan with this creation (cf. chapter 2.2). That starting point will find its completion in the new heaven and new earth. It reminds us of the original creation in Genesis 1–2, but is of a different quality: it is the glorified original and redeemed creation.

8.2 JESUS AND THE WILD ANIMALS

8.2.1 Christ Was with the Wild Animals

The ultimate peace of which Isaiah speaks "can only be completed in a radical new creation of people and animals," according to the German Old Testament historian Otto Kaiser (1924–2017).[10] A unique phenomenon is that the Gospel of Mark mentions that the wild animals were with Jesus after the temptations in the wilderness:

> He was in the wilderness forty days, tempted by Satan; and he was with the wild beasts; and the angels waited on him. (Mark 1:13)

This particular situation is only found in this Gospel. What Mark writes remains premature and requires clarification. What exactly happens after the temptations in the wilderness? Does this demonstrate the hostile nature of the wilderness to humans? Do wild animals threaten Jesus?

Interpreters assume that the latter is the case.[11] Because the biblical text states that Jesus is with the wild animals and not the other way around (that the wild animals are with Jesus), there is a chance that Jesus will have to take on these animals. The attack of the wild animals then follows the attack of Satan. This idea can be substantiated by the fact that the expression "wild beasts" (θηρίον, *thērion*) has a negative connotation. We think of the snakes and scorpions that lived in Israel's wilderness. They face the angels serving Jesus as dangerous animals.

Did these angels protect the Messiah from the animals? Then what Psalm 91:11–13 states would come true:

> For he will command his angels concerning you to guard you in all your ways. On their hands they will bear you up, so that you will not dash your foot against a stone. You will tread on

---

10. Kaiser, "Die ersten und die letzten Dinge," 82. My own translation.
11. Heil, "Jesus with the Wild Animals"; France, *Mark*, 87; Caneday, "Mark's Provocative Use," 27–33; Gibson, *Temptations of Jesus*, 65–67; Gundry, *Mark*, 58–59.

the lion and the adder, the young lion and the serpent you will trample under foot.

Many Christians have recognized themselves in this situation later on. Many of them would fall prey to wild animals because they continued to follow Jesus Christ. They may derive courage from the idea that Christ also stood face-to-face with wild animals during temptations. The Lord knows their fear and supplication for a speedy redemption in such circumstances.

At the same time, numerous interpreters do not see wild animals as opponents but as servants of the Messiah.[12] Nowhere in Mark 1:13 is there any mention of struggle or enmity. The conjunction "and" (καί, *kai*) even puts the wild animals alongside the angels. The wild animals come to Jesus to be subservient. Possibly the word "with" (μετά, *meta*) indicates this servitude. Elsewhere in Mark, this word has the meaning of proximity (Mark 3:14; 5:18; 14:67). Both angels and wild animals then positively address Jesus.

Is this a strange situation? Not directly. From Isaiah 11 and 65 there is the expectation that the Messiah will reign peacefully over animals and creates a paradisiacal atmosphere of salvation around him, causing wild animals to lose aggression. So, they could live in peace when Christ was in their midst. Through the work of the Messiah, not only the blind would see, and the paralyzed would walk. His service would extend further and lead to wild animals being brought to peace. The Messiah would do what God traditionally commanded humans to do: subdue creation from God's image and likeness. Followers of Christ were allowed to hold on to this. The hope that a time of peace and harmony in the future would come, in which both humans and animals would share, would not be ashamed. Thanks to Christ, animals and people would live in peace with each other.

In Jewish and Christian tradition it is stated that this peace and harmony among humans and animals was also present in the garden of Eden, because both lived vegetarian lives (see chapters 4 and 13). So, at the beginning of his service, Christ immediately restored peace among animals, which had previously been taken from earth by humans disobedience. This event would be repeated several times in history.

---

12. Donahue and Harrington, *Gospel of Mark*, 66; Moloney, *Gospel of Mark*, 38–39; Marcus, *Mark 1–8*, 168–71; Bauckham, "Jesus and Animals II," 58; Bauckham, "Jesus and the Wild Animals," 3–21; Guelich, *Mark 1–8*, 38–39.

8.2.2 Legends about Jesus and the Animals

Early on, Christian tradition chose to place two animals in the manger to connect it from the very beginning with Christ's redemption. The Gospel of Pseudo-Matthew from the fifth century recounts:

> On the third day, after the birth of our Lord Jesus Christ, Mary went from the cave to the stable. There she put the child in a food bowl while an ox and a donkey worshipped it. This fulfilled what the prophet Isaiah said, "The ox knows its owner and the donkey knows the feeding bowl of its master" [Isa 1:3]. Therefore the ox and donkey worshipped him when he was in their midst. This also fulfilled what the prophet Habakuk said, "Between two living beings you have revealed yourself" [Hak 3:2(LXX)]. Joseph and Mary stayed in this place for three days. (ch. 14)[13]

For many Christians, the presence of the ox and the donkey in the birth story of Jesus is so obvious that one no longer realizes that its source comes from outside the Bible. The tradition of both animals at the manger can already be found on various sarcophagi from the fourth and fifth centuries and ivory works of art from the fifth and sixth centuries.[14] In this same extrabiblical gospel, we learn that the holy family, fleeing from Herod, takes a short rest in a cave. In that cave, they are overwhelmed by a large number of dragons. But they do not come to devour them, but to worship Christ. Christ calls on the dragons not to kill any of those present. To his frightened parents, he says:

> Don't be afraid and don't treat me like a child, because I have always been perfect, and all the animals of the forest should bow down before Me. (Gospel of Pseudo-Matthew, 18:2)

This event recalls Psalm 148:7: "Praise the Lord from the earth, you sea monsters and all deeps." Other animals, such as lions and panthers, also meet the holy family in this extrabiblical literature. They help them on their flight to Egypt. Each time this is accompanied by the worship of the Messiah:

> The lions walked with them, while the oxen carried the donkeys and other pack animals that took the supplies. They did not attack any of them and were tame with the sheep and rams they

---

13. A German edition of the Gospel of Pseudo-Matthew was consulted; these are all my translations.

14. Schneemelcher, *New Testament Apocrypha*, 65.

had brought from Judea. They were further accompanied by wolves and had no fear. None of them was injured by the other. This fulfilled what the prophet said, "The wolf and the lamb will graze together, and the lion will eat straw" [Js65:25]. (Gospel of Pseudo-Matthew, 19:2)

These kinds of stories underline the expectation that the Messiah would bring peace to the whole of creation. His redemption would not be limited to humans. It would also include the animal world, as the prophets proclaimed. Jesus would bring life on earth back into harmony and get rid of the violence between the creatures. Nor were animals rejected by God. The Creator would not destroy his creatures if he founded the kingdom on earth. He would complete creation and make it as God had always had in mind. God did not want the horrible nature of chaos and violence. He longed for a creation in which peace, harmony, and order would reign. Many Christians were inspired and motivated in lifestyle by this future peace of God's kingdom. This caused legendary stories to appear in history, strongly reminiscent of the harmony between people and animals of which the Old and New Testament testified.

8.2.3 Legendary Stories of Animal Peace

Lions, Crocodiles, and Other Animals

Confronted with wild animals, Isaiah 11 and Mark 1 made Christians realize that this should not be the end of their lives. Particularly concerning lions, various testimonies were created that gave an impression of the coming peace between animals and humans. Christians believed that God could deliver them from the lion pit just like Daniel. God then sent his angel to muzzle the lions (Dan 6:23a). Imposing lions that were considered formidable predators could demonstrate compassion, sympathy, and empathy in unimaginable ways. Sometimes this led people to think that the peace of which Isaiah 11 and 65 spoke was already present on earth. With the coming of Christ, the promise of the messianic realm became a reality for those who believed. God could protect his children from the violence of wild animals.

Thus, lions laid themselves at the feet of Saint Thecla of Iconium (~30–100), of Saint Agapitius (d. 274), and of Saint Vitus of Sicily (d.

304), when they were let loose on them by enemies.[15] The church father Tertullianus (~160–230) tells the tale of Perpetua and Felicitas that Saturus, one of Perpetua's friends, was tied to a wild boar in the arena of Carthage. The boar dragged Saturus along but refused to devour him with his teeth. Instead, it attacked the animal fighter and killed him. The organizers were furious. They tied up Saturus and sent a bear at him. However, the bear refused to come out of his cage. Only at the third attempt, the bear managed to get out of his cage. In the end, a leopard tore Saturus to pieces.[16]

Another story tells that a lion appears to the church father Jerome of Stridon (347–420) when he eats outside at a table with fellow Christians. All the believers flee, screaming, but the lion has no evil intentions. Jerome recognizes this and calls them back. The lion had a thorn in his front legs and was hoping to find help from Christians. Jerome helped the lion, and out of gratitude, the lion stayed as a pet in the monastery.[17]

This story has several parallels with other events. We hear that the Roman slave Androclus, who fled the church, meets a lion, crying loudly and showing him a thorn in his paw. When Androclus is later sentenced to death by the animals, he meets the lion again in the arena. Both embrace each other. This leads people to call for their release.[18] It is also told that a certain Elpis from Samos experienced that a lion opened his mouth so wide that Elpis could remove a strong bone that was stuck between the teeth.[19]

Another story is that of a mother who addresses the bishop of Augsburg because a wolf took her child. On the bishop's intercession, the wolf brings the child back to its mother in good health.[20] Also, animals in the early church would sometimes obey the orders of the monks. This ensured that animals did not destroy the plants of the Christians and served them when they were called. Wild donkeys, snakes, and crocodiles thus served as carriers or guardians of Christians. Crocodiles carry the Egyptian monk Pachomius (~292–348) to the other side of a river.[21] A hyena

---

15. Braun, *Tracht und Attribute*, 36, 686, 729–30.
16. Meijer, *Hond*, 88.
17. Schulze, "Der Heilige," 281.
18. Aelianus, *Natura Animalium*, 5.14.
19. E.g., Meijer, *Hond*, 79; Pliny the Elder, *Naturalis Historia*, 8:56–58.
20. Braun, *Tracht und Attribute*, 667.
21. Schenderling, *Mens en dier*, 147.

brings her blind offspring to a Christian, upon which the Christian heals the animal.[22] And a wild boar becomes the servant of the Irish abbot Ciaràn of Clonmacnoise (516–49).[23]

Nowhere in the New Testament is this peace between Christians and wild animals found. Instead, we learn that the apostle Paul has to fight the wild animals in Ephesus (1 Cor 15:32). Nevertheless, these testimonies remain special. For example, the Roman soldier and scientist Pliny the Elder (AD 24–79) tells us that the lion is one of the few animals that can grant mercy to a supplicant. He who kneels is spared. The lion expresses his anger towards men rather than women and children. Libyans believed that the lion understands the supplication of a human being. For example, Pliny the Elder learned that a Gallic prisoner calmed many lions in the forest by telling them she was a weak, fleeing woman. To choose her as prey would be unworthy of the lion, who likes the reputation of the king of the wild. Whether this story is true or made up, Pliny doesn't know for sure. Opinions about it are divided.[24]

The Modern Age

In recent times, there are curious situations among animals that remind us of the future promise of Isaiah 11 and 65. For example, on June 22, 2005, a twelve-year-old girl in Ethiopia was abducted by seven men. Their goal was to force her to marry one of them. Sergeant Wondmu Wedja declared to the press that they had found the girl alive, but in shock. Three lions had emerged during her abduction. They caused the seven kidnappers to flee.

Wedja testifies that the lions guarded her until they found her. They left her as a gift and retreated into the forest. If these lions had not turned up, the situation would probably have ended badly. Often young girls are raped and beaten multiple times to force them into marriage. Everyone sees the attitude of the lions as a miracle because they usually attack people.

A wilderness expert from the Ethiopian Ministry of Agriculture said the girl was probably spared because she cried fiercely during this traumatic abduction. "Maybe this young, softly wailing girl reminded the lions of the gentle meowing of a lion cub. That would explain why they

---

22. Lietzmann, *Geschichte 4: Kirchenväter*.
23. Waddell, *Beasts and Saints*, 104.
24. Pliny the Elder, *Naturalis Historia*, 8:48.

didn't devour her," he says. Four of the seven men were captured by the police in the meantime.[25]

In addition to this peace between lions and humans, there is peace between animals. For example, there are recent stories in which carnivores build up relationships with tame animals. In the 165 km² large nature reserve Samburu National, it was observed in 2002 that a lioness took care of a young oryx in the north of Kenya. Typically these skewers are a favorite meal for lions. Still, the lioness adopted the animal as her baby and protected it from other predators, including a leopard. For the discoverer Herman Mwasaghu, this was the eighth wonder of the world on earth. According to wildlife expert Vincent Kapeen, this happened because animals are instinctively encouraged to take care of other young animals. However, while drinking together by the river, the lioness fell asleep, and another lion killed the oryx. After waking up, the lioness was torn over what had happened. She furiously went to the lion and growled several times. Then she left the area.[26]

A curious phenomenon also occurred in the famous Mutsugoro Okoku Zoo of the Japanese capital Tokyo. A snake made friends with a dwarf hamster. The snake refused to eat mice from the freezer. Animal keepers thought that a hamster would probably arouse the snake's appetite. They gave it the name Gohan, which means "meal." However, the snake also refused this meal. They seemed to prefer to share the cage with the hamster. The hamster even sometimes slept on the back of the snake. Although the snake started to eat rodents from the freezer, she still showed no interest in devouring her boyfriend. An animal keeper testified that he never had seen such a scene in his life.[27]

---

25. Mitchell, "Three Lions"; Associated Press, "Lions Save Girl"; British Broadcasting Corporation, "Kidnapped Girl."

26. British Broadcasting Corporation, "Lioness and the Oryx."

27. Associated Press, "Hamster."

9

Prophetic Images

A REFLECTION ON HOW to deal with prophetic texts is essential for those who want to elaborate on God's future for animals. At the same time, such a reflection is not easy. Human thoughts can be quite tricky. In concrete terms, this means that this chapter is somewhat more abstract than the other ones in this book. However, we should not take our reflection on the prophetic biblical language too lightly. That is why I have included this reflection. At the beginning of it, we will reflect on the importance of image and speech in the interpretations of biblical images. In this context, we will discuss the impact of conceptual and metaphorical speaking (chapter 9.1). After that, we look more concretely at similarities and differences between the current creation and the new creation (chapter 9.2).

9.1 TAKING A CLOSER LOOK AT PROPHETIC SPEAKING

9.1.1 The Physical World and Biblical Images

Attention to the Physical

In the testimony of Jesus, the promise of future peace gives us a wonderful foretaste. Together with many other descriptions of the future, they call for a reconsideration of the anthropocentrism that originated in the time of the Enlightenment. This anthropocentrism placed the human being as the only central being. However, the biblical expectation of the future shows that God's future is more holistic than is often thought.

Besides the future for humanity, it also includes a future for the animal kingdom. There will be a "super paradise" that far surpasses the glorious descriptions of Genesis 1–2. God, as Creator, chooses not to let the work of his hands be lost. Not only the spiritual, invisible part of this creation belongs to God; also, the physical, material part of creation is taken into renewal by the Creator.

Scholars often search for a hermeneutic key that can help unlock prophetic and apocalyptic texts for Christian doctrine. Particularly the current social interest in the physical side of creation is causing question marks to be placed where prophetic or apocalyptic texts are stripped of any physical meaning. It has already been pointed out on several occasions that systematic theology paid little attention to this kind of texts when it spoke about the Christian expectation of the future.[1] After all, the kingdom Jesus is not only looking forward to subjective, individual, spiritual, and internal matters. It is also about objective, collective, physical, and external things. The German theologian Hans Küng (b. 1928) writes that a renewed listening to the prophetic earthly-human images can make us realize again

> what a mental impoverishment it would imply if we tried to rationalize these images out of existence or reduce them to a few concepts and ideas. Jesus himself speaks of the feast at the end of time with new wine, of the marriage, of the banquet to which all are invited, of great joy on all sides. . . . All metaphors of hope, not yet "sicklied over with the pale cast of thought."[2]

Although John writes that it is not yet revealed what we would be (1 John 3:2), this does not mean that this hope is unknown. This verse is often used for that purpose, but John points out that what Christians know has not yet come to light in this reality. This will only happen later when all things are renewed. Then the sons of God will be revealed (Rom 8:23). A parallel with this is the coming of Christ. At his first coming, he was exposed to Israel (John 1:31). At his second coming, he will be revealed to the whole world (1 John 2:28). So, it is a known expectation that has not yet been fulfilled, but about which the Christian faith testifies many times.

---

1. Hausoul, *New Heaven*; Wilkinson, *Eschatology*, 24–26, 54–57; Braaten, "Significance of Apocalypticism," 482–83.

2. Küng, *Eternal Life?*, 218.

Image and Speech: An Inseparable Duo

The Roman Catholic theologian Karl Rahner (1904–84) pleads in the interpretation of prophecy to make a distinction between form (*image*) and content (*speech*), without disconnecting the two. Every human thought about the future automatically creates imagery. There is no "understanding" without "proposals."[3] Therefore, it is impossible in Christian doctrine to speak about the future in an imageless way. Anyone who tries to do so will discover that the original biblical imagery then merges into a speech that is separate from the biblical imagination. The original "image" is then lost and replaced by the interpretation of the interpreter, which in itself forms a new image. This strips the original biblical-prophetic image of its imaginative character and records it too unambiguously and conceptually. Whoever reads in biblical prophecies about a rainbow sees more than a color arch. The rainbow reminds the reader of God's promises and therefore carries with it a symbolic value. It is about more than colors.

At the same time, we must not imprison the future in one prophetic image. That would also be too short of the original biblical message. For this reason, Rahner pleads for the various images we encounter in the Bible about the future to be interpreted as one coherent whole.[4] They are different voices of the same orchestra. Both the prophetic images of the Old Testament and those of the New Testament should participate in them.

Nor should we lose our "speech" in our dealings with biblical imagery. There is otherwise a danger that we will interpret the images as paintings that correspond to future reality down to the smallest detail. The prophecy then resembles a doctor's prescription or construction manual, which must be followed precisely and where no differences in emphasis are possible. In such an approach, a text in which God announces that he strikes bow and arrow out of the hands of the superpower Gog (Ezek 39:3) is conceived as a future war in which Gog attacks others with the military armor of bow and arrow. But the prophets do not want to present their visions as photorealistic paintings, doctor's prescriptions, or construction manuals of the future in such a detailed manner.[5] These are historically, culturally situated images, which the prophet expresses concretely to point to a future reality. This is why Gog's weapons can be

---

3. Rahner, *Hörer*, 201–2; Rahner, "Prinzipien," 426–28.
4. Rahner, "Prinzipien," 427–28.
5. Thiselton, "Future," 14; Sandy, *Plowshares*, 83–102.

interpreted as the weapon of war that Gog is deprived.[6] So prophecy is not the same as looking into a crystal ball. It is looking through colored stained glass windows. It is not the same as exact historiography. It is looking ahead in images, which offer a sketch of a new physical and spiritual reality.

So, image and speech remain indispensable in speaking about the Christian expectation of the future. The biblical images are of theological value because of what they say (*content*) and how they say it (*presentation*). The form influences the content cognitively and emotionally.[7] In explaining this, image form and image content must match. Neither should exclude each other. The image remains an image that refers to its full richness, to a reality that cannot be replaced with words.

Methodology for Imagery

We want to take this into account in the explanation of prophetic texts. Gregory Beale (b. 1949) offers a method in the interpretation of biblical symbolism and imagery. He does this by working from a fourfold division: (1) the description of the vision in its context, (2) the references present in the vision, (3) the symbolism present in the vision, and (4) the meaning of the vision. Thus the vision of the beast in Revelation 13 refers to one or more persons in history (point 2). The symbolism of the beast refers to a power that resists God and his people in a brutal and demonic way and reminds us of the beasts in the visions of the Old Testament (point 3). From this form, the meaning of the vision can be deduced (point 4).[8]

Through this method, different images in the Bible can be dissected. We want to take care not to merge the image visions thoughtlessly into one image. The images should enrich each other and make the different perspectives of the expectation visible.[9]

In his reflection on salvation, the famous preacher Tim Keller (b. 1950) sees these images as the "languages" or "grammars" that help us explain what God's salvation means. When it comes to the work of the

---

6. Sandy, *Plowshares*, 90, 184; Block, *Ezekiel 25–48*, 461–62; Cooper, *Ezekiel*, 341; Allen, *Ezekiel 20–48*, 207.

7. Beale, *Book of Revelation*, 55, 68; Rahner, "Eschatologie," 1097; "Prinzipien," 410.

8. Beale, *Book of Revelation*, 52–54, 67.

9. Beale, *Book of Revelation*, 57, 66; Rahner, "Prinzipien," 408, 416–19, 423–24.

salvation of Jesus Christ, this is done in the battlefield's language, in which the power of Christ conquers the forces of evil: In the marketplace's language, where Christ buys us loose and frees us from slavery and exploitation. In the language of exile, about Christ who was banished to earth to free us from our exile and bring us home. In the temple's language, about Christ's sacrifice that cleanses us and makes us acceptable to a holy God. In the court's language, where Christ stands before the judge and carries our punishment so that he can remove our guilt and process our acquittal. In the language of a deputy, where Jesus, as our deputy, carries the punishment, goes into exile, so that we may receive freedom and security. In the same way, the future visions of redemption can be interpreted.

In this way, biblical theology can provide valuable elements for systematic theology in its interpretation of biblical images. It can analyze the biblical images in depth and place them in the broader thematic context of the biblical storyline. The whole of Christian theology is involved in this. After all, while popular faith designs use this imagery too quickly and thoughtlessly for their representations, official theology can respond to this by sufficiently implementing the imagery in their eschatological framework.

9.1.2 Concepts and Metaphors

Speaking in Terms

In general, the handling of biblical imagery remains reserved in Christian doctrine. We also encounter this reluctance with the German Protestant Jürgen Moltmann (b. 1926). Although Moltmann mentions several biblical images of the new creation in his works, he is careful not to visualize the new heaven and the new earth concretely. As a result, his reflection remains mainly philosophical-ideal and can come across to many as rather abstract. A concrete description of hope, however, is unthinkable, according to Moltmann. That would capture things too conceptually. Concepts enclose, are unambiguous, and always mean the same thing. They are definitions which record how something exactly is. That has the danger that ideas become rigid and become idols. The future is then squeezed into its description.[10]

---

10. Moltmann, *Erfahrungen*, 100, 156.

We also see this when we speak conceptually about God. A concept of God turns out to be a dead idol that we control. God is then as fixed as $2 + 2 = 4$. Whoever defines everything conceptually in speaking about the future thus captures it entirely in a photo. The future is then tightly defined and bounded and excludes the possibility that new biblical-theological insights bring other elements forward.

Speaking in Metaphors

Speaking in terms is opposed to speaking in metaphors. Metaphors unlock, are ambiguous, and create surprise effects. That is why God's Spirit speaks to the biblical prophets through images, analogies, and comparisons, in an "as if." Doing so, they offer physical and spiritual elements about the coming world, which we can better characterize as "ideas" instead of "concepts." An idea is a boundary concept, representing things that are of founding meaning to us but transcending reason and escaping precise definition.[11]

An example of this is love. If you ask someone what love is, you will find that this word is difficult to capture conceptually. It is not so easy to define love in fixed terms. Therefore, we speak of love in a more ideological sense: Love is warm affection, a sense of dedication to someone else. Love can address an animal or an object. Exactly how love expresses itself differs in every situation. Love has several meanings and cannot be captured with one term.

It is good to let these reflections affect us as we think about God's future for animals. Even if we speak only metaphysically about the future, we realize that this transcends our present perception, but this does not abandon the prophetic image or discard it. After all, the other danger is that a too great emphasis on speaking in metaphors leads to a blurring of the prophetic vision because everything is understood metaphorically. The prophetic image can then no longer be explained concretely and becomes a mystery with great vagueness. A healthy balance in dealing with biblical imagery is a challenge. In this respect, prophecy is butterfly theology for caterpillars.

---

11. Caird, *Language and Imagery*, 259; McFague, *Metaphorical Theology*, 16–19.

9.1.3 Positive Progress and Negative Removal

Prophetic texts in the Bible look ahead to what has yet to be done, to what is possible and promised. The view on the continuity and discontinuity between this life and the future life is thus limited. Anyone who interprets the visions of the new creation has to take the similarities and differences between the present creation and the new creation into account. So things are the same and things are different. The biblical expectations thus open the present to God's liberation and renewal and bring about more than just an extension of the present creation.

In Revelation 21–22, we see these two aspects of similarity (continuity) and difference (discontinuity) in the prophetic descriptions of the new heaven and the new earth. We discover how this biblical text about the future magnifies, on the one hand, the positive, uplifting, and rejoicing from this creation (continuity) and, on the other hand, the negative, sad, and only wholly exorcised (discontinuity).

After all, Christian hope, which resembles today's world domination too much, is losing the redemption that the crucified and resurrected Christ brought to creation. Nor should we forget that the biblical expectation places this and the future age in conflict with each other. This is expressed in contrast-images, contrast-histories, and contrast-worlds. For example, the heavenly Jerusalem as an image of the new creation is contrasted with the earthly Babylon as an image of the present cases and transient creation (Rev 18–21). Through Christ's resurrection, various things are an extension of the past: a new land, a new Exodus, a new David, a new covenant, a new Mount Zion. These are all terms that indicate continuity. Besides, there are negative things that find an end in the new creation (Rev 21:4). To achieve this, God's intervention is necessary. After all, the present creation cannot develop into the new heaven and the new earth. Only a radical intervention from above can bring us to that goal.

The many positive elements in the prophetic imagery of the new creation, which are in line with the first creation and remain present in the new creation, help us to assume that we cannot know anything about the future. Otherwise, the boundaries are set so sharply that any talk about the new creation becomes impossible.

An example of this reluctance can be found at the Swiss Reformed theologian Emil Brunner (1889–1966). He writes that we know nothing about the new heaven and the new earth and can only speculate about it.[12] In this regard, Emil Brunner is a follower of the German philosopher Immanuel Kant, who previously stated that humans should be content with only that which could be intellectually determined. Any expectation that went beyond this recognizable world could and should be avoided.[13]

With this attitude, we have to ask ourselves what to do with the biblical statements about the new heaven and the new earth. That is why it is not advisable to set limits to the biblical messages or speculate about them in detail. A deeper reflection on speaking in terms of continuity and discontinuity is necessary to gain insight into the theme of the new creation.

9.2 CONTINUITY AND DISCONTINUITY

In Christian doctrine, God is confessed to be the Creator of heaven and earth. That choice is not self-evident. For example, the ancient Greeks thought that shapeless matter, such as water, wind, and fire, existed forever. The Bible testifies that God made the world and cared for it. This led to animals having a higher value in Judeo-Christian culture than in Greek philosophy. It was unthinkable for a Jew or Christian that nature, animals, or plants had no value for God. As Creator, God is elevated above creation and redeems creation to realize his excellent plan.[14] That prospect is not only found in the Old Testament. The New Testament also looks forward to the restoration of all things, as Peter testifies after the healing of a disabled person when he speaks of Jesus, "who must remain in heaven until the time of universal restoration that God announced long ago through his holy prophets" (Acts 3:21). Faith in a future for God's good creation is inextricably linked to the Messiah's work of redemption. Jesus Christ redeems body and soul, and that is what the disabled at the Beautiful Gate discovered (Acts 3:1–26).

In the proclamation of the gospel, this belief in physical salvation was under tremendous pressure. It was a curse for Greeks and other contemporaries to learn that there was a resurrection of the dead (Acts 17; 1 Cor 15). For them, the body was a prison for the invisible soul. The testimony of the resurrection was under pressure. According to

---

12. Brunner, *Lehre von Glauben und Vollendung*, 491; Brunner, *Das Ewige*, 221–22.
13. Kant, "End of All Things," 79.
14. Graf, *Moral Dimensions of Animal Life*, 11; Thiel, "For What May We Hope?," 527; Attfield, *Ethics*, 26.

Acts, the apostle Paul was rejected on the Areopagus when he spoke about the resurrection:

> When they heard of the resurrection of the dead, some scoffed; but others said, "We will hear you again about this." At that point Paul left them. (Acts 17:32–33; see also chapter 2.2)

Even in the centuries that followed, the belief in resurrection would often be erased as a children's fable.[15]

This hostile attitude towards the resurrection caused the Christian proclamation to keep silent about the resurrection theme. Christians missed the biblical testimony and adopted ideas of a future in heaven in which bodiless souls resided. Talking about a future new earth became unfamiliar in the church. People knew about a new heaven, but no one seemed to be waiting for a new earth. Also, the infrequent mentions of "new heavens and new earth" or "the renewal of all things" in the New Testament caused this gap to widen. Few biblical texts explicitly dealt with the renewal of creation. This seemed to confirm that the Old Testament was concerned with earth and the New Testament with heaven.

Only texts like Romans 8, Colossians 1, and Revelation 21–22 still reminded us of the Old Testament expectation of a new heaven and a new earth, in which God's plan with the original creation was completed. The doctrine of the first things (*protology*) and the doctrine of the last things (*eschatology*) was seen from there as two hinge sheets, which found their central axis in the theme of Christology.[16]

Together with the teaching of the Gospels and the book of Acts, this apostolic testimony allowed humanity to see salvation as part of the greater redemption of God's creation. Through Christ, everything is created, the visible and the invisible. And through him and for him, everything is reconciled with him, everything on earth, and everything in heaven so that he is first in everything (Col 1:16–20).

So how should we imagine the relationship between the present creation and the new creation? Did the biblical writers believe in a new heaven and new earth that—just like the original creation—would be created entirely out of nothing (*ex nihilo*)? Or did they think that God would change this old creation, renovate it, or transform it into the new creation (*ex vetero*)? From theology, various biblical testimonies about

---

15. Bynum, "Material Continuity"; Bynum, *Resurrection of the Body*; Moo, "Nature in the New Creation," 453, 461–62; Wright, *Resurrection*.

16. Cf. Hausoul, "Protologie," 11–29.

the new creation can be divided into two groups: a group that emphasizes the continuity of all good things and a group that emphasizes the discontinuity of all negative things.

9.2.1 Discontinuity in Continuity

The Testimony of 2 Peter

In his Christian doctrine, the American systematicist Lewis Chafer (1871–1952) opts for the idea of a new creation that emerges ultimately from nowhere: "The present heaven and the present earth are to pass away and disappear forever."[17] In the Bible, we find several texts that emphasize this discontinuity between this creation and the new creation. A classic text, which is often quoted in conversations about this, is 2 Peter 3. It is a good idea to use this as the primary text for this idea:

> But the day of the Lord will come like a thief, and then the heavens will pass away with a loud noise, and the elements will be dissolved with fire, and the earth and everything that is done on it will be disclosed. Since all these things are to be dissolved in this way, what sort of persons ought you to be in leading lives of holiness and godliness, waiting for and hastening the coming of the day of God, because of which the heavens will be set ablaze and dissolved, and the elements will melt with fire? But, in accordance with his promise, we wait for new heavens and a new earth, where righteousness is at home. (2 Pet 3:10–13)

This biblical text emphasizes God's intervention and the associated fire-judgment. The heavenly spheres perish on that day, and the earth's elements melt away because of the fire. The fire on the day of the Lord cannot be underestimated. It scorches the earth and everything that grows there, and it will devour the foundations of the mountains (Deut 32:22). Then "the host of heaven shall rot away, and the skies roll up like a scroll" (Isa 34:4). With the murmur of a flying arrow, the rolling of thunder or mighty waters, the world's fire engulfs everything.

This fire is a catastrophe for creation, like the great flood that was in the past. The author of 2 Peter writes about this flood in Noah's time before the fire flood is mentioned. In the days of Noah,

---

17. Chafer, *Systematic Theology*, V:362.

the world of that time was deluged with water and perished. But by the same word the present heavens and earth have been reserved for fire, being kept until the day of judgment and destruction of the godless. (2 Pet 3:6–7)

The Jews liked to characterize the creation after the flood as "new creation."[18] God made everything new, and the evil that previously dominated the world order was no longer thought.

This context illustrates that the writer of 2 Peter mentions the threat of fire in response to the mockers and the wicked, who reject God and his promises (3:3, 7). It should encourage believers to live holy and pious lives (3:11, 14) and look forward to the fulfillment of God's promises (3:12–13). While mockers ignore the coming of God, Christians live in joyful expectation. Peter emphasizes that what he says is related to the writings of Paul, who also points to God's promises (3:16). That reference makes it possible to make a bridge in speaking about the new heaven and the new earth between 2 Peter and the writings of Paul. The author recognizes that "the corruption that is in the world" (2 Pet 1:4) is over. The triune God gave his Son to deliver people from this destruction so that they would not come under judgment.

God Fulfills His Promises

From this context and background of 2 Peter 3:10–12, interpreters chose to reject the idea that Peter teaches that God's creation perishes.[19] God's promises for creation are not nullified like evil desires. God's promises are fulfilled and lead to the new heaven and the new earth. The fire does not burn the positive works of God. God does not let his creation destroy itself. Only evil powers do that. Instead, God destroys those who destroy the earth (Rev 11:18). Therefore, the Son of God has appeared to destroy the deeds of the devil (1 John 3:8). The day of the Lord stands in continuity with this, and the elements of the earth are destroyed by a flood of fire, in a similar way to the flood of water. Just as the flood in Noah's days put an end to the evil worldly system, so it will be in the future. In the words of the Dutch systematic theologian Anthony Hoekema (1913–1988),

---

18. Beale, *New Testament*, 60.

19. For the early church: Irenaeus of Lyon, *Adversus Haereses*, I.7.1; V.35.2–36.1; Origen of Alexandria, *Contra Celsum*, II.11–21; IV.13. Cf. Hausoul, *New Heaven*; Raabe, "'Daddy,'" 148–60; Caird, *Revelation*, 265; Scott, *Revelation*, 418; Lenski, *Epistles of St. Peter*, 350.

> If God would have to annihilate the present cosmos, Satan would have won a great victory. For then Satan would have succeeded in so devastatingly corrupting the present cosmos and the present earth that God could do nothing with it but to blot it totally out of existence. But Satan did not win such a victory. On the contrary, Satan has been decisively defeated. God will reveal the full dimensions of that defeat when he shall renew this very earth on which Satan deceived mankind and finally banish from it all the results of Satan's evil machinations.[20]

Several texts emphasizing the discontinuity confirm this line of thought. When God intervenes, the earth and heaven flee: "Then I saw a great white throne and the one who sat on it; the earth and the heaven fled from his presence, and no place was found for them" (Rev 20:11). There is no place anymore for what used to terrorize and smear the earth: "Then I saw a new heaven and a new earth; for the first heaven and the first earth had passed away, and the sea was no more" (21:1). All evil will disappear, and the good of God's creation will remain.

The impact of evil in creation is so significant that the whole earth and the entire sky disappear. It is not a fungus that can be banished from creation. God sent his Son because creation is corrupt to the root of its existence and is marked by sin. Against the biblical texts that emphasize the decay of heaven and earth stand the promises of God that the earth and heaven will not perish. As the heavenly bodies lose their orbit and even fall to earth (Rev 6:14–15), we hear at the same time that they must praise God, for "he established them forever and ever; he fixed their bounds, which cannot be passed" (Ps 148:6), "You set the earth on its foundations, so that it shall never be shaken" (Ps 104:5). Destruction of God's creation is unknown in the Bible. This creation is redeemed and renewed by God. That is why Peter, in his first sermon, looks forward to "the time of universal restoration" (Acts 3:21). These words are in harmony with the difficult statement in 2 Peter 3.

The End of the World System

Creation emerges after a fierce and not to be underestimated fire even more tested and cleansed than the world after the flood of water. The image used by 2 Peter recalls gold that is melted down and purified by fire.

---

20. Hoekema, *Bible and Future*, 281.

The "elements" (στοιχεῖα, *stoicheia*) that perish are the evil world spirits, but also the negative governments and their social influences, traditions, and precepts. We don't have to think about raw materials or the periodic elements from chemistry in the context of 2 Peter. Those elements are good and do not have to perish.[21] What perishes is the sinful world system. The power with which that happens and the discontinuity which it produces is apparent from the terms "passing," "burning," "loosening," and "melting." So, Peter's statement should not be taken too lightly. It should not give the impression that there is only a small bump between this creation and the new creation. The work of Jesus Christ is too precious to be taken too lightly. The Gospel is about a gigantic struggle against the most dangerous and pernicious powers this creation has ever known.

The author of 2 Peter declares: there is an extreme discontinuity in continuity. But the believer realizes that this is not the end of God's creation. God has made promises for creation. Christ is the firstborn of all creation because he created everything. All is created for him, and through him, God wants to reconcile everything (Col 1:15–20). But just as Jerusalem was judged and no stone was left on the other, this will also happen with creation. And just as God resurrected Jerusalem from the dust based on his promises, he will resurrect creation from the dust like he promised. Therefore, the new heaven and the new earth are not an extension of the historical misdeeds in creation. They are straight in line with the promises and in the light of an new creation where justice dwells permanently. Now righteousness still suffers, but in the coming messianic kingdom righteousness will rule, so that righteousness will dwell eternally in the new creation. Then the words from Isaiah are fulfilled:

> Shower, O heavens, from above, and let the skies rain down righteousness; let the earth open, that salvation may spring up; and let it cause them righteousness to sprout up also; I the Lord have created it. (Isa 45:8)

> For as the earth brings forth its shoots, and as a garden causes what is sown in it to spring up, so the Lord God will cause righteousness and praise to spring up before all the nations. (Isa 61:11)

---

21. Delling, "Στοιχέω, Συστοιχέω, Στοιχεῖον," 686.

Confirmation of 2 Peter

Several shorter texts that talk about the passing of creation are in line with these statements in 2 Peter. Think of the words of Jesus, "Heaven and earth will pass away, but my words will not pass away" (Matt 24:35). Jesus pronounces these words in the context of the judgment on the day of the Lord and the promise (v. 34). The separation between good and evil is expressed with the same power as in the above mentioned second letter of Peter. The present earth and heaven, just like the righteous, will have to go through a complete process of rebirth.

Paul, too, is familiar with this idea about the new creation and discontinuity. The righteous live in this world "as though they had no dealings with it. For the present form of this world is passing away" (1 Cor 7:31). From the context, it is clear that life in the world is more than life in creation. The apostle, in this context of his marriage instructions, refers primarily to life in this world. The righteous must realize that the world has no eternal abode to offer. It is as temporary as the present life the righteous one leads on earth. This does not exclude the possibility that in the afterlife, there will no longer be a world. However, it will be a radically different world, the world of the new creation, in which the righteous can already participate. In the end, we can also think of the words in the prayer of the unfortunate one, who succumbs under the power of evil:

> They will perish, but you endure; they will all wear out like a garment. You change them like clothing, and they pass away; but you are the same, and your years have no end. The children of your servants shall live secure; their offspring shall be established in your presence. (Ps 102:26–28)

The psalmist recognizes that the world, as he perceives it, does not last forever. It wears away like clothes through transience. At the same time, the psalmist realizes that God will replace the worn-out clothes. Because God is eternal and not subject to impermanence, he intervenes and does not foresake the work of his hands.

This emphasis on discontinuity is essential. Anyone who realizes that the early Christians had to strongly oppose Gnosticism, which denied a future for the physical, realizes how important the emphasis on physical restoration was. Gnostics did not want to know anything about a future for creation. The idea of a "new creation" was out of the question.

Despite these choices, the prophets and apostles did not hesitate to speak of a flood of fire over creation and the collapse of heavens and earth. At the same time, in their works, they turned fiercely against gnostic influences. An example of this is the rejection of the physical-bodily recovery by Gnosticism. The apostles did not want to follow in those footsteps. They did not want to replace physical reality with spiritual reality. If that happened, the incarnation and resurrection of Jesus Christ would be under fire. Christians resisted this. Whoever left out the resurrection of Christ from the proclamation did not have a gospel left. Gnosticism was wrong in its expectation of the future. Christ had not come to deliver us from creation. He liberated an excellent creation, including matter. Therefore, Gnosticism's redemptive doctrine did not do justice to God's redemptive, creative, and future doctrine. In the discontinuity, it no longer had an eye for continuity. We now want to go into that in more detail.

9.2.2 Continuity of Discontinuity

The Testimony of Romans

Just as 2 Peter 3 is the core text for discontinuity between this creation and the new creation, Romans 8 is the core text when it comes to continuity. We will take a closer look at this text and relate it to other similar biblical statements.

> I consider that the sufferings of this present time are not worth comparing with the glory about to be revealed to us. For the creation waits with eager longing for the revealing of the children of God; for the creation was subjected to futility, not of its own will but by the will of the one who subjected it, in hope that the creation itself will be set free from its bondage to decay and will obtain the freedom of the glory of the children of God. We know that the whole creation has been groaning in labor pains until now. (Rom 8:18–22)

These verses contain the good news that God will deliver creation from the forces of evil and transience. Central to this is the continuity in discontinuity. Creation looks forward to the day of redemption.

The biblical text of Romans 8 is a climax in Paul's writing. After the apostle has written in Romans 5 about the moral bankruptcy of the first Adam, he reflects in Romans 8 on the victory of the second Adam, Jesus Christ. The outcome is that through the work of Christ, the whole of creation will be set free. Thus, the liberation and glorification of the righteous (8:12–17, 23–24) find a parallel in the liberty and glorification of creation (8:18–22). Together with creation, Christians wait for their complete redemption (8:19, 23). They are both saved in hope (8:20, 24), may know that they will be set free (8:21, 23), and often still groan deep in their hearts at this moment (8:22, 23). This is understandable for those who realize that we are still often subject to fruitlessness in this world. But in the end, the whole creation of transience will be liberated.

This is delightful news for those who realize that the suffering in this creation is immense. During the minute I use to write this sentence, thousands of animals worldwide are eaten alive. Other animals flee for their lives, die of thirst, or starve to death. At the same time, what Romans 8 claims is an immense expression of faith in this transitory world. The German New Testament scholar Rudolf Bultmann (1884–1976) realized the impact of these words and could not believe them. These were mythological speculations about the future that were inappropriate to him.[22] Humans today recognize that creation around them is not hopeful and in line with what the apostle writes. It is faith that has great expectations of God and is based on God's promises. Sometimes it is impossible to hold out in creation. Therefore, we sigh along with creation, and even the Spirit of God agrees with that sighing (Rom 8:26). At the same time, we confess that creation is not on the deathbed but on the childbed. There is the expectation of a new birth: "We know that the whole creation has been groaning in labor pains until now" (8:22).

Confirmation of Paul

Concerning these texts from Romans 8, several other texts emphasize the continuity between this creation and the new creation. As with the discontinuity, we can refer first to a word of Jesus:

> Jesus said to them, "Truly I tell you, at the renewal of all things, when the Son of Man is seated on the throne of his glory, you who have followed me will also sit on twelve thrones, judging the twelve tribes of Israel." (Matt 19:28)

In the first part of the verse Jesus mentions the renewal or rebirth of all things. This rebirth is connected in Jewish tradition with the renewal of life, the renewal of the earth, and Israel's restoration. We also find a parallel of what Paul writes in Romans 8 expressed by the apostle

---

22. Bornkamm et al., *Christliche Hoffnung*, 57.

Peter, when he testifies of Jesus, "who must remain in heaven until the time of universal restoration that God announced long ago through his holy prophets" (Acts 3:21). Peter realizes that Jesus Christ is glorified in heaven by God. However, that is only his temporary abode. The Messiah returns at the restoration or cosmic renewal of the creation. Then he will restore the kingdom of God (Acts 1:6). In this way, the voices of the New Testament complement each other. Jesus, Peter, and Paul testify of a radical discontinuity and remarkable continuity between this creation and the new creation.

If the new creation were utterly different from the current creation or the original creation of Genesis 1–2, the powers of evil would have destroyed the work of God. There would be nothing left of what God created. Animals, plants, people, and so much more would have been ruined and eventually destroyed. Little would remain of a Christian doctrine of salvation. Only a positive part of the invisible things that God created would stay in an immaterial heaven. All the physical would have disappeared or been transformed into the spiritual. Also, the positive part of creation would have perished forever and would not have been redeemed by God. God would make a new creation from nothing, as was the case in Genesis 1. The discontinuity between this creation and the new creation would then be the main point in the Christian proclamation. This proclamation leaves its impact on the care for this creation. It also influences speaking about material recovery, which includes the confession of faith in a resurrection of the body, which we mentioned at the beginning of chapter 9.2.

Opposite this attitude is the choice to see the new creation concerning the present creation. The new creation is then a renovation of the old one. But if the new creation is precisely the same as the current creation or the original creation, little would have changed through the work of the Messiah. There would only be continuity between now and later. There would be no glorification or renewal. The whole would linger at a resurrection of the physical and the spiritual part of creation. Continuity between this creation and the new creation would then be the main point in Christian proclamation. The Christian doctrine of the future, the eschatology, would then essentially not differ from general futurology.[23]

This field of futurology originated mainly after the Second World War in America and France. It is practiced by companies to develop

---

23. Moltmann, "Is the World," 131. See also Hausoul, *New Heaven*, 72–81, 104–5, 121–25, 203–46.

strategic policymaking. Choices are made based on well-considered future projections. For example, a company in futurology can choose to focus on Japan in the global market because the forecasts indicate that America and Europe will play a subordinate role on a global level in the future. This can also be applied to a complete continuity between this creation and future creation. Nothing new can then be expected for the future.

9.2.3 The Grain and Ear of Corn

The apostle Paul knows the field of tension evoked in conversations about the continuity and discontinuity between this creation and the new creation. In his first letter to Corinth, he discusses the resurrection body. There are critical noises in Corinth about the question of whether the dead are raised. The resurrection of the dead is unimaginable and is immediately swept off the table. The apostle defends himself:

> But someone will ask, "How are the dead raised? With what kind of body do they come?" Fool! What you sow does not come to life unless it dies. And as for what you sow, you do not sow the body that is to be, but a bare seed, perhaps of wheat or of some other grain. But God gives it a body as he has chosen, and to each kind of seed its own body. . . . So it is with the resurrection of the dead. What is sown is perishable, what is raised is imperishable. It is sown in dishonor, it is raised in glory. It is sown in weakness, it is raised in power. It is sown a physical body, it is raised a spiritual body. If there is a physical body, there is also a spiritual body. (1 Cor 15:35–38, 42–44)

Paul indicates with his metaphor of seed and corn that the present body and the resurrection body are not separated (continuity) and that, at the same time, there is a difference between the earthly and heavenly bodies (discontinuity). The "spiritual body," however, is not a thin, immaterial body. Literally, the apostle speaks of a "soul-controlled body" (σῶμα ψυχικόν, *sōma psychikon*) and a "spirit-controlled body" (σῶμα πνευματικόν, *sōma pneumatikon*). The former is of a lower order than the latter. The body that is led by the Spirit follows to glorify God and can be classified as the highest (cf. 1 Cor 2:14–15).

So Paul makes a comparison that resembles that between a sailing ship and a steamer. The "soul-controlled person" often does not accept the things of God. He is self-centered and guided by his own "self." The "spirit-controlled person" allows himself to be led by God's Spirit. That is the body that Jesus received as firstborn of the resurrection. It is a body that could be touched and took food (chapter 9.2). The future body and the present body relate to the glory of the ear of corn and grain or the glory of the great oak and the acorn. In the less beautiful looking seed, the beautiful plant is already locked up. This plant is not totally different from the seed. It is also not the same. There is a resurrection from the seed and a renewal.

The large oak does not look like the acorn, but has emerged from it. The acorn contained all the elements that the large oak had. So it is with the new creation—it will come from the current creation, which in principle contains the elements that will characterize the new creation. Therefore there is radical continuity and radical discontinuity between the two. It is just as with the future resurrection body that will be imperishable (1 Cor 15:42; 2 Cor 5:1), glorious (1 Cor 15:43), powerful (v. 43), spiritual (v. 44), heavenly (v. 48; 2 Cor 5:2), and immortal (1 Cor 15:53; 2 Cor 5:4). There will be no more pain, no more sorrow, no disease, no death, and so on. The identity between the two is thus inseparable. That makes God the ultimate Creator and Redeemer of creation. It is this proclamation that meets resistance in the world of the New Testament.

This is still the case today. When astrophysics proclaims a devastating end to this universe, we cannot imagine a renewal of this new heaven and new earth. There has to be an end, in which only immaterial souls remain with God.[24] However, when environmental researchers call upon society to pay more attention to creation and look admonishingly at the history of Christianity (see chapter 3), we dare not proclaim a future without paying special attention to the earth. In both cases, critics may point out to us the lack of measurable evidence for such a faith representation. They then urge us to reduce the Christian faith to what is provable. That is the choice for some values and norms that have a psychological, social, and moral function.

The influence of our historical-cultural Zeitgeist cannot be underestimated for our future expectations. We see this with the Christians of Corinth, who from a Hellenistic culture chose to say goodbye to the faith and hope of a physical resurrection. When Paul writes to them about this, he does so faithfully to the teaching of Christ that the dead will resurrect physically.

---

24. Hausoul, "Theology and Cosmology," 324–36.

We see the same influence with the church fathers Irenaeus of Lyon (~140–202) and Methodius of Olympus (d. 312). In the first centuries of church history they resisted gnostic and Hellenistic ideas about the resurrection. The struggle between what God's Spirit reveals and what mutilates the ideas of our time is thus a fact. Examples of this are the descriptions of Adamantius Origenes (~185–254) and Gregory of Nyssa (~335–94) about the future resurrection. These descriptions are made in such a way that any relation with the biblical imagery is missing. What remains are speculations, which remain attractive until there are changes in the time and culture in which they arose.

However, the aforementioned Irenaeus and Methodius join the prophets in talking about the future in the same richness of earthly concrete representations. Although the future has not yet been revealed, the biblical writers indicate the direction in which we should think. In many cases these descriptions go beyond our thoughts and proposals. Yet at the same time the prophetic language of hope ensures that their vision of the future remains richer and more vivid than the philosophical-speculative wishes of many a theologian influenced by the Zeitgeist. Bram van de Beek therefore rightly writes, "With Gregory of Nyssa no one is going to sing and no one is going to hope. Isaiah, Micah, Zechariah and John do."[25]

In our biblical speaking about the new heaven and the new earth we have to take into account the material and immaterial renewal of creation. Thereby we may emphasize the continuity between this creation and the new creation from the belief in the resurrection of the body. Jesus Christ, as firstborn of the new creation, makes it true that the resurrected body is in continuity with the crucified body. Good examples of this are the crucifixion wounds, which are still present in the resurrected body of Christ. Those who read the resurrection stories in the Gospels discover a diversity of continuity between what Jesus did before his resurrection and what he did after his resurrection.

At the same time there is also discontinuity between this creation and the new creation. We are not talking about a *renovation* of the creation, but about a *transformation* of it. There will be a new, glorified heaven and a new, glorified earth. This element of the glorification emphasizes the discontinuity that will be there. Resurrection and glorification, continuity and discontinuity, should therefore be present in speaking about the new creation, without the one cancelling the other. A powerful example

---

25. Van de Beek, *God doet recht*, 94.

of this can be found in the firstborn of the new creation: Jesus Christ personally. From this testimony we will again listen to the church fathers Irenaeus of Lyon and Methodius of Olympus, and their contemporaries Adamantius Origenes and Gregory of Nyssa.

10

Jesus, Firstborn and Protector

10.1 THE FIRSTBORN AND THE NEW CREATION

10.1.1 Christ as Firstborn of the New Creation

CHRISTIAN THINKING ABOUT THE new heaven and the new earth is inextricably linked to the resurrected Christ as firstborn of the new creation. Christ's resurrection is a hopeful testimony that gives certainty to the future. It is the beginning of the new creation and testifies that decay and transience in this world will come to an end. The resurrection shows God's intervention and reveals what the new world will be like. It is thus a fixed point of reference in speaking about the new creation. This is especially the case when it comes to the transformation of creation. Just as Christ died and rose from the dead in a glorified body, this creation will die completely and be transformed into the new creation. Therefore, the Bible connects the new creation with the resurrection (e.g., Rom 8:18-23; 2 Cor 5:14-17; Col 1:15-18). Jesus also connects his words and deeds with the kingdom of God, the new creation. The King and his empire are thus the heart of world history. As the last Adam, Christ represents what the new creation has to offer. That future goes beyond what Adam was able to realize in primal history. It far surpasses the primeval and what Christians now know. This, what we know about the future, finds its foundation in Christ.

For those who want to take Jesus Christ seriously as the physical, resurrected Messiah of the coming kingdom, the soteriological doctrine of creation is inseparable from the eschatological doctrine of creation. After all, Christ is not only the center of humanity, but the center of all creation. Through him the first creation was made and he is also the first-born of the new creation, the alpha and omega. In the light of this, the biblical hope sees a future for this creation. That future is connected with the revelation of God's kingdom.

10.1.2 Plea for the Cosmos

Anthropocentrism

In the past, Western theology mainly emphasized God's way with humans. This ensured that creation as a whole, with its flora and fauna, received no attention. Today, many theologians point out that a belief in God as Creator cannot be reconciled with a hope of destroying creation. Humans are never released from creation. Creation is always redeemed with humanity. Western theology started to think differently in this, mainly due to the influence of an anthropocentrism that was inspired by the Renaissance or Enlightenment philosophy. Contrary to Judeo-Christian anthropocentrism, which emphasizes human responsibility with regard to creation, Enlightenment anthropocentrism opted for the view that the nonhuman world was created solely for the sake of humankind.[1]

This caused humanity to place itself too much at the center of the universe and forget that it was part of a greater whole: the creation, the work of God's hands that the Almighty does not want to abandon. The accompanying influence of Hellenism and Platonic ideas strengthened that thought. Creation was seen as a temporary backdrop for the relationship between God and humans. This led to the fact that God's dealings with the cosmos received little attention in Christian doctrine. An example of this is the medieval theologian Thomas Aquinas (1225–74). Inspired by a Hellenistic worldview, he presents the future creation as an earth without plants and animals.[2] For many, this points to an eternal impoverishment compared to the expectations of the future in the early church. As mentioned in the previous chapter, the church father Irenaeus of Lyon addresses in his theological reflections all kinds of Hellenistic, Platonic, and gnostic currents, which qualified the physical side of

---

1. Moltmann, *Geschichte*, 176–77.
2. Aquinas, *Summa Theologiae*, IIIa.supp.q91.5.

creation as evil and attributed it to a false deity or demonic intermediate power. Irenaeus pleads to call the physical aspect of creation good and to believe in a resurrection of the body. According to him it was normal that the good things of creation were also present in the new creation. He thought of wine, which Christ promised to drink again (Matt 26:29), of fields and houses, which Christ promised to his followers (19:29), of prosperity and fertility, which God promised to the righteous (Gen 27:28; Isa 26:19; 65:19–23; Ezek 28:25–26), and of peace among animals (Isa 11:6–10; 65:25). Irenaeus took all the biblical talk about this earthly-physical expectation, without wanting to make closed-photo reportage of it. They were open paintings that gracefully expressed what the future would be like. He rejected a symbolic interpretation of biblical speaking, which dissolved the imagery into philosophical-abstract spirituality.[3]

Everlasting Earth

This approach is particularly sensitive for those who in their explanations choose in advance to reinterpret physical fulfillment of the prophetic (image) promises as spiritual fulfillment.[4] An example from the previous chapter was Origen of Alexandria. He disputed the earthly-concrete ideas of Irenaeus and many others and developed the principle of allegorical interpretation, which distinguished the earthly-physical meaning of the Bible from a deeper, spiritual meaning. To this the church father Methodius of Olympus reacted,

> It is not satisfactory to say that the universe will be utterly destroyed, and sea and air and sky will be no longer. For the whole world will be deluged with fire from heaven, and burnt for the purpose of purification and renewal; it will not, however, come to complete ruin and corruption. For if it were better for the world not to be than to be, why did God, in making the world, take the worse course?[5]

However, after Irenaeus and Methodius, creation would for many remain only a temporary backdrop on which the history of God and humanity took place. The Roman Catholic Karl Rahner (1904–84) turned sharply against the theologians in the twentieth century who failed to

---

3. Irenaeus of Lyon, *Adversus Haereses*, V.33–35.
4. E.g., Waltke, "Kingdom Promises," 272.
5. Methodius of Olympus, "From the Discourse," I.8.

reflect critically on such thoughts.[6] From his reflection on Christ's resurrection, Rahner emphasizes that material creation does not disappear into completion. Whoever confesses this "loves the absolute," but not God, who is the creator of heavens and earth. In principle one hates the created reality.[7]

For Rahner, a separation between the immaterial and the material is as unchristian and despicable as a polytheism that worships the created powers and forces as gods. The God whom the Christian confesses is a God-with-the-creation, who shows his unconditional love to this creation and does not leave it Godless or remove it, as Gnosticism does.[8]

This impact of Hellenism, Platonic thinking, and Enlightenment philosophy explains to a large extent why Christian doctrine of faith in church history focused mainly on individual eschatology and why there is little interest in cosmic or universal eschatology. Yet, in the Bible, people and nature are part of the same created and God-oriented reality. Thus, in Genesis 1, humans receive the same blessing as animals, "Be fruitful and multiply" (v. 22, 28). Together with animals, people receive a living soul, living space, food, and the blessing of fertility.

In Christ, God reconciles men with nature, as the biblical references to the Sabbath for animals (Exod 20:10), the Sabbath year for the land (Lev 25:1–7), and Christ's stay with animals (Mark 1:13) seem to clarify. The Swiss evangelical theologian Eduard Thurneysen (1888–1974) writes,

> So the world in which we come into the future of Christ is no other world. It is this world: this heaven, this earth, which both perished and became new. These forests, these fields, these cities, these streets, these people will be the place of salvation.[9]

The new creation in Revelation 21–22 is explicitly connected with the kingdom of God and the first creation in Genesis 1–2. The future of this creation has been locked in from the beginning. God gives the creation a future in which humans may fulfill the commission from Genesis 1:28. The garden that God establishes in Eden is the first temple and the prototype of the new creation. Humans must expand this sacred space all

---

6. Rahner, "Leib," 407–8, 420; Rahner, "Einheit von Geist und Materie," 338; Rahner, *Auferstehung*, 27; Rahner, "Auferstehung," 224. Cf. Hausoul, *New Heaven*, 107–9.

7. Rahner, "Ewige Bedeutung," 53–54.

8. Rahner, "Einheit von Geist und Materie," 183–84, 187–95; Rahner, "Immanente," 609. Cf. Hausoul, *New Heaven*, 107–9.

9. Thurneysen, "Christus und seine Zukunft," 209.

over the earth by faithfully fulfilling God's commission in Genesis 1:28. The completion of the world does not consist of the resurrection of single individuals, but of the whole creation. The Dutch theologian Gerrit Berkouwer (1903–96) writes in his dogmatic reflections:

> Better the extreme concreteness of Thurneysen than dualistic spiritualizing of the expectation, which is foreign to the works of God and wraps the future in impenetrable darkness.[10]

10.1.3 Body, Space, and Time

Resurrection Body Space

In the previous chapters, the importance of the future of the physical in speaking of the Christian future expectation has already been pointed out. The German Lutheran theologian Paul Althaus (1888–1966) emphasizes that our questions about the future resurrection of the body must be connected with the questions about God's new world.[11] This leads to necessary consequences. Bodies are material and take up space. The same goes for a body which is glorified. A representation of future life without relationships, without surroundings, and without space can hardly be typified as a "resurrection of the body." Such a representation, according to the Christian physicist Blaise Pascal (1623–66), would only be an existence in endless "nothingness."[12]

In my book *The New Heaven and the New Earth*, I have gone deeper into these kinds of questions about the presence of time, space, and matter in the new heaven and the new earth. It is impossible to repeat those discussions here. What can be established is that there has often been a great tendency in church history to perceive time, space, and matter as something negative. But we do not encounter this thought in the biblical storyline. Looking at Jesus Christ as firstborn and reference of the new creation, one sees that Christ's glorified resurrection body remains connected with matter, space, time, and all the relations that go with it.[13] One thing that stands out is that Jesus suddenly appears with his glorified body in the room while the windows and doors are locked (John 20:26).

---

10. Berkouwer, *Return of Christ*, 231.
11. Althaus, *Letzten Dinge*, 344.
12. Pascal, *Pensées*, §206. Cf. Ladd, *Theology of the New Testament*, 631.
13. Hausoul, *New Heaven*, 230–46.

But this doesn't mean that he walked through walls or doors with his body. Jesus, like the angel Gabriel in the birth story, does not need to walk through anything in order to appear. That the resurrected body is also a real physical body is apparent from the invitation to Thomas to touch the wounds of the Messiah (John 20:27). A spirit cannot be touched and is not considered as "resurrection body" either.

The Resurrection Body of Jesus

In a similar way, other events of Christ's resurrection body can be explained. For example, we read that Jesus is unrecognizable to the disciples at Emmaus—not because he has a different form, but because God obscured their gaze (Luke 24:16, 31). There is also talk of Mary of Magdalene, who does not recognize Jesus in the tomb garden because at the dark dawn at the tomb she assumes that it is the gardener who speaks to her, so that she only looks at him sporadically (John 20:1, 14–16).

It is remarkable that Luke and John, who are the only two Evangelists to mention these two events, emphasize that the resurrection body of Jesus Christ is the same as the crucified body. Both do so by mentioning that Jesus Christ showed his wounded body to the disciples to reveal his identity.

> See my hands and my feet, that it is I myself. Touch me, and see. For a spirit does not have flesh and bones as you see that I have. (Luke 24:39)

> [Thomas:] Unless I see in his hands the mark of the nails, and place my finger into the mark of the nails, and place my hand into his side, I will never believe. . . . [Jesus:] Put your finger here, and see my hands; and put out your hand, and place it in my side. Do not disbelieve, but believe. (John 20:25, 27)

The resurrection body of Jesus serves as an identity marker for the authenticity of Christ's bodily resurrection. In this, the continuity between the crucified body and the resurrection body comes to the fore. The resurrection is the proof that Jesus has conquered death. The bodily resurrection is the ultimate proof of everything Jesus said and did during his service on earth.

Space and Time in the New Creation

Because physicality is connected with space and time, Christians who are convinced of the physical resurrection of Jesus Christ accentuate the physical, spatial, and temporal side of the new heavens and earth. The new creation is then concretely presented and not limited to abstract thinking. For this reason, "How can we imagine the resurrection of the body?" forms a key question. With that question we do not mean whether someone can imagine that there is a resurrection. The question is how that resurrection actually happens in reality. Anyone who is less able to imagine Christ's physical resurrection from the grave will often be less inclined to speak about its physical, spatial, and temporal side.

This has not only been the case since the rise of critical theology during the Enlightenment; examples of this can also be found in earlier times. The Hellenistic-inspired Origen dismissed the earthly-concrete representations of Irenaeus as naïve and remained vague about the exact nature of the resurrection body. Gregory of Nyssa went further and ignored the talk about the bodily resurrection. For Gregory the central Christian hope was the ultimate return of the immortal soul to God.[14]

A new creation can only be imagined by both as the absence of any physical reality. As a result, speaking of a cosmic eschatology is impoverished and no account is taken of a resurrection of all things. In the case of the new heaven and the new earth, it is no longer an earthly reality that reminds us of this existence, but *God's* reality and its inescapable dimensions. But it is unclear how the two can be separated from each other. Is not earthly reality the reality given by God? Or does one mean that creation differs from deity? But that distinction, according to the Christian faith, also continues to exist in eternity. Creature does not become deity. The new creation is not God. In biblical speech the distinction between Creator and creation persists and any form of pantheism is rejected. Humans do participate in the eternal divine life, through the rebirth from above and position in Christ. But that does not mean that people become God. It was from this thought that the misery of humanity began, and not their glory.

---

14. Gregory of Nyssa, *De Anima et Resurrectione*.

Resurrection Naïve

In contemporary Christian theology it is often seen as naïve to believe in a physically-concrete resurrection of corpses at the resurrection. That kind of belief is like believing in fairies, elves, trolls, and gnomes. However, the Dutch Reformed theologian Bram van de Beek (b. 1946) asks the question why the one is more credible or humanly conceivable than the other. What, for instance, do we mean by "the soul" or "with God"?[15] For many people, these expressions are as naïve as the earthly paradisiacal representations of Irenaeus and Methodius. Why can't we accept the prophetic descriptions of the future with a physical credibility? Is the confession of new heaven and new earth in which there is a form of flora and fauna so naïve? Is the confession of new heaven and new earth in which a form of flora and fauna is absent, but which only speaks of a soul in remembrance of God, not equally naïve? Jürgen Moltmann characterizes this last performance as a pathetic existence for a human being who wants to avoid the resurrection of the physical at all costs.[16] Closely watched, it is not even really an existence as "human being." Whoever perishes as a corpse can hardly speak of his "human existence." The Christian confession of the resurrection therefore encompasses the idea of a resurrection of the whole human being: body, soul, and spirit.[17] Mind and matter form a complex, inseparable unity with each other. That connection is so strong that any separation in it is inadmissible.

After all, it is not as easy for human beings to divide themselves into soul and body forever. That is why Karl Rahner denies any separation between soul and body in the eschaton. He does so by invoking the resurrection of Jesus Christ, who remains the eternal God-man even after his resurrection.[18]

While the idea of the immortality of the soul relies on "something" immortal in humans and accepts death as a liberating friend, faith in the resurrection of the dead is based on the hope of a God who creates in life what does not exist and who makes the dead alive by overcoming death as the last enemy. Thus, Christian faith is not about spiritualization, but about transformation. We see this continuously in the history

---

15. Van de Beek, *God doet recht*, 86.

16. Moltmann, *Weg Jesu*, 279; Moltmann, "Liebe," 843.

17. Moltmann, *Kommen*, 74–95; Moltmann, *Weg Jesu*, 279; Moltmann, *Gott in der Schöpfung*, 250–53.

18. Rahner, "Neue Erde," 590.

of salvation: God created humans physically as masculine and feminine from the physical earth. God's Messiah became flesh and lived physically among people. God poured out his Spirit on all flesh. From this salvific historical perspective, Moltmann poses the question, "Why should God's history with his creatures not end in a resurrection of the flesh and an eternal physical life?"[19] After all, what God unites universally is not reduced to individualism or spiritualism in salvation. The suffering in this creation does not ask for salvation from this creation, but for the removal of all evil. The new heaven and the new earth may therefore see the many victims of history as an answer to prayer: "Your kingdom come, your will be done, on earth as it is in heaven" (Matt 6:10).

10.2 THE MESSIAH AND THE PROTECTION OF ANIMALS

10.2.1 Jesus Stands Up for a Groaning Donkey

Those who are familiar with the Gospels know that animals occupy a special place in the teaching of Jesus (cf. Matt 6:29; Luke 12:24). In chapter 8.2.1 we already saw how the wild animals came to Jesus after the temptations in the desert. Jesus takes a loving attitude towards what God created. That attitude is strengthened by an old apocryphal story that is handed down from the Coptic. In it we read,

> It happened that the Lord left the city and walked with his disciples in the mountains. There they came to a mountain. The way up was steep. There was a man with a mule. However, the mule had collapsed because the man had loaded it too heavily. The man hit the animal, so it bled. Jesus went up to him and said, "Man, why are you hitting the animal? Can't you see that it is too weak to carry the burden and don't you realize how it suffers?" The man answered, "What business is it of yours? I'm allowed to hit the pack mule as often as I want. It is my property. I bought it for a large sum of money. Ask those who are standing there with you. They know me and they know enough about this." Some of the students responded, "Yes, Lord, what he says is true. We saw how he bought the donkey." But the Lord said, "Don't you see how the animal is bleeding and don't you hear how it groans and cries for mercy?" They responded, "No, Lord, we don't hear that it groans and cries." Jesus was sad and said, "Woe to you that you do not hear how it groans and cries for

---

19. Moltmann, *Sein Name*, 62–63.

mercy with its Creator in heaven. And a triple woe to him about whom the donkey complains and speaks in his pain." Jesus went and touched the animal. It rose up and the wounds were immediately healed. Jesus then said to the man, "Go on and don't hit the animal again, so that you may receive mercy."[20]

This event is connected with the statutes of God to care for animals and not burden them heavily (Exod 23:4; Deut 22:4; cf. chapter 7.1). From this legend it can be concluded that early Coptic Christians did not limit the loving and merciful attitude of Jesus only to humans. It implies that if people do not show respect for animals, they should not expect mercy from God. Christ, like God, had an eye for the whole of creation. Animals were part of this.

10.2.2 Jesus and the Battle between Pigs and Demons

A great challenge in this is the event in the life of Jesus in which about two thousand pigs are killed. In the land of the Gadarenes the Messiah frees a man from various demons. These demons beg him to be sent into a herd of pigs nearby. Jesus gives grace to the demons and allows them to go into the pigs. Then the herd moves and plunges from the steepness into the sea, causing them to perish in the water (cf. Matt 8:23–34; Mark 5:1–20).

By giving grace to the demons, the lives of two thousand pigs are completely destroyed. Doesn't this event draw a red line through Jesus' love for animals? Does Jesus care more about demons than pigs, created by God? Why does Jesus allow this animal-unfriendly event to take place in his presence? Is Jesus amoral?[21]

This event presents us with a challenge. In the past, interpreters tried to separate the death of the pigs from Jesus' choices. They offered the following explanations for the event:

1. *The pigs die to show how bad the demonic power is and to show that the possessed one has been freed.*[22] But that is superfluous. The demonic power was already sufficiently visible before the liberation of the man took place (Mark 5:3–5) and the liberation is visible because of the big difference. People in the vicinity recognize that (v. 15–16).

20. Translated and adapted from Boehmer, *Neutestamentliche Parallelen*, 26–27.
21. See the criticism in: Plummer, *Luke*, 228–29; Fitzmyer, *Luke I–IX*, 734.
22. Lane, *Mark*, 186; Manson, *Luke*, 96; Schlatter, *Matthäus*, 294; Zahn, *Lucas*, 355.

2. *Pigs are unclean animals that were not allowed to be kept by Jews.* But keeping pigs is allowed in the Bible. Eating pigs is forbidden for Israelites (Lev 11:7–8).

3. *Jesus has to make a choice between the man and the pigs. So he allows a lesser evil.*[23] But nowhere is Jesus forced to make that choice. The evil that happens is unnecessary. Jesus can also send the demons somewhere else.

4. *It is not Jesus, but the demons that drown the pig herd.*[24] But this happens because Jesus allows them to do so. He could also punish them and send them elsewhere.

5. *Jesus allows this in order to be able to point to his own death through the death of the pigs. Both lead to the liberation of people.*[25] But a relationship with Jesus' crucifixion is unclear in this context and the pigs do not die to redeem the possessed. The man is already redeemed by the powerful word of Jesus. The pigs do not change that situation.

These different proposals do not help to take away the critical questions in Jesus' attitude. A less common explanation that does mitigate them is that it is not the pigs but the demons that are drowning. This may sound strange, but there are several indications for this proposal:[26]

1. There is no need for the demons to let the pigs die. If that happens, they destroy their "new home." In their conversation with Jesus it was expressed that they were anxiously longing for a "home" to escape pain (Matt 8:29, 31; Mark 5:17; Luke 8:31). Also, the demons were not interested in killing the man before. However, they did choose to hurt the man thoroughly.

2. Pigs are good swimmers. Several videos on the internet show this. In the Bahamas I found an attraction of a group of pigs that swam every day from the beach to different sea boats. Also, when the pigs fall from the steepness into the water, this does not necessarily mean that they die. If the quay is not too long, they can go ashore again.

---

23. Witherington, *Gospel of Mark*, 183; Bauckham, "Jesus and Animals I," 48; Lane, *Mark*, 186.

24. Bauckham, "Jesus and Animals I," 47.

25. Craghan, "Gerasene Demoniac," 522–36.

26. Cf. Gilmour, *Eden's Other Residents*, 85–86; Eve, *Jewish Context*, 380–83; Anderson, *Mark*, 147; Rienecker, *Matthäus*, 110–11.

3. Jesus nowhere fulfills the request of demons to go into a body. He frees people without giving grace to the evil powers. He came precisely to destroy the powers of evil and not to kill pigs (1 John 3:8). The mysterious statement that unclean spirits pass through "waterless regions" (Matt 12:43; Luke 11:24) may indirectly indicate that they cannot stand water. This would argue in favor of the way in which they perish.

4. The term "steepness" (κρημνός, *krēmnos*) indicates a bank or slope. It is not necessary to think of a steep cliff. The pigs throw themselves into the water from the mountain. The Greek language leaves open the possibility of thinking of either the "unclean spirits" or of the "pig herd" when "they drowned" (Matt 8:32; Mark 5:13; Luke 8:33). Often the herd is chosen because it is mentioned last in the text. However, it is not impossible to think of the unclean spirits.

5. The land dwellers beg Jesus to leave their territory when they learn what happened to the possessed and the pigs (Matt 8:16–17; Mark 5:34; Luke 8:37). If about two thousand pigs had come to the end of their lives, we would expect a different reaction. The freed man is even sent to the city and area of the Decapolis to testify of God's mercy (Matt 8:19; Luke 8:39). This is not an obvious response if the Messiah has just robbed you of your fortune.

6. Jesus teaches his followers several times about the care God has for this creation. He points out God's care for the sparrow (Matt 10:29) and the care of men for their animals (Luke 14:5). His attitude towards the pigs is therefore strange.

It would be worthwhile to develop this alternative explanation even further and to link it to geographical data on the area (steepness of the mountains), biological data on the pigs (swimming distance), and theological data (relationship between demons and water).

If the explanation that the demons drowned is correct, God would be using the pigs in judging the evil forces. The pigs would then not be victims, but fellow fighters against demonic supremacy. This immediately explains the use of the militaristic word ὁρμάω/*hormaō*, which in classical Greek refers to the advancement of an army. The pigs choose not to spread in their fear, as they would normally do. They trot like an army in one direction. The herd moves from the mountain to the bank.

The name of the unclean spirit, "Legion" (λεγιών, *legiōn*), is also a militaristic term. It reminds us of an occupying power. In Decapolis this was not hard to imagine. Roman legions had settled widely in that area. Just as the demonic power held the man in its grip, the Romans held the country in their grip.

Jesus then consents to the demons (ἐπιτρέπω, *epitrepō*; Mark 5:13; Luke 8:32), as a higher army commander does to his subjects (cf. Matt 8:21). Again, a militaristic term sounds like that. Because of the pigs the demons eventually come to an end. Their new home is destroyed. Instead of the demons arbitrarily pushing the pigs into the lake, the pigs do so as an army in battle order. Because they are good swimmers, it remains to be seen whether they commit suicide in the process.

That demons beg not to be sent out of the place is also unique.[27] Are they dependent on this piece of nature reserve? The land plays an important role in the story. Who has a claim to this area? Is it the Romans with their *Imperium Romanum*, the Greeks, the demons, or Jesus? The militaristic terms show that the coming of Christ means the end for every other power. The storm at sea, which precedes this event, is then no coincidence. It is a struggle that is related to the land and the events that will take place there.

The population hears what happened next and discovers that Jesus comes from the other side, from which the people of Decapolis have long distanced themselves. They want to keep that distance. Again, the country comes up for discussion and the inhabitants ask Jesus to leave their area. Gadara stays for the Gadarenes. They want to remain boss in their own country—especially now that the madman has become calm.

However, this redeemed man is left behind in the area by Jesus. The eastern-Jordan area that once belonged to Og, king of Basan, may now be reclaimed by grace before the God of Israel. The former resident becomes a preacher in Decapolis, an alliance of cities east of the Sea of Galilee.

---

27. Garroway, "Invasion," 64.

11

Revelation: Creation Destroyed?

11.1 GOD'S DEALINGS WITH CREATION IN REVELATION

11.1.1 The Book of the Birth Pangs

THE BOOK OF REVELATION has often been used to justify the destruction of creation. James G. Watt, who was secretary to Ronald Reagan from 1982 to 1983, shouted that the end times were near. For Watt, it would be no problem if people chose to uproot large forest areas.[1] Many followed this thought. God gave the earth to humanity to rule over plants, animals, and trees. The world was made for humans. Men and women were allowed to use it for their good.

Inspired by the book of Revelation the "use it or lose it" principle was applied. We also get this impression from video games like *Left Behind: Eternal Forces* (2006). The player of this game is called up to send his troops into the end-time battles around New York. As a soldier with various firearms in his hand, he witnesses spectacular attacks by angels and demons on this earth, while in the background, the melody of the famous Christian song "Amazing Grace" is played.

From this approach, it is not strange that the Jewish researcher Yehezkel Landau pronounced the sentence, "God loved the world so much that he sent her the Third World War."[2] The book of Revelation is for many a basis to keep the military industry awake. Not the

---

1. Boyer, *When Time Shall Be No More*, 141.
2. Landau, "President and the Bible," 475.

redemptive talk about the renewal of the earth, but the violent war at Armageddon is central.

The early church did not look forward to the destruction of all things. At the risk of their lives, the first Christians proclaimed their faith in a resurrection and the realization that there would be a renewal of everything God had made. Those who spoke about the future of the earth did so in terms of the birth pangs (Matt 24:8). Judgment hung only above those who turned against God's plan with creation. God's wrath would come upon evil. The book of Revelation was seen as the call to global justice.

It is impossible to deny that there are terrible natural disasters and ecological devastations that affect both flora and fauna in Revelation from this proclamation. We think of, among other things, heavy terrible earthquakes (Rev 6:12a; 11:13; 16:18), the changing and moving of the celestial bodies (6:12b–14a; 8:12), the moving of the mountains and islands (6:14b), hail and fire that is thrown on the earth mixed with blood and the burning of a third of the land with its trees and all greenery (8:7), turning the water into blood, causing all creatures living in the sea to die (8:8–9; 16:3), and the damage it causes to the rivers and springs of water when they become bitter and turn into blood (8:10–11; 16:4).[3]

Hail and Fire on the Earth, the Trees, and the Grass

Because the doom over the trees and the water also affects the animals in them, it is good to elaborate on these two events (Rev 8:7–9; 16:3–4). In Revelation 8, the first angel blows the trumpet, and disaster strikes the trees:

> The first angel blew his trumpet, and there came hail and fire, mixed with blood, and they were hurled to the earth; and a third of the earth was burned up, and a third of the trees were burned up, and all green grass was burned up. (Rev 8:7)

The old English biblical scholar John Gill (1697–1771) already mentions the suggestion that the "trees" in this verse symbolically refer to earthly rulers (cf. Rev 7:3; Targum: Isa 2:13; Zech 11:2).[4] A disadvantage of this explanation is that it is difficult to fit the "all green" at the end of the verse, where the original Greek text reads "the yellow-green grass."

---

3. See in detail: Adams, *Stars Will Fall*, 241–42.
4. Gill, *Exposition*.

Because the parallel thematic text in Revelation 9:4 also speaks about plants, shrubs, and trees, it is obvious to think of hail and fire affecting nature in the judgment in Revelation 8:7. In Revelation 8:7, a third of the trees and all the yellow-green grass burns. Then, in Revelation 9:4, it is obvious that the locusts should leave the plants, shrubs, and trees untouched. The grasshoppers should target only people. The plague is a reminder of the ancient plague over Egypt.

> Then Moses stretched out his staff toward heaven, and the Lord sent thunder and hail, and fire came down on the earth. And the Lord rained hail on the land of Egypt; there was hail with fire flashing continually in the midst of it, such heavy hail as had never fallen in all the land of Egypt since it became a nation. The hail struck down everything that was in the open field throughout all the land of Egypt, both human and animal; the hail also struck down all the plants of the field, and shattered every tree in the field. (Exod 9:23–25)

In both cases, the plague affects three earth elements: the land, the field crop, and the trees. Each time it involves a part of it. Not the whole world is affected. In the book of Exodus, only Egypt is concerned, and in the book of Revelation, it is one-third of the earth or the land. Exodus further emphasizes the impact of hail, while Revelation emphasizes the effects of fire. The blood is only present in Revelation. In Exodus, only the Nile changed into blood at the first plague. It is not easy for interpreters to explain the blood at the fire and the hail in Revelation 8:7.

The Dutch theologian and philosopher Willem J. Ouweneel (b. 1944) thinks that the blood refers to the moral death, but does not substantiate it.[5] So why does not the writer of Revelation immediately write, "mixed with death"? Anyone who physically explains the blood feels this difficulty. We are unfamiliar with such a phenomenon.

From the context of this plague, the blood reminds us of the blood of the Lamb in heaven (Rev 5:6). After all, people on earth realize that the wrath of God and the wrath of the Lamb come upon them (6:16). During the plague, people are reminded of the work of salvation of the Lamb. The evil that takes place on earth is an event that God must endure to make creation utterly free of all evil through the blood.

---

5. Ouweneel, *Offenbarung Jesu Christi*.

The Sea, Rivers, and Water Sources

After the first trumpet, a second and third trumpet sounds in Revelation. These affect a third part of the sea, the rivers, and the water sources:

> The second angel blew his trumpet, and something like a great mountain, burning with fire, was thrown into the sea. A third of the sea became blood, a third of the living creatures in the sea died, and a third of the ships were destroyed. The third angel blew his trumpet, and a great star fell from heaven, blazing like a torch, and it fell on a third of the rivers and on the springs of water. The name of the star is Wormwood. A third of the waters became wormwood, and many died from the water, because it was made bitter. (Rev 8:8–11)

It is impossible to discuss this verse in full depth. We focus on elements that are important for the theme of our book. Because the great mountain loses its stability and is thrown into the sea, one-third of the water turns to blood. This reminds us again of the plagues in Egypt, where the Nile turns to blood (Exod 7:20). At the second scale, in Revelation 16:3, the entire sea will eventually become blood, and every living creature in the water will die. The doom in these verses is disastrous and affects the animals in the sea and the ships that sail on the sea (8:9). This will bring a sudden end to the trade with Babylon (18:17–19). The sea, as the origin of the first beast in Revelation 13, of the creatures in Daniel 7, and of the primeval flood in Genesis 1:2, will experience a gigantic judgment.

At the third trumpet, a big star falls on the rivers and water sources. Contrary to the big mountain, it is not thrown, but it falls. This big star is often related to the heavenly powers behind the big mountain Babylon. According to the Jewish Midrash, a similar phenomenon happened with the heavenly power of Egypt at the Red Sea (cf. Isa 14:12–15).[6] This idea was included in the Judeo-Hellenistic *Sibylline Oracles*: "A great star falls from the sky onto the divine sea and burns the depths of the sea, Babylon, and the land of Italy" (V.158–60). The star in Revelation makes the waters bitter and undrinkable. Only the water that the Lamb offers creation remains fresh and invigorating in the biblical book of Revelation (Rev 7:17; 21:6; 22:1).

---

6. Freedman and Maurice, *Midrash Rabbah: Exodus*, 23:15.

11.1.2 God's Judgment through Intermediaries

Those familiar with the book of Revelation know that the judgments in this book are often not carried out by God himself. There are always angels who bring justice to the earth. As a result, God does not act in the active, but in the passive form. In the book of Revelation, power is mainly given to intermediate beings. There are four living beings (Rev 6:1–8), four angels (7:1–3), seven angels with trumpets (8:2—11:19), a star (9:1), locusts (9:3–5), and seven angels with scales (15:7—16:21). Although the judgments are related to God's anger (15:1) and there are commands from God's temple (16:1), these judgments occur through intermediate beings. The passive form "was given" is characteristic (6:4, 8; 7:2; 9:3, 5; 13:5, 7, 14–15; 16:8; 17:12).

So, God is not connected with every shortcoming in the book of Revelation. For example, we learn from the four apocalyptic horsemen that they only appear when the Lamb breaks the seals, but that they are given power and victory by others (Rev 6:1–9). Who these "others" are, who give power to the horsemen, is not said. Presumably, they are the people who live on earth.[7] Thus the "ten horns" are disgusted by the whore and ruin her (17:16). Humanity is always faced with the choice of renewing or destroying creation. Former defense analyst Daniel Ellsberg (b. 1931) shows in his book *The Doomsday Machine* how often such a threat has been hanging over people's heads in recent history.[8] In the time to which the book of Revelation refers, this will not be much different.

Revelation and the Pharaoh

Because the book of Revelation depicts scenes that remind us several times of Egypt, this relationship is not strange. Just as the pharaoh resisted God's plan and called for severe disasters over Egypt, the people in the book of Revelation also resisted God's plan. They called for severe disasters over their homeland. Both the pharaoh and the people who live on earth choose through their resistance against creation. This leads to destruction in their residential area. It becomes visible how much their existence depends on creation. Those who turn against the plan of the Creator turn against creation. This is because creation looks forward to

---

7. Caird, *Revelation*, 82–83.
8. Ellsberg, *Doomsday Machine*.

redemption and completion, which God as Creator brings. In the Bible, we encounter situations in which creation connects with God and turns against the thought of unbelievers (cf. Ps 18:7–15; Isa 29:6–7; Hag 2:6–7).

In the testimony about the pharaoh, the choice for death and anti-creation is already visible. At the beginning of Exodus, pharaoh chooses to kill the children of the Israelites (Exod 1:8–22; cf. chapter 7.2.2). Later biblical books connect the pharaoh of Egypt with the evil forces of chaos (Ps 74:12–14; Isa 30:7; Jer 46:7–8; Ezek 29:3–5; 32:2–8). The plagues over Egypt are cosmic because the sins of Egypt are cosmic as well.

The same essential attitude is also found in Revelation. The earth's rulers are compared with evil forces of chaos (Rev 12–13) and judged by cosmic disasters (8–10, 15–16). The introduction, at the beginning of the throne scene, is reminiscent of what happened on Mount Sinai when God appeared to the people in glory and holiness:

> Coming from the throne are flashes of lightning, and rumblings and peals of thunder, and in front of the throne burn seven flaming torches, which are the seven spirits of God. (Rev 4:5; cf. Exod 19:16; 20:18)

At the seventh seal, we hear of "thunder, rumblings, flashes of lightning, and an earthquake" (Rev 8:5), at the seventh trumpet, we hear of "flashes of lightning, rumblings, peals of thunder, an earthquake, and heavy hail" (11:19), and at the seventh scale "flashes of lightning, rumblings, peals of thunder, and a violent earthquake . . . and huge hailstones" (16:18, 21) are mentioned. Each time the enumeration of natural disasters becomes more massive. The goal of all these natural disasters and the related judgments lies, just like during the situation in Egypt, in the liberation of God's people. Not the destruction, but the redemption of creation from evil and destructive counter-powers stands in the foreground of the Bible.

The Impact of Evil

Creation has become completely sick and weakened by the influence of humans. There is global warming that is disproportionate. In the Arctic, gigantic tons of ice are melting away, causing the sea level to rise to such an extent that other regions on earth are being flooded. In Greenland, a soccer field of ice disappears every day from the surface. The demand for recovery and healing is thus becoming louder and louder on our planet.

Revelation offers a message of hope for this creation. That is why the whole creation worships the slaughtered Lamb when it takes the scroll in Revelation 5. Despite the many contractions that the present creation still has to go through, the book of Revelation reminds its readers that the birth of the new creation is near. There will be a tree of life in the new heaven and the new earth, of which the leaves will serve to heal. So, it is essential to see the testimony of Revelation not as an attempt to destroy this creation. The book of Revelation bears witness to the hope of salvation that this creation through the Messiah may know. This Messiah is, just like creation, drenched in blood.

That does not mean that God is separated from judgment. People acknowledge in Revelation 6:16 that this is the "wrath of the Lamb." In Revelation 16:19, God testifies that he gives Babylon the wine cup full of his wrath and makes her judgment (cf. Rev 18:5, 8, 20; 19:2). Although the book of Revelation mainly avoids bringing God into direct relation with judgment, the recognition that God judges sounds several times. The Lamb and God are the only just Judges who can universally fulfill the call for justice for this creation. In the book of Revelation, this is recognized several times: "Just and true are your ways" (15:3), "Your judgments are true and just" (16:7), "His judgments are true and just" (19:2). In these statements, it is recognized that the judgment of God is faithful and righteous.

> Then I saw heaven opened, and there was a white horse! Its rider is called Faithful and True, and in righteousness he judges and makes war. (Rev 19:11)

When God justly punishes people by pouring blood on the water through an angel, it sounds, "You are just, O Holy One, who are and were, for you have judged these things" (Rev 16:5). The punishment with blood is righteous because people also shed the blood of the saints and prophets:

> Because they shed the blood of saints and prophets, you have given them blood to drink. It is what they deserve!" And I heard the altar respond, "Yes, O Lord God, the Almighty, your judgments are true and just!" (Rev 16:6–7)

In Revelation 11:18, it sounds, "Your wrath has come, and the time for judging the dead . . . and for destroying those who destroy the earth." God does not destroy creation, but those who destroy creation. Their actions come down on their heads (cf. Ezek 22:31).

These observations do not conclude that God is presented in Revelation as a horrible tyrant with a bloodthirsty desire to hurt people. God is a righteous Judge who delivers his creation from all evil done to it by humans.

11.1.3 The Lamb That Frees Creation

The choice to have judgment primarily carried out through intermediate beings ensures that it is God's active will to save people. This element comes to the fore in the book of Revelation, because when it comes to salvation, no intermediate beings are used in the book of Revelation.[9] The Messiah is directly connected to the blessing in this book. Where there is a passive form ("was given"), it is explicitly refers to God or his Messiah. We see an example of this in the seven epistles to the churches in Asia Minor (Rev 2:7, 26; 3:9, 21) or in the assignment to the two witnesses to prophesy (11:3). Elsewhere in the book of Revelation, God acts active when it comes to aspects of salvation. The Lamb will bring the great crowd out of oppression to the springs of life (7:17a; 21:6), and God will erase all tears from their eyes (7:17b; 21:4). So, the Almighty is directly connected with the restoration and redemption work. At the same time, God distances himself in the execution of judgment. Only at the end of the book of Revelation comes a moment when the author dares to threaten with the active judgment of God if someone adds or omits something from the book (22:18–19).

The vision of Babylon presents itself as a prophetic critique of injustice against creation. There are global deforestation and ecological imperialism. However, the new Jerusalem promises an entirely new world, where God will live among people on earth. There are remarkable differences between these two cities. The new Jerusalem has no sea and, therefore, no economic shipping, which is criticized early in the book (Rev 8:9). Also, the trade in luxury products, which is prominent in Babylon, is lacking in the new Jerusalem. At the beginning of the new Jerusalem, we find for a second time that God speaks personally as "I am the Alpha and the Omega" in the book of Revelation (21:6). The first time appears in Revelation 1:8, "'I am the Alpha and the Omega,' says the Lord God, who is and who was and who is to come, the Almighty." These words return in large part the second time: "It is done! I am the Alpha and the

---

9. Bauckham, "Judgment," 5–6.

Omega, the beginning and the end. To the thirsty I will give water as a gift from the spring of the water of life" (21:6).

Two Ways

Revelation is thus characterized as a book that shows two ways: (1) the blessing of salvation and eternal life that comes from God's throne and leads to God's eternal kingdom, and (2) the way of evil and the power of death that is judged from God's throne. The judgments connected with the seven seals, the seven trumpets, and the seven scales ultimately lead to the fall of the fornicating city of Babylon and the coming of the new Jerusalem from heaven. In the storyline of the book of Revelation, the followers of God and the Lamb play a leading role. We hear several times of their testimony or prayers (Rev 5:8; 8:3). However, nowhere do the followers of the Lamb pray to God to carry out the judgment. Their prayer goes out to the coming of God's kingdom, to the desire that God's will be done on earth as it is in heaven. Even the prayers of the martyrs under the altar do not initially beg for judgment. They beg for righteousness about what has been done to them (6:9–10).

The four horsemen, who precede the begging of the martyrs, are not directly related to their martyrdom. Their prayers are heard in Revelation 16:6–7. There we hear under the altar that God is trustworthy and righteous because he made people on earth drink blood: "Because they shed the blood of saints and prophets, you have given them blood to drink. It is what they deserve!" (16:6). This same testimony is heard in Revelation 19:2, where the writer, just as in 6:9, uses the term "avenge" (ἐκδικέω, *ekdikeō*). This term appears only in these two verses and indicates the desire for righteousness on earth.

Intermezzos

So-called interludes further characterize the judgments described in the book of Revelation. They often separate the last seventh judgment from the previous six. For example, after the sixth seal, we hear of the redeeming God (7:1–17), after the sixth trumpet, there is an opened book and two witnesses (10:1—11:13), and after the sixth scale, the victor and his followers are seen (15:1–8). So, between the judgments, there are moments of rest in the book of Revelation, so that the reader experiences that these judgments do not follow each other. Also, judgments never touch people directly. Primarily the military, political, and economic system, maintained by the beasts and whores of Babylon, is affected. Only those who commit themselves to this ungodly system and identify themselves with it by worshiping the beast and trading with the whore come under judgment.

That explains why a voice from heaven shouts, "Come out of her, my people, so that you do not take part in her sins, and so that you do not share in her plagues" (Rev 18:4). Then the followers of the Lamb applaud her judgment (18:20), as many did in the past during the fall of National Socialism in Germany (1945), the fall of the Berlin Wall (1989), or the fall of various other degrading systems. The cheers of the fall of the city of Babylon sound because "in her was found the blood of prophets and of saints, and of all who have been slaughtered on earth" (18:24). It is not only about the followers of the Lamb, but also about all other people that the Babylonian system falls. The writer of the book of Revelation also relates these other people to the Lamb by using the term "slaughtered."

11.2 THE DISAPPEARANCE OF THE SEA

While creation in the book of Revelation suffers the consequences of evil, God intervenes through his servants. The Lamb has come to deliver all creation from evil. Consequently, Revelation ends with the beautiful prospect of the new heaven and the new earth. However, it is not easy to describe the relationship between the present creation and this new creation. The statements in the book of Revelation about what will no longer exist in the new heavens and earth offer some direction: "Death will be no more; mourning and crying and pain will be no more, for the first things have passed away" (Rev 21:4b).

Most challenging for many readers is that even the sea will no longer exist (21:1). How should we understand this absence? This is especially interesting for those who are engaged in a book on animals and God. Will the new creation no longer know the rich flora and fauna that enriches our oceans? Does the author of the book of Revelation prepare his listeners for this striking absence of the sea? The book of Revelation is more concerned with water than any other book of the Bible. Besides, it is striking that the Jewish work Assumption of Moses mentions that "the sea will retreat into the abyss, the water sources will cease, and the rivers will dry up" (10:6). However, the book of Revelation concentrates only on the sea. What is the reason for this?

11.2.1 The Sea as a Physical Element of Nature

The sea is part of this globe, as are the land, the sky, rivers, and water sources. It contains its creatures that praise and worship God and the Lamb (Rev 5:13; cf. 8:9; 10:6). Like the earth, the sea is used by evil (12:12), and is connected with the judgments that follow the trumpets (8:8–9) and the scales (16:3). This leads us to think of the seas of this earth in Revelation 21:1. A sea separated John from his congregations in Asia Minor and was a dangerous obstacle for humans in the past. Plutarch (AD 46–120), a famous Greek historian in antiquity, saw the sea as an element that did not belong to this creation. It was a "corrupt and pernicious remnant of a strange nature."[10]

Until modern times, the sea would remain a frightening phenomenon. Many rough fishers prayed fearfully for a safe passage during his sea voyage. Many of them did not even go out to sea without giving their children a cross on their forehead and encouraging their wives to regularly visit the chapels and the fisherman's mass. Everywhere in fishing harbors, we find chapels to pray for the fisherman. The sea was grim, and many would die there. The fact that their bodies were not found caused many sleepless nights with their relatives. There was a chance that the ship's sailor was still alive but lost on an island. So, love for the sea was always accompanied by fear of the sea. When a new ship went into service, it was baptized and the ship's crew was blessed. This is still the case in many places today. Certain areas, such as the Bermuda Triangle or the Formosa Triangle, also arouse many fears. These areas are known for the mysterious disappearance of ships (and planes). Whoever travels through them with his ship can experience frightening moments.

11.2.2 The Sea as a Source of Evil

In Revelation 12–13, the sea is related to evil. For example, it mentions that the dragon stands on the sea beach when a terrible beast emerges from it (13:1). This dragon is similar to the ancient serpent and refers to cosmic evil. In Revelation 11:7 and 17:8, we learn that the beast emerged

---

10. Plutarch, *Moralia VII*, 353E.

from the sea from the ἄβυσσος/*abyssos*. That is the "abyss" or "subterranean depth." So, the sea does not point to the Mediterranean or one of the oceans. It is about the primeval flood in Genesis 1:2, from which all seas traditionally sprung. In Psalm 106:9, the Septuagint translates this depth as ἄβυσσος/*abyssos*. In Hellenistic myths, this refers to the realm of the dead, where the disobedient spirits were imprisoned. Also, in Revelation, evil spirits come out of these ἄβυσσος/*abyssos* (Rev 9:1–11; 20:1–3).

From this approach, interpreters relate the sea in Revelation 21:1 to the source of evil.[11] The primordial sea's depth is then opposite to the highest heaven, from where redemption is realized. This sea will no longer exist in the new heaven and the new earth. A difficulty here is that the book of Revelation does not present the sea as hostile to God. That makes us cautious to see an evil opponent of God in the sea.[12] This is only possible if the sea is a symbolic reference to the unbelieving peoples of the earth. The sea has that meaning in Revelation 17:15: "The waters that you saw, where the whore is seated, are peoples and multitudes and nations and languages." The streams of water refer to the sea. It is then human evil and the associated forces of chaos that must disappear. As the new Jerusalem relates to the believers, to God's highest holy place, and to God's omnipresence, the sea in Revelation refers to the unbelievers, to the highest unholy place, and to God's absence.

In the book of Revelation, the sea is also a medium the sea trade of Babylon. However, Babylon is destroyed and thrown into sea like a millstone (Rev 18:21). The sea is a place of judgment and death. Just as the sea washes away Tyre, Babylon will be washed away (Ezek 26:19–21; cf. Rev 8:8–9). The sea is the realm of the dead (ᾅδης, *hadēs*), and soon these dead will be released (Rev 20:13). In these descriptions the sea carries a negative connotation.[13] The absence of the sea then testifies that the new creation will be a place of joy. It will then be a place without evil or danger, and without the primeval flood as the ancient source of evil. This stimulates us to reflect some more on the sea as a theological motive.

---

11. Osborne, *Revelation*, 731; Beale, *Book of Revelation*, 1042–43; Aune, *Revelation 17–22*, 1119–20; Mounce, *Revelation*, 381; Bauckham, *Theology*, 53; Roloff, *Revelation*, 235; Ford, *Revelation*, 361.

12. Moo, "Sea That Is No More," 158.

13. Bauckham, *Fate of the Dead*, 280–81.

11.2.3 The Sea as Primeval Flood

The book of Revelation first mentions the sea in Revelation 4:6 as "something like a sea of glass, like crystal" (cf. Rev 15:2). This sea is reminiscent of the copper laver that stood in the court outside the temple. When the new heaven and the new earth come, this court with its objects will be absent, because everything will belong to God.

> The court outside the temple ... is given over to the nations, and they will trample over the holy city for forty-two months. (Rev 11:2)

The court will no longer be present at the beginning of the new heaven and the new earth.[14] That the laver stands, in Revelation 4, "before the throne" of God is explained as the laver being located in the court, outside the Most Holy Place, where the throne of God is. Nevertheless, the location of it cannot be deduced from the text.[15] Then the absence of the sea indicates that a laver to clean oneself is no longer necessary. The way to God is entirely open. The veil of the sanctuary is torn from top to bottom. This event is a reminder of the exodus from Egypt, where the Red Sea was also an obstacle for Israel. This theme of the exodus plays an essential role in the book of Isaiah, where the theme functions as a motive for God's redemption in the future (Isa 10:26; 11:15; 43:16; 51:10; cf. Zech 10:11).

Because Revelation 21 takes up the theme of the new heaven and the new earth from Isaiah 65, it is quite possible that this background of Isaiah also plays a role in its description. The absence of the sea in Revelation 21:1 is then an echo of Isaiah's biblical-theological descriptions of the new exodus. This exodus theme can already be found in the Old Testament in the books of Isaiah, Ezekiel, and Zechariah. It is also discussed in Revelation, which builds heavily on these works.[16]

In total, there are seven things which the prophet testifies "passed away" in the new heaven and the new earth (οὐκ ἔσται ἔτι, *ouk estai eti* or οὐκ ἔστιν ἔτι, *ouk estin eti*): the sea (21:1), death, mourning, lamentation, pain (21:4b), every curse (22:3), and the night (22:5). The middle

---

14. Snyder, *Combat Myth*, 162–68.
15. Moo, "Sea That Is No More," 153.
16. Cf. Jauhiainen, *Zechariah in Revelation*; Kowalski, *Rezeption des Propheten Ezechiel*; Mathewson, *New Heaven*; Beale, *John's Use*; Fekkes, *Isaiah and Prophetic Traditions*.

five elements (death through curses) cancel the consequences of human disobedience in Genesis 3. The outer two elements (sea and night) cancel the hostile powers that are already present from Genesis 1 and never received the predicate "it was good" (see chapter 2.2). Also in ancient Egyptian literature, the sea and darkness are elements that go against creation (anti-creation). Therefore, they are strange and malicious spheres of power.

We see the same thought in other biblical books. From a biblical theology, sea and night are fundamental sources of evil in creation. We saw in chapter 2.2.3 that this was expressed in Genesis 1:2: "The earth was a formless void and darkness covered the face of the deep, while a wind from God swept over the face of the waters." The waters of the primeval flood and the darkness of the night form a potential from which evil and the forces of chaos emerge. In the middle of the day, the sudden darkness of the night comes over the land and is considered as a judgment (Amos 8:9; Joel 2:2, 31; Zeph 1:15). Also, deep darkness covers the earth during the crucifixion of Jesus Christ (Mark 16:33). It is reserved for the evildoers of whom Jude speaks in his letter (Jude 1:6, 13). The same applies to the sea. In Daniel 7, we learn that four beasts rise from the sea and build kingdoms on earth opposite to the realm of the Son of Man from heaven. This same pattern is continued in Revelation 13. There the beast from the sea also turns against the kingdom of the Messiah.

It would be impossible for this evil to emerge from a sea that bears the predicate "good." By clinging to the striking negative connotation from Genesis about the night and the sea, Revelation builds further on this biblical theology. It shows how creation in Genesis 1 finds its rest and completion in the new creation of Revelation 21–22, where the sea, the night, and all evil are gone forever. This means that the good has conquered evil that was present in creation from the beginning. The slaughtered Lamb testifies that God faithfully supports his creation in achieving its goal: the rebirth of the whole creation.

12

Animals in the New Creation

12.1 RELATIONSHIP BETWEEN HUMANS AND ANIMALS

12.1.1 Life and Death

PETS ARE AN INTEGRAL part of our society. For more than a thousand years, living together has shown that people and animals know how to build a special bond with each other. On average, half of all families in Western countries have a pet. This shows how precious animals are to people. Many older adults who lost their former friends enjoy their pet immensely in their senior years of life. Their dog or cat is their only friend. Scientific research has been done on how pets and older people improve each other's lives.[1]

In our care for the elderly, we discovered that the maintenance of pets is often a motivation to postpone the relocation to a retirement home. The well-being of the pet then takes precedence. Society may still be generous and subsidize the rent for the care home. If the move implies a separation between the older person and the animal, the action is not done. The bond between the animal and the owner is not free to buy or solve. The social challenges this entails cannot be taken lightly. Psychology points out possible challenges that arise when people think they can have a relationship with animals in the same way they do with people. It is striking, for example, that dogs and their owners grow similarly together after several years as human partners normally do.

---

1. E.g., Geisler, "Companion Animals," 285–88.

This shows how intensive the relationship between animals and humans can be. It is good to be attentive to this when we address the sincere question of whether animals also go to heaven. Animals are more than living robots. We see a confirmation of this in the use of the well-known Tamagotchi. The Japanese developer Aki Maita (1967) offered everyone a virtual pet with his design in November 1996. He sold several million copies of Tamagotchi. But, to this day, real pets for young and old remain a much more tremendous success than these game consoles.

The pet is often kept as part of the family. Because pets have a shorter life than humans, children are often confronted with losing their favorite pets at an early age. It may seem strange, but the grief and mourning over the death or loss of a beloved pet can weigh as heavily as the death or loss of a family member or friend.[2] Often the death of a pet occurs without prior warning. The contact with the animal then ends abruptly. A time to say goodbye to our dear friend is missing. To say that we just have to move on is easier said than done. Nor is it what the owners of the deceased animal want to hear. Human beings even process the death of an animal in the same way as a fellow human being's death. There can be sleepless nights, difficulties in daily activities, and other psychological and social challenges.[3] Therefore, it is irresponsible to ignore or ridicule the pain of losing a pet. It often happens that parents, together with their children, take a moment to reflect on the animal's life when they bury it in the garden. The goldfish or parakeet is buried, and some feel they want to say a prayer at that moment. "May you rest in peace." Then the place is marked, and nobody comes to the thought of digging a hole on that spot.

For many, the death of a beloved pet is even the first time they are confronted with death. This loss raises all kinds of questions about the death and further existence of the animal. Silent witnesses to this are the diaries of children and elderly:

> Meanwhile, a few sad days have passed. I miss him wherever I am. I feel a great emptiness in my heart, mostly because I don't know if we will ever see each other again. I would like so much to know if I will see him again. If God made Cooper and knew and loved him more than we loved him as a family, will he then

---

2. Cf. Kaufman and Kaufman, "And Then the Dog Died," 61–76.

3. See, in detail: Cowles, "Death of a Pet," 135–61; Field et al., "Role of Attachment," 334–55; Sharkin and Knox, "Pet Loss," 414–21; Gerwolls and Labott, "Adjustment to the Death," 172–87; Quackenbush, "Death of a Pet," 395–402.

also accept the desire to make Cooper alive again? Jesus once said that God does not forget a swallow.

In medical science, there is a growing research into the influence that a pet's death has on humans.[4] "I played with Rocky every day. He immediately jumped up to me when he saw me from afar," it sounds in other diaries. Most children did not have those extraordinary, joyful experiences with their grandparents. Children realized that their pet had unconditional love for them. It was a dear friend who was always available. The ancient Egyptians had already chosen to mummify specific domesticated animals at the death of their owner. The owner could then continue to enjoy his animals in the afterlife. They could serve him as companions in the realm of the dead.

So children like to ask their parents whether their dead pets are in heaven. If so, it offers hope to see their beloved pet again. There will come a day when the child can run his hands through the animal's soft fur, place his face on his warm back, dash with him across the fields, and teach him new tricks.

12.1.2 Hero Francis of Assisi

Animal lovers have always been associated with the religious hero Francis of Assisi (1181–1226). In the basilica at Assisi (Italy), we find the famous little painting in which Francis preaches the gospel to the birds. The Italian painter and architect Giotto di Bondone (1266–1337) painted the canvas around 1297–99. Surrounded by a golden halo, Francis calls on animals to continue praising God with their songs. Francis understood God's love for creation. In 1980 Pope John Paul II chose him as the patron saint of ecology. Every year on October 4, his blessing of animals is commemorated as World Animal Day is celebrated. The life of St. Francis is marked on this day in Christian tradition.

Francis treated animals kindly and spoke to them as brothers and sisters. When he stayed for a time in complete solitude in a vault, a falcon woke him up at night and in the morning to say his prayers in time. At another moment, Francis enjoyed the singing of a cricket. However, when swallows suddenly disturbed one of his sermons with their loud

---

4. E.g., Harrison and Harrington, "Adolescents' Bereavement Experiences," 159–69; Adams et al., "Predictors of Owner Response," 1303–9; Archer and Winchester, "Bereavement," 259–71; Sharkin and Knox, "Pet Loss," 414–21.

twittering, he silenced them. Another time, Francis received a waterfowl from a fisherman. The bird sat in his garden for a while. It subsequently flew away after Francis had given it the order to do so. When a sow killed a lamb, she was cursed by Francis. The sow died shortly afterward, and prey animals did not touch her carcass.[5]

Furthermore, Francis freed a rabbit caught in a snare, threw captured fish back into the water, and bought a lamb so that it was not killed and eaten. He also refused to eat a pheasant, which he got as a present. Yet Francis did not choose to impose vegetarian coercion on people. During the Christmas party preparation, he was asked if meat should be prepared because the Christmas party took place on a Friday. He answered that they indeed had to prepare a luxurious meat meal. Christmas was the most beautiful feast of the year.[6] That moment rose above the tradition of eating fish on Fridays.

In general, there are few theological texts left by Francis. According to traditional imagery, Francis's extremely positive approach to nature and the animal world is a new Christian traditional element. But his choices in dealing with animals are not unique. Numerous other Christians of his time also point to the joy that animals can bring to life. An example is the Anglo-Saxon Bishop Cuthbert (634–87). When he said his prayers at night, he was standing with his feet in the waves of the lake. Then in the morning, two otters came out of the lake to dry his feet with their fur. Other times, birds ate from his harvest. He ordered them to leave, and they obeyed immediately. The English hermit Goderik of Finchale (1065–1170) rescued a deer chased by hunters and freed animals caught in snares.[7] In chapter 8.2.3, we also mentioned several other examples in which humans and animals specially dealt with each other.

Francis admires animals and plants, stones, and a candle flame as God's creation, in addition to the nuances mentioned above. As a result, his praise goes beyond the animal world. It is a life in recognition of all that God created. But to what extent does this animal world also have a future?

---

5. See, for these illustrations, Habig, *Francis of Assisi*, §§59, 80–81, 111, 167–68, 171.

6. Habig, *Francis of Assisi*, §§60–62, 79, 170, 199–200.

7. See for these illustrations, Schenderling, *Mens en dier*, 147–50.

12.1.3 Reflections on a Systematic Approach

The idea that animals are present in the new creation is often new for many people. This is because for a long time Christian doctrine paid almost no attention to the new heaven and the new earth's themes. Also, the theme of animals was hardly addressed in Christian theology. That may cause this proposal to be rejected in advance. But, already in the eighteenth century, the British theologian and preacher John Wesley (1703–91), called upon his listeners not to be guided by social philosophies but by biblical revelation. So, it is not new to Christianity that certain biblical truths have been pushed into the background. When we rediscover them, they often initially sound like heresies.

Another challenge in the reflection on the future of the animals on the new earth is that the Bible contains few clues about this. The only text in which the terms "new heavens and the new earth" are directly related to animals is Isaiah 65:

> "For I am about to create new heavens and a new earth; the former things shall not be remembered or come to mind.... The wolf and the lamb shall feed together, the lion shall eat straw like the ox; but the serpent—its food shall be dust! They shall not hurt or destroy on all my holy mountain," says the Lord. (Isa 65:17, 25)

At the same time, the belief that there are animals on the new earth clashes with other Christian proclamations. Christians confess that people who believe in Christ will participate in the new heaven and the new earth. This is a problem with animals. They are not called upon in the Bible to repent, change their minds, and dedicate themselves to God's kingdom. There is no altar call for animals in the Bible.

Although several Christians in church history went to church on a donkey or horse, nowhere did these animals enter the church to praise God or give their hearts to Christ. The expectation of a future reunion with pets seems from a Christian proclamation nothing more than wishful thinking.

It has also been pointed out that animals have no part in salvation and resurrection because they have no soul. An example of this can be found in the work of the Italian philosopher and theologian Thomas Aquinas (1225–74). In his time, he was intensively concerned with the place of animals in this creation. Nevertheless, Aquinas saw only humans as creatures directly involved with God.[8] Only people lived to serve God. The calling of animals to God in biblical books such as Jonah or Joel (see chapter 7.2.3) was not considered. Animals belonged to a lower class of creation and seemed to express themselves only to God. They served the higher creation class of people just as plants or "immobile animals" (e.g., oysters) existed for animals.[9] Characteristics of the animal were its impulsive, unconcerned urges and the absence of a free will.[10] From this, many concluded that animals had no soul and, therefore, no future.

Also, according to Augustine (354–430), animals had only a "living soul" (*anima*), but no "rational spirit" (*spiritus, intelligentia, ratio*).[11] An animal would cease to exist when it died. According to this philosophical line of thought, it was only useful in this present creation to provide people with food and help.[12]

Nevertheless, these philosophical ideas about the future of animals had been questioned already ages before Thomas of Aquinas. The Celtic father of scholasticism, Johannes Scotus (810–877), and the English philosopher Benedict Adelard of Bath (~1080–1152) were among those who did so. In Aristotelian philosophy, the lower (plants, animals) was only there for the sake of the higher (animals, humans), without taking into account the value for the whole. That led to the question of what the meaning of the lower classes of creation was for God. Was there a biblical hope for a cosmological perspective? What would it be like if everything in heaven and everything on earth, the invisible and the visible, was reconciled by the Son of God (cf. Col 1:16–20)? This is remarkable for those who realize that Thomas Aquinas also believed that creation was an expression of God's wealth. How could a temporary, transient creation be a testimony to that eternal, permanent wealth?

---

8. Aquinas, *Summa Theologiae*, I.78.1; Aquinas, *Summa Contra Gentiles*, III.22, 112.

9. Aquinas, *Summa Contra Gentiles*, III.22; Aquinas, *Summa Theologiae*, I.96.1. In this, Aquinas followed the Greek philosopher Aristotle (384–22): Aristotle, *Politics*, 1256b. Cf. Happ, *Die Scala Naturae*.

10. Aquinas, *Summa Theologiae*, I.81.3; I.83.1; IIa.6.2; IIa.15.2; Chrysostom, *Homilies on Romans*, Sermon 92.

11. Augustine of Hippo, *De Natura et Origine Animae*, 4.23.

12. Aquinas, *Summa Contra Gentiles*, II.82; Aquinas, *Summa Theologiae*, I.75.3, 6; Supp.91.5.

Also, the view that animals did not have a soul was critically questioned.[13] How was this proven? To what extent did the biblical authors make such a distinction between humans and animals? It turned out that they used the term "soul" for both humans and animals. Both were called, without any merit, a "living soul" (נֶפֶשׁ חַיָּה, *nefesj hajāh*; Gen 1:21, 24, 30; 2:7, 19; Rev 16:3). The question about the future of animals was not thought through in-depth from a biblical-theological and systematic-theological reflection. Those who argued that there were no animals in the new creation because no repentance of animals was expected could argue from similar reasoning that there would be no angels in the new creation because no repentance of angels was expected. After all, even to them, there is no call of repentance in the Bible. Nevertheless, I have not yet come across any Christian work that argues that there will be no angels in eternity.

That is why more is needed in Christian doctrine than just reflection on biblical texts that directly or indirectly touch upon the theme. We need an examination from the perspective of a biblical theology. An example of this can be found in the Christian reflection on the Trinity. Although the word "Trinity" or its equivalent cannot be found in the Bible, Christians realize that faith in the Trinity is part of the scriptural witness. Although a statement such as "animals go to the new heaven and the new earth" is not present in the Bible, there are several indications that Christ's work of salvation includes the animal world. Indeed, for those who believe that God let humans evolve from the animal world, the question of whether animals have a future expectation is essential. So what can be said from biblical discourse about animals' eventual future in the new heaven and the new earth?

12.2 BIBLICAL-THEOLOGICAL REFLECTIONS

The arguments for believing in a future for the animals in the new heaven and the new earth can be brought together from different approaches: (1) biblical texts that connect a cosmological function to the work of salvation of Jesus Christ; (2) biblical texts that relate animals to salvation

---

13. Cf. Kurz, *Cold Noses*, 81–85; Hagencord, *Gott und die Tiere*, 30; Habermas and Moreland, *Beyond Death*, 79–82; Clark, *Moral Status*; Hartog, *Sin, Redemption, and the Animal Kingdom*.

and the future; and (3) biblical texts that show God's care for animals in salvation history.

12.2.1 Cosmological Reflections

Throughout church history, several Christians expressed the idea that humans and animals would find a place on the new earth. It was unacceptable to them that Christ's work of salvation only affected humans. John 3 emphasized that God gave his Son for all creation, namely the cosmos:

> For God so loved the world [κόσμος, kosmos] that he gave his only Son, so that everyone who believes in him may not perish but may have eternal life. Indeed God did not send the Son into the world to condemn the world, but in order that the world might be saved through him. (John 3:16)

Christ was the Lamb who took away the sin of the cosmos: "Here is the Lamb of God who takes away the sin of the world [κόσμος, kosmos]!" (John 1:29).

The British philosopher and theologian Keith Ward (b. 1938), for example, found it unacceptable that animals should be dragged along in the destruction by the first Adam, but not in the glorification by the last Adam. The horrible pain that animals had to go through in salvation history would never be alternated with peace.[14]

Many see this peace fulfilled in the messianic realm of peace, which is expected for the new heaven and the new earth. After this time, the animals could still disappear on earth.[15] However, the question is how plausible this proposition is within a salvation doctrine that holds cosmic significance. Indeed, the New Testament's impression is that the cosmic impact of Jesus Christ is not limited to a few years but has eternal value.[16] "Creation itself will be set free from its bondage to decay and will obtain the freedom of the glory of the children of God" (Rom 8:21). To argue that this would only be temporary would be as hard as saying that humanity's redemption would only be temporary and pass after a few years. That would be immensely deficient compared to the work of Jesus Christ

---

14. Ward, *Pascal's Fire*, 255–56; Ward, *Rational Theology*, 202; Ward, *Concept of God*, 223.
15. Southgate, *Groaning of Creation*, 85.
16. Kärkkäinen, *Hope*, 87.

and still allow the powers of death and destruction to respond to God's creation.

The French theologian John Calvin (1509-64) correctly writes in his commentary on Romans 8:21 that the context of this biblical text speaks not only of the glory of the sons of God but also of the renewal of all creatures. Thereby the Reformer notes that the apostle Paul does not automatically mean that animals have the same glory as of the sons of God. However, they will share their way into the better state of the future because God renews creation.[17] Also, John Wesley expressed in a sermon on Romans 8:19-22 ("The General Deliverance") the idea that animals are part of the new creation:

> After death for these poor creatures also; that these, likewise, shall one day be delivered from this bondage of corruption, and shall then receive an ample amends for all their present sufferings.[18]

The work of Christ's salvation would bring peace to *all* creation. The New Testament emphasizes this "all" or "everything" several times in the proclamation of the work of redemption.

> He is the head of the body, the church; he is the beginning, the firstborn from the dead, so that he might come to have first place in everything. For in him all the fullness of God was pleased to dwell, and through him God was pleased to reconcile to himself all things, whether on earth or in heaven, by making peace through the blood of his cross. (Col 1:18-20; cf. Eph 1:9-10)

In the Bible, the redemption that Jesus Christ brings is redemption for all creation, everything on earth, and everything in heaven. That means that the salvation a person personally receives through Christ is inextricably linked to the greater whole. There is no salvation in the Bible; no social and personal life separated from creation as a whole. From Genesis to Revelation, there is attention to all creation's redemption so that Christ may be firstborn in all things. This does not mean that the personal aspect of salvation is absent. It means that in its great importance, it is part of a greater whole.[19] The Jewish thinker Moses Maimonides illustrates this relationship between the personal and the whole as follows:

---

17. Calvin, *Romans*.
18. Wesley, "General Deliverance," III.3.
19. Gunton, *Christ and Creation*, 33-34.

Some citizens may imagine that it was for the purpose of protecting his house by night from thieves that the king was chosen. To some extent this is correct; for when his house is protected, and he has derived this benefit through the king whom the country had chosen, it appears as if it were the object of the king to protect the house of that man.[20]

If these individual citizens would realize that the government also has to protect the city's inhabitants' homes, this would not force them to reject the idea that the government protects the home of the individual. However, this idea does not take into account the government's primary purpose for the greater good. The government not only protects the house of the individual but of all inhabitants.

There is hope for this creation's future from the reflection on the cosmic meaning of the work of salvation of Jesus Christ. In the history of salvation, we see at length that God takes care of his work and does not surrender it into the hands of his enemies.

12.2.2 Eschatological Reflections

The Completion and the Kingdom of God

In Isaiah 65:17, the prophet announces that God will create new heavens and earth. The context speaks about the renewal of the human world and the animal world:

> "For I am about to create new heavens and a new earth; the former things shall not be remembered or come to mind. But be glad and rejoice forever in what I am creating; for I am about to create Jerusalem as a joy, and its people as a delight. I will rejoice in Jerusalem, and delight in my people; no more shall the sound of weeping be heard in it, or the cry of distress. No more shall there be in it an infant that lives but a few days, or an old person who does not live out a lifetime; for one who dies at a hundred years will be considered a youth, and one who falls short of a hundred will be considered accursed. They shall build houses and inhabit them; they shall plant vineyards and eat their fruit. They shall not build and another inhabit; they shall not plant and another eat; for like the days of a tree shall the days of my people be, and my chosen shall long enjoy the work of their hands. They shall not labor in vain, or bear children for

---

20. Maimonides, *Guide of the Perplexed*, 3.13.

calamity; for they shall be offspring blessed by the Lord—and their descendants as well. Before they call I will answer, while they are yet speaking I will hear. The wolf and the lamb shall feed together, the lion shall eat straw like the ox; but the serpent—its food shall be dust! They shall not hurt or destroy on all my holy mountain," says the Lord.(Isa 65:17–25)

Because this text refers to the city of Jerusalem (Isa 65:18–19), to people who die young (v. 20) and who have children (v. 20, 23), they are explained as descriptions of the future messianic kingdom. That kingdom will be temporary, and creation will still not be perfect. Revelation 20 suggests that the messianic kingdom will last a thousand years and end after a war with Gog and Magog. After the millennial kingdom, Revelation 20 speaks about the judgment, and Revelation 21 heralds the coming of new heavens and a new earth. In Isaiah 65, the description runs the other way around: from the new heaven and the new earth to the time in the messianic kingdom where death is not yet gone (cf. Isa 25:8; 26:6–9; Ps 110:2).

There is nothing wrong with this explanation. What is striking is how the prophet introduces this description of the temporary states of peace: "For I am about to create new heavens and a new earth" (Isa 65:17). In Christian proclamation, this strange introduction often leads to these words being nuanced or changed into, "Behold, I am creating a temporary messianic kingdom."

But the prophet does not choose that salutation. He decides to see the descriptions of this kingdom in the light of eternity. Whoever does not accept this process perspective will often pick out of one of the three phases: (1) Isaiah 65 describes the present state of God's kingdom on earth; (2) Isaiah 65 describes the millennial kingdom in the future; or (3) Isaiah 65 describes the eschatological new creation. The challenge then remains the opening words "new heavens and earth," which refer to the completed new creation (phase 3) and the references to death and curse (65:20), which belong to phase 1 and 2 (cf. 25:8).

We do not want to solve this field of tension, which was consciously created by the prophet. Together with the Old Testament scholar John Oswalt (b. 1940), we choose that the prophet, when announcing "new heavens and the new earth," thinks of completion and the whole process of transformation.[21] What happens in the millennial kingdom is a foretaste of what happens next. Thus the context testifies to forgetting and

---

21. Oswalt, *Isaiah 40–66*, 656–57.

rejoicing. First, God forgets (Isa 65:16b), then humans forget (v. 17b), then humans rejoice (v. 18a), and then God delights (v. 19a). Central to the description of the future is the joy in the city, which God chose for glory (v. 18), the fulfillment of the years of life (v. 20), the enjoyment of the home, the garden, and the family (v. 21–22), the safe living of old and young (v. 23), the deep connection with God (v. 24), and the harmony between animals (v. 25). Rejected are thoughts of the negative, complicated past (v. 17), weeping and moaning (v. 19), the cursed (v. 20), and the robbing of earthly blessings and offspring (v. 22–23). The creation of the new heaven and the new earth is then closely connected with the future redemption and renewal of the chosen city of Jerusalem. This is not a strange phenomenon. Elsewhere, the themes of the new creation, Jerusalem, and the royal Davidic house are also connected (Ps 132:11–14). It is a beautiful description of what will happen in the holy city.

Connection with Isaiah 11 and Hosea 2

In this description, the animal peace, which the prophet has already mentioned in Isaiah 11, is discussed again. In chapter 8, we already elaborated on that part of the text. The first pair of animals (wolf and lamb) and the fifth pair of animals (lion and cow) from Isaiah 11 return in Isaiah 65. It is also possible to see in the serpent of Isaiah 65 (נָחָשׁ, *nāchāsh*) a reference to the adder (פֶּתֶן, *peten*), and the poisonous snake (צִפְעֹנִי, *tsif'oni*) of Isaiah 11:

> "The wolf and the lamb shall feed together, the lion shall eat straw like the ox; but the serpent—its food shall be dust! They shall not hurt or destroy on all my holy mountain," says the Lord. (Isa 65:25)

Wolf and lamb eat harmoniously from the same meal. There is no more evil and injustice. All animals feed on vegetable products. Then God's new covenant with animals is fulfilled. Of this the prophet Hosea testified:

> I will make for you a covenant on that day with the wild animals, the birds of the air, and the creeping things of the ground. (Hos 2:18a; cf. chapter 6.2.3)

However, the serpent continues to crawl on its belly and is not restored to its original shape (cf. Gen 3:14). While every creature, wolf and lamb, lion and cow, is freed from the curse, the seducer has no part in salvation.

The New Creation as a Theater of God's Glory

Let's take Isaiah 65 and see this as a weak reflection of what God wants to work towards in eternity. This means that there is also hope for animals. It would be strange to restrict this very fact to the messianic kingdom or interpret it symbolically. The basis for doing so would not be present in the text but would originate from a choice made in advance. However, it is crucial to recognize how earthly the whole vision in Isaiah 65 is, material and tangible.[22] It is God's promise for life in the real world with real houses, gardens, and births.

Isaiah 65 testifies of the fulfillment of God's plan with creation. Those who do not want to know anything about a lasting recovery in the animal kingdom will do everything to discard this text. Because the prophet introduces his description of the future renewal concerning the "new earth" and ends his description with the coming harmony among animals, this does not seem the right choice. On the contrary, Isaiah 65 argues that God's new creation does not only include human society. It brings blessing to the whole creation. Both the opening and closing of Isaiah 65:17–25 testifies intensely to the radical cosmic change that will eventually take place in creation.

For this reason, the British writer and Christian apologist C. S. Lewis (1898–1963) speculated that at least the tame animals would be present in the new creation. They have an intense relationship with humans and are not hostile to them.[23] In the future new city garden, of which Revelation 21–22 testifies, everything would then be renewed. In that future all-embracing temple, there may be room for animals, as was the case in God's old temple:

> Even the sparrow finds a home, and the swallow a nest for herself, where she may lay her young, at your altars, O Lord of hosts, my King and my God. Happy are those who live in your house, ever singing your praise! *Selah*. (Ps 84:3–4)

All creation gives honor to God and testifies of his beauty and greatness.

---

22. Brueggemann, *Isaiah*, 250.
23. Lewis, *Problem of Pain*, 145–46.

Animals around the Throne

From this theological perspective, it is not strange that there is attention for animals around the throne of the Lamb at the end of Revelation 5:

> Then I heard every creature in heaven and on earth and under the earth and in the sea, and all that is in them, singing, "To the one seated on the throne and to the Lamb be blessing and honor and glory and might forever and ever!" (Rev 5:13)

This verse is an excellent expression of the universal praise the Lamb will receive in eternity. However, questions arose about whether this part of the text refers to universal praise. Because interpreters believed that only humans and angels had the intelligence to sing, "every creature" could only refer to these two categories.[24] For this reason, Gregory Beale thought of "every creature" as opponents of God, who now had to pay homage to the Lamb (cf. Phil 2:10–11).[25] Challenges for this explanation were: How were the opponents connected to the "heaven"? How could people or angels be connected to everything in the sea? And weren't the people already mentioned in Revelation 5:8–10 and the angels in 5:11?

Revelation 5:13 indicates the presence of animals praising God, alongside humans and angels.[26] The descriptions suggest the whole of creation: the birds in the sky, the land animals on earth, the crawling animals under the earth, and the sea animals on the sea and in the sea (cf. Exod 20:11; Job 11:8–9; Ps 146:6; Neh 9:6; Rev 5:3; 10:6). This communication between animals and God was not strange. The prophet Isaiah already wrote,

> The wild animals will honor me, the jackals and the ostriches; for I give water in the wilderness, rivers in the desert. (Isa 43:20a)

Furthermore, in the Psalms:

> Let heaven and earth praise him, the seas and everything that moves in them. (Ps 69:34)

> Let the heavens be glad, and let the earth rejoice; let the sea roar, and all that fills it; let the field exult, and everything in it.

---

24. Yeatts, *Revelation*; Easley, *Revelation*, 96; Alford, *Alford's Greek Testament*, 611; Ladd, *Revelation*, 93.

25. Beale, *Book of Revelation*, 365.

26. Patterson, *Revelation*, 175; Osborne, *Revelation*, 264; Kistemaker, *Revelation*, 213–14; Aune, *Revelation 1–5*, 366; Morris, *Revelation*, 102.

> Then shall all the trees of the forest sing for joy before the Lord.
> (Ps 96:11–13a; cf. 98:7–9a)
>
> Let everything that has breath praise the Lord! Praise the Lord!
> (Ps 150:6)

This is the testimony which entirely fills Psalm 148:

> Praise the Lord! Praise the Lord from the heavens; praise him in the heights! Praise him, all his angels; praise him, all his hosts! Praise him, sun and moon; praise him, all you shining stars! Praise him, you highest heavens, and you waters above the heavens! Let them praise the name of the Lord, for he commanded and they were created. He established them forever and ever; he fixed their bounds, which cannot passed. Praise the Lord from the earth, you great sea monsters and all deeps, fire and hail, snow and frost, stormy wind fulfilling his command! Mountains and all hills, fruit trees and all cedars! Wild animals and all cattle, creeping things and flying birds! Kings of the earth and all peoples, princes and all rulers of the earth! Young men and women alike, old and young together! Let them praise the name of the Lord, for his name alone is exalted; his glory is above earth and heaven. He has raised up a horn for his people, praise for all his faithful, for the people of Israel who are close to him. Praise the Lord!

It is a beautiful testimony that fits in with the old idea that animals were created as a tribute to the deity.[27] The whole creation brought honor to the Creator.

Unjustified Separation

We can interpret these biblical statements about laudatory animals metaphorically, but what motivates us to that view?[28] Is this based on the biblical testimony or is it based on other ideas? I think the latter is the case. An unintentional separation that came out of Enlightenment thinking between humans and animals made the biblical relationship between animals and God unimaginable (cf. chapter 3). In that case, this is as strange as Balaam's donkey being able to see an angel. Such biblical stories were

---

27. Beyerlin, *Near Eastern Religious Texts*, 22; Keel, *Symbolism of the Biblical World*, 47; Hillers, "Psalm 148," 331.

28. A metaphorically perspective can be found in Allen, *Psalms 101–150*, 393.

meant to spiritualize modern humans. After all, animals did not have the same intelligence as people; they had no soul and could not relate to God or angels. This darkened the realization that the whole creation took part in the redemption work of the Messiah.

According to the English New Testament scholar Richard Bauckham (b. 1946), biblical references to the praise of animals point precisely to the fact that "all creatures bring glory to God simply by being themselves and fulfilling their God-given roles in God's creation."[29] For example, the book of Jonah testifies that God uses a large fish and a small worm for his honor (Jonah 2:1; 4:7). "The Lord, the God of heaven, who made the sea and the dry land" (1:9) cares for animals. The importance they have for God is shown in the final question God asks in this book:

> And should I not be concerned about Nineveh, that great city, in which there are more than a hunderd and twenty thousand persons who do not know their right hand from their left, and also many animals? (Jonah 4:11)

Thus, the praise of the animals is connected with creation, God's way of salvation, and God's purpose with creation. God's creation does not only praise its Creator for the past and present. The praise of creation is also deeply related to God's purpose for creation: the future glorification, the new heaven and new earth. In the way God goes from the original creation to the new creation, animals get their special place. So, humans and animals are gathered around the throne to pay homage to the Lamb for this creation's redemption and glorious future.[30]

12.2.3 Soteriological Reflections

God's Intense Care for Animals

God created creation as an expression of his glory. Several times, inspired writers point out the unique characteristics of animals: "O Lord, how manifold are your works! In wisdom have you made them all; the earth is full of your creatures" (Ps 104:24). These animals are primarily not made for humans. They are made for God: "For every wild animal of the forest is mine, the cattle on a thousand hills. I know all the birds of the air, and

---

29. Bauckham, "Joining Creation's Praise," 47.

30. Horrell and Coad, "'Stones Would Cry Out,'" 29–44; Patton, "He Who Sits," 406; Wessels, "Spiritual Link," 31–32.

all that moves in the field is mine" (Ps 50:10–11). God is in relationship with animals and takes care of them (Ps 104:21, 27–28, cf. chapter 4.1.2). The psalmist exclaims, "May the Lord rejoice in his works" (v. 31). It is good to be aware of the good care God has for animals.

In this book on God's future for animals, God's place and care for animals in the history of salvation have been mentioned many times. It would be superfluous to repeat them all in this section. We can refer to the relevant chapters in this book. Even since the beginning, people and animals have been closely connected. God creates the land animals and the people on the same day (Gen 1:24–30, chapter 2) and lets humanity give names to animals (2:19–20, chapter 3). Through disobedience, humans and animals are subjected to the forces of evil and to transience (6:1–12, chapter 4). However, God chooses to have Noah build an ark for humans and animals (6:18–20) and makes a covenant with both groups (9:8–17, chapter 6). The same attitude can be heard in the setting of the Sabbath on Mount Sinai: God wants humans and animals to enjoy rest (Exod 20:8–11, chapter 7.1.1). In history, humans and animals were intensely involved with each other. This happened both peacefully and cruelly (chapter 5). God later confronts Jonah because of his nasty attitude. Jonah does not take into account the many animals in Nineveh (Jonah 4:11, chapter 7.2.3). God's choice to save animals from calamity and to give them life also emerges here.

Salvation history thus shows that God sees more than the redemption of humanity. In the way that God goes with this creation, animals are also given a particular place, as David states, "You save humans and animals alike, O Lord" (Ps 36:6b). This path of salvation will be continued in the future. Isaiah 11 and 65 bear witness to the renewal that God brings in the animal kingdom. Many Christians hold on to the physical-concrete explanation of this future expectation (chapters 8–10). Would completing God's plan with this creation be a step backward when it comes to animals? Does the life of animals remain forever in the clutches of death, even though animals are different from humans?

From the intense relationship that the Bible describes between God and animals, it is not surprising that animals are also allowed to know a place in the new heaven and the new earth. Too easily, this idea is dismissed as childish. Nevertheless, it is essential that biblical speaking has the highest authority in this. It testifies to a future kingdom of God. The Messiah is at the center, in which also spiritual and physical beings are present. In the Bible, the testimony is repeated that God wanted this creation with its time and space, but evil forces subjected it to transience. We hear of a new earth where righteousness dwells (2 Pet 3:13). When all iniquity is gone by the coming fire, the time of the new heaven and the new earth begins. That is the time when creation will be liberated from all impermanence and the negativity that plagues it today. It will be a time when the wolf will be with the lamb, and the leopard will be with the small cattle (Isa 11:6).

New Animals or Resurrection?

It is a legitimate question whether the animals in the new creation are new animals, which God will create, or if these animals are dead animals, which God awakens from the power of death. Are the animals in the new heaven and the new earth a consequence of God's act of creation or God's act of redemption? If the latter is true, does this mean that dinosaurs that plagued the past will be present on the new earth?

The vast majority of the theologians, reflecting on the new heaven and the new earth, will find it unthinkable that there are no animals on the new earth. A world without animals, trees, flowers, and many other beautiful things that this creation knows would be a massive regression. It would be a creation which only consists of "new heavens" with angels and spirits, but no longer a "new earth," in which all the promises of God can be fulfilled. That would be entirely beyond the hope of the biblical righteous when they looked forward to a time when they could enjoy the wine and rest under the fig trees.

Simultaneously, because many cannot imagine that every animal that ever lived on earth would rise from the dead, most Christians believe that God will create *new* animals for the new earth.[31] One difficulty with this is that we never had a relationship with these *new* animals before. We had a specific relationship with our *old* dog or cat and not with a general category of *new* dogs or cats. Will we never see the pet we loved again? From biblical revelation, there is currently no clear answer to this.

Immortal Animals

From the promise that humans may eat again from the tree of life (Rev 2:7; 22:2), the thought is permitted that this food will ensure that humans

---

31. E.g., Polkinghorne, *Science and the Trinity*, 152.

regain access to eternal life. In chapter 4, we reflected on whether animals, just like humans, were also mortally created. We discovered a reasonable basis for stating that this was the case. Humans and animals were mortally created in Genesis 1–2. Humans had the opportunity to live eternally by eating from the tree of life. Those who did not eat from the tree of life would not live forever.

> Then the Lord God said, "See, the man has become like one of us, knowing good and evil; and now, he might reach out his hand and take also from the tree of life, and eat, and live forever"—therefore the Lord God sent him forth from the garden of Eden, to till the ground from which he was taken. He drove out the man; and at the east of the garden of Eden he placed the cherubim, and a sword flaming and turning to guard the way to the tree of life. (Gen 3:22–24)

In the future, the path to the tree of life will be reopened. Like in Genesis, we do not hear that this road will be opened for animals. This may mean that the animals in the new creation, just like the animals in the original creation, do not suffer or hurt but die. Another possibility is that God takes care that the animals will not die in the new heaven and the new earth. Death as the enemy of life will then be over. Then a statement like "Death will be no more; mourning and crying and pain will be no more, for the first things have passed away" (Rev 21:4) applies to both humans and animals.

A challenge with this mortality is—as in the conversation about original creation—the meaning and usefulness of the tree of life. Why is a tree of life needed when people and animals receive eternal life? And if animals no longer die in the new creation, does this mean that we humans will no longer eat meat? What does biblical revelation or Christian doctrine tell us about our ways of eating in the future? Will all human beings then be vegetarian and will all delicious summer meat barbecues disappear forever from history when the new heaven and the new earth arrive?

13

Vegetarian Meals in the Eschaton

13.1 VEGETARIANS AND THE BIBLE

13.1.1 Christians and Vegetables in History

ENJOYING VEGETARIAN DISHES IS one of many culinary trends. Worldwide, top chefs offer vegetarian menus in restaurants that meat eaters can also appreciate. Western Christians like to associate this choice for vegetarianism with ancient philosophies or Eastern religions. The Greek philosopher Plato (427–347 BC) wrote that people would live as vegetarians in an ideal state.[1] He was not alone in this idea. A century earlier, Pythagoras (~570–500 BC), the famous mathematician, also fought off the meat from his plate and threw the greengrocer's bean off it. His choice not to eat meat became so well known that those who ate vegetarian were "followers of Pythagoras." Yet, it was not until the year 1850 that the term "vegetarian" came up.

In Christianity, we find similar scenes. At the time of the church father Augustine, the Manichaeans refused to eat meat. The tribe of the Sassas even killed Mani from Persia in AD 276 because he refused to eat meat. According to Manichaean beliefs, meat was evil. It had to be considered corrupt and bad for humans. For the church father Tertullianus (~160–230), those who ate too much meat chose to make their belly a god. For this reason, he strongly criticized those who abused selfishly

---

1. Plato, *Republic*.

the biblical statement that all food was pure to overfill their bellies (Rom 14:20–21; 1 Cor 10:25).²

Clement of Alexandria (~125–215) and Ambrose of Milan (339–97) called on people to rejoice at the many vegetables and fruits that creation provided.³ In the description of what a "spiritual diet" is, Clement closely follows thinkers such as the Greek philosopher Plato (428–348 BC), the Greek historian Plutarch (46–120), and the Roman philosopher Gaius Rufus (30–102).⁴ A balanced diet consisted of "onions, olives, some vegetables, milk, cheese, seasonal fruit, and cooked food without sauce." Distinguishing himself from his contemporaries, Clement added, "And if roasted or cooked meat is needed, let him receive a portion." He wants to handle this with care because meat and wine would darken the human soul as a food of pleasure and fill it with evil lusts. They would awaken the "demons of the belly."⁵ It was better to remove both from the menu and keep the soul clean to remain healthy and wise. Clement referred to Paul for this, who wrote, "You better leave meat, wine, or anything else that offends your brother or sister" (cf. Rom 14:21).⁶ However, the context in which the apostle uttered these words was omitted by the church father in his reference.

Furthermore, the church father Athanasius of Alexandria (295–373) writes that Antony of Egypt (251–356), the founder of the first Christian monastery, only ate bread with salt and drank water. Meat and wine did not enter the mouth of this saint.⁷ The Greek church father and great monastic Basil of Caesarea (330–379) followed that trend. He pointed out that Genesis 1 showed that God's original plan with humans and animals was that both would live vegetarian lives. Both humans and animals left those divine instructions in the time of Noah and the flood. However, in the new heaven and the new earth, humans and animals would return to the principle from Genesis 1 and live vegetarian. Then humanity would "no longer be a slave to the flesh. Humans would be free and, like the

---

2. Tertullian, "On Fasting," §15–16.
3. Clement of Alexandria, *Paedagogus*, II.1; Ambrose of Milan, *Hexameron*, III.28.
4. Shaw, "Vegetarianism," 79.
5. Clement of Alexandria, *Paedagogus*, II.1.15–16.
6. Clement of Alexandria, *Paedagogus*, I.11.1; II.2.29.
7. Athanasius, *Life of St. Antony*.

angels, live in deep intimacy with God." At the same time, Basil recognized that many Christians did not take much notice of these insights.[8]

Later, Benedict of Nursia (480–547) forbade his monastic order to eat meat. Only in the case of serious illness did the monk dare to turn a blind eye. With Augustine, we hear a more nuanced thought about this:

> I fear not the uncleanness of meat, but the uncleanness of lust. I know that Noah was permitted to eat every kind of flesh which was useful for food; that Elijah was refreshed by eating flesh; that John, who was gifted with marvelous abstinence, was not defiled by the creatures, that is the locusts, which became his food. I know also that Esau was ensnared by his desire for a pottage of lentils, and that David rebuked himself for his longing after water, and that our King was tempted not with meat, but with bread. And so likewise, the people in the desert deserved to be condemned not because they desired meat, but because in their desire for food, they murmured against God.[9]

Not everyone followed the choice to live strictly vegetarian. Irenaeus of Lyon (~140–202) already pointed out that a persistent rejection of eating meat was more connected with the fallacy of Gnosticism than with the Christian faith.[10] The Benedictine monk, preacher, and mystical writer Eckbert von Schonau (~1120–84), proclaimed in the year 1163 ten errors about the so-called Cathars. One error was that they refused to eat meat. And in the year 1208, Pope Innocent III (1160–1216) declared war on those who learned vegetarianism. Thousands were exterminated in the name of carnivorous Christianity.

Nevertheless, vegetarianism would not disappear. Many celebrities would put the flesh aside: Gautama Buddha (~563–483 BC), Leonardo da Vinci (1452–1519), Emanuel Swedenborg (1688–1772), John Wesley (1703–91), Ellen G. White (1827–1915), Vincent van Gogh (1853–90), Mahatma Gandhi (1869–1948), Albert Schweitzer (1875–1965). In 1809 William Cowherd (1763–1816) founded the Christian Church in England, which included its doctrines to live vegetarian. He relied on the Swedish Lutheran theologian and mystic Emanuel Swedenborg, according to whom eating meat had led to the first sin in paradise.

Although there are new societal tendencies today to promote vegetarianism, churches often pay little attention to it. Food seems to be of

---

8. Basil of Caesarea, "De Hominis Structura," II.6–7.
9. Possidius of Calama, *Life of Saint Augustine*, 31.
10. Irenaeus of Lyon, *Adversus Haereses*, I.28.1.

secondary importance in the Bible. Didn't the famous apostle Paul write, "For the kingdom of God is not food and drink but righteousness and peace and joy in the Holy Spirit" (Rom 14:17)? So, Christians parked vegetarianism too quickly as a theme that came from the East into the pluralistic world.

Nevertheless, Christians ask themselves whether their moral responsibility is to be more frugal in eating meat. The question is then asked whether the high consumption of meat, which characterizes the wealthy West, is not an expression of its sinful gluttony. In doing so, it ties in with an old Christian tradition.

Is it a good idea to consume meat grown in bulk in the food industry three times a day? As Christians, why do we choose to participate in a livestock industry that produces meat products with the highest possible efficiency and minimum welfare for the animals we keep? Is this production process worth it to buy cheaper pork ribs, steaks, and other meat products? To what extent may we show a change as God-appointed rulers of this creation? These kinds of questions ensure that vegetarianism should not function as an unknown concept in the Christian tradition.

13.1.2 Biblical Arguments

The Creation Story

Those who want to live vegetarian lives as Christians today like to refer to the biblical story of creation and the biblical scenes of the future in which people and animals are close to each other and live in peace with each other (Gen 1:29; 2:19–20; Isa 65:25).[11] These texts can show that God's original instructions were to let people eat only fruit and vegetables. In the story of creation, we read that God intended the fruits of plants and trees for people:

> God said, "See, I have given you every plant yielding seed that is upon the face of all the earth, and every tree with seed in its fruit; you shall have them for food. And to every beast of the earth, and to every bird of the air, and to everything that creeps on the earth, everything that has the breath of life, I have given every green plant for food." And it was so. (Gen 1:29–30)

---

11. Southgate, "Protological," 247–65; Linzey, *Animal Theology*, 33–34.

These verses have led many people to the conclusion that God initially gave humanity only vegetarian food.[12] They received the seed-bearing plants and the fruit trees. Thus, humanity was allowed to enjoy fruits, vegetables, grains, legumes, nuts, and many other seeds. The consumption of other living creatures is not mentioned.

For others, it was not easy to imagine that humans in Genesis 1 did not eat meat. The human body was equipped to eat meat.[13] Questions about this arose early on in Judeo-Christian tradition. For example, the French Reformer John Calvin (1509–64) thought that God allowed humans from the beginning to kill animals and make tents and clothes for themselves. According to Calvin, there were no valid reasons to suppose that humans could not eat animals.[14] According to Jewish medieval commentaries, the first humans consumed only the flesh of animals that died a natural death.[15] Hunting an animal to kill and eat was not what Adam and Eve did. Another life did not have to be ended to feed someone. Eating animals that had died a natural death was more dignified. The thought was that animals could die before Genesis 3 (see chapter 4).

Another Jewish legend thought that eating dead animals was not a reasonable proposition, given its rejection in later food laws (Lev 11:1–47; Deut 14:1–21). So, it chooses to explain that God caused the first people to receive flesh from heaven. According to the Jewish rabbi Judah ben Tema:

> The first man reclined in the garden of Eden, and the ministering angels roasted meat for him and strained wine for him.[16]

We don't find this kind of fable anywhere in the Bible. Instead, the testimony of Genesis 1–2 shows the harmony between the creatures in God's original creation. All formed one large family and ate vegetable food. An animal was not killed to feed a human being or any other animal. All creatures were vegetarian and enjoyed the peace of creation. It was only after the disobedience of humanity that this peace was disturbed,

---

12. Neusner, *B. Sanhedrin*, 59b; Waltke, *Old Testament Theology*, 296–97; MacDonald, "Food and Diet," 18; Hamilton, *Genesis 1–17*; Keil and Delitzsch, *Pentateuch*, 102; Freedman and Maurice, *Midrash Rabbah: Genesis*, 34:13.

13. Luzzatto, *Genesis*, 27.

14. Calvin, *Genesis*.

15. Neusner, *B. Sanhedrin*, 56b.

16. Neusner, *B. Sanhedrin*, 59b.

and a war of everyone against everyone began. From then on, people and animals ate each other.

Only after the expulsion of the people from the garden and the coming of the great flood of water did God agree that humans could also eat meat:

> Every moving thing that lives shall be food for you; and just as I gave you the green plants, I give you everything. Only, you shall not eat flesh with its life, that is, its blood. (Gen 9:3–4)

However, this consent was a gift from God after the increasing disobedience of humans towards one another (see chapter 6.2). The encore did not arise in an optimal situation. God made concessions in a period that had dramatically gotten out of hand in terms of murder and destruction. Already from Genesis 3, it became clear that humans chose to take what was available. That negative attitude towards God and creation would only increase in the time after that. When preparing the ark, Noah already had to make a distinction between pure and unclean animals. After all, the animal kingdom was involved in the violence that raged on earth. This fact determines God's choice to make his first explicit covenant in Genesis not only with humans but with humans and animals. Both are called to account when God's rulings are violated. Eating animals, therefore, develops a bad aftertaste, reminding one of the life of the animal that had to die. It is allowed in a covenant that pleads for protecting all life on earth in the future. We already pointed out in chapter 6.2 that God's purpose with this extension is to control the human tendency to violence.

Another conception of God's choice in Genesis to allow humans to eat meat is that God only temporarily allowed humans to eat meat after the flood. The reason for this was that the flood destroyed all plants and trees. In that situation, humans could do nothing more than eat animals. Then the permission to eat animals was lifted again after the flora recovered.[17]

Manna and Dietary Laws

Later, God gives Israel manna in the desert. The descriptions of that manna point to a vegetarian dish. When the infidelity rises among the strangers and the Israelites, they call for meat. The people then yearn back to the meat pots of Egypt and shout lamentingly, "If only we had meat to eat!"

---

17. Schwartz, *Judaism and Vegetarianism*, 4–5.

(Num 11:4). Then they are given quail to eat, "a whole month—until it comes out of your nostrils and becomes loathsome to you" (v. 20). Later, the people call down God's wrath upon themselves, and God inflicts a great blow on them (v. 34). That choice is understandable. God desires that the people respect creation and not—like pharaoh—call judgment on themselves by elevating themselves above creation. From Genesis 1–2, God's dealings with creation instead testify of dealings in mercy and love. The Lord, therefore, chooses not to kill all living things after the flood (Gen 8:21).

This theme of meat-eating also plays a role in the later food laws of Israel. These insertions acquire a particular weight because they are at the forefront of the so-called laws of purity and sanctification (Lev 11; cf. Deut 14). Animals who are mainly herbivores are mentioned as pure animals. Most of the carnivores get the stamp "impure," which Israel is not allowed to consume. Partly inspired by these food laws, Jews choose to keep fish and meat separate. Although meat and fish are abundantly provided during the Sabbath and other holidays, both are prepared in different cooking pots. Those present then choose either the fish or the meat. A combination of both is not applied.[18] According to the Babylonian Talmud, this happens because the combined eating of fish and meat causes bad aroma and/or skin disorders. However, according to this source, eating fish on a meat dish is not problematic.[19]

Meat and Bad Desires

Vegetarians also refer to events in which flesh causes separation between God and people. These situations confirm the idea that eating meat can evoke immoral lusts in a human being. Jewish legends tell us that Nimrod was the first human being on earth who started hunting animals and eating meat.[20] He was considered a tyrant, a term that carries a negative connotation (cf. chapter 6.1.1).

That relationship between food and violence was also assumed in the rebellious son in Deuteronomy 21:18–21. According to Jewish tradition, this son was a carnivore and wine-sucker.[21] Meat stimulates the

---

18. Cf. Rosner, "Eating Fish," 36–44.
19. Neusner, *B. Pesahim*, 76b.
20. Teugels, *Aggadat Bereshit*, Gn10:8.
21. Neusner, *B. Sanhedrin*, 70a; Neusner, "M. Sanhedrin," 8.2.

body and increases the human temperament. Until the beginning of the twentieth century, meat was seen as the source of excessive alcohol consumption, sexual excesses, and gruesome wars. Vegetarian life was the remedy for all these ailments which could arise in a human body. Not eating meat cultivated the desire for purity, kindness, peace, pacifism, sobriety, and control over the passionate lusts.[22] After a vegan Adolf Hitler had unleashed a Second World War with all its atrocities, this thought quickly lost credibility. Shortly after the death of his cousin Geli Raubal (1908–31), Hitler chose to live vegetarian.[23]

A further difficulty with the view that Christians should live vegetarian lay in this statement of God:

> When the Lord your God enlarges your territory, as he has promised you, and you say, "I am going to eat some meat," because you wish to eat meat, you may eat meat whenever you have the desire. If the place where the Lord your God will choose to put his name is too far from you, and you slaughter as I have commanded you any of your herd or flock that the Lord has given you, then you may eat within your towns whenever you desire. (Deut 12:20–21)

God does not impose restrictions on Israel concerning eating meat. For Israel, this was a great pleasure. It was widely believed that fruits and vegetables were mainly intended for land animals and birds. The average Israelite did not highly value either. Because vegetables were mentioned in the Bible in the context of Egypt (Num 11:5) and the godless king Ahab (1 Kgs 21), people felt supported in this.

On the other hand, there was the saying of wisdom, "Better is a dinner of vegetables where love is than a fatted ox and hatred with it" (Prov 15:17). Also, in the Babylonian Talmud, the Jews were advised to apply the instructions mentioned above of Deuteronomy 12:20 only when they had enough cattle. It was then considered a virtue to slaughter some of one's animals and not those of their neighbor.[24]

---

22. Walker, *Pulling*, 185; White, *Testimonies for the Church*, II:71; White, *Education*, 203.

23. Spencer, *Vegetarianism*, 287.

24. Akiva ben Joseph, *Sifre Devarim*.

13.1.3 Was Jesus a Vegetarian?

Supporters and Opponents

Vegetarians like to point out the love of Christ for creation. The love of God the Father is expressed in the example of sparrows (Matt 10:29; Luke 12:6), God takes care of the birds in general (Matt 6:26; Luke 22:24), and Jesus compares himself to a hen who wants to protect her chicks (Matt 23:37). Even the cleaning of the temple, in which Jesus strikes the animal traders, is gladly interpreted from a plea for vegetarianism as an actual messianic act of animal protection and liberation. With it, Jesus would oppose the unnecessary mistreatment and death of the animals.[25] After all, God the Son took care of the whole creation and gave his life so that he freed creation from the powers of death. Therefore, killing and consuming animals is the opposite of this attitude of the Messiah, who gave himself to give life to creation.[26]

Based on this loving approach of Jesus towards the animal world, it is often a disaster for Christians who want to live vegetarian that Jesus participates in the Passover, where lamb is served. Some vegetarians point out that none of the evangelists implicitly writes that Jesus ate lamb during this meal.[27] The thought that Jesus ate meat during this meal can, therefore, not be proved.

People who claim that Jesus was a vegetarian are shortly after the Passover confronted with another challenge. After his resurrection, we learn that Jesus eats a fish (Luke 24:41–43). When Jesus meets his disciples again at the lake of Tiberias, he serves the barbecue on the shore, on which soon dozens of fish are grilled, which Jesus gathered. Besides, already at the beginning of his service, Jesus called the fishermen to follow him. It is these fishermen that he miraculously helped with fish (Luke 5:3–10), and one also remembers the multiplying of fish to feed a crowd (Mark 6:38–43). We also learn several times in the New Testament that Jesus was invited to the meal with considerable persons (Mark 2:15; Luke 7:36; 11:37; 14:1; 19:5). He is even taken for "a glutton and a drunkard" (Matt 11:19).

---

25. Webb, *Good Eating*, 93–97; Akers, *Lost Religion*, 113–34; Vaclavik, *Vegetarianism*, 260–71.

26. Southgate, "Protological," 255; Cobb, "All Things in Christ?," 173–80; Frear, "Caring for Animals," 5.

27. Webb, *Good Eating*, 129–31, 150.

It is possible that meat was also eaten during these moments, even though it was a luxury product in ancient times (cf. Sir 39:26–27). Therefore, it is almost impossible to base on these data that Jesus was a vegetarian. For those who want to stick strictly to a vegetarian Jesus, only these possibilities remain: (1) to state that the texts in the Gospels in which Jesus eats fish or meat are later additions,[28] (2) to state that Jesus was not perfect because he was not a vegetarian, (3) to state that killing and eating fish is not the same as killing and eating other animals, (4) to state that eating animals is only allowed in emergencies, or (5) to state that Jesus gave a loose interpretation of vegetarianism.[29]

During a PETA advertising campaign (People for the Ethical Treatment of Animals), this testimony was thrown overboard. On a large billboard, a Jesus could be seen with an orange disk as a halo in the background. Next to it was written in big letters, "Jesus was a vegetarian." The goal was to win Christians for vegetarianism. On the website All-Creatures.org, everything was done to get rid of events in which Jesus multiplied fish.[30]

This is reminiscent of the ancient Jewish sect of the Ebionites, who also advocated vegetarianism and chose to change John the Baptist's menu from "locusts" (ἀκρίς, *akris*) to "cake" (ἐγκρίς, *enkrides*).[31] Although many Westerners would much prefer this last dish, the fact remains that all Greek manuscripts of the Gospel speak of "locusts" when it comes to the meals John the Baptist consummated.

Fortunately, vegetarians are also critical of this kind of controversial propaganda. The positive attitude of Jesus towards creation should not necessarily imply that he followed a vegetarian habit.[32] This is even less true of his apostles. For example, many see Peter's vision in which he is called upon to slaughter and eat animals (Acts 10–11), as well as Paul's statements that Christians may eat anything (1 Tim 4:3; cf. Rom 14:14; Gal 2:1–10; 1 Cor 10:25–26), as a significant obstacle in the plea to combine the Christian faith with a forced vegetarian lifestyle. These apostolic testimonies are in line with the statement of God to Noah:

---

28. E.g., Akers, *Lost Religion*, 129; Vaclavik, *Vegetarianism*, 258–82.

29. For the first four points see Linzey, *Animal Theology*, 132–35. The fifth point is taken from Webb, *Good Eating*, 134–35.

30. Murti, "Loaves and Fishes."

31. Luomanen, "Nazirenes," 292.

32. Linzey, *Animal Theology*, 135; McDonagh, *Passion for the Earth*, 140; McDonagh, *Greening of the Church*, 158–59.

Every moving thing that lives shall be food for you; and just as I gave you the green plants, I give you everything. (Gen 9:3)

The reaction of John T. Ferrier (1855–1943) to the statements of the apostles is therefore abrupt. As the spiritual founder of the Christian sect Order of the Cross, he writes, "Paul did not know Master Jesus."[33]

Nevertheless, the apostolic data clarifies that several tensions arose related to food in the time of the first Christians. Were Jewish Christians allowed to sit together at the table with gentile Christians? Were the gentile Christians, like the Jews, supposed to abide by the food laws? In what way did Christians have to deal with meat associated with idolatry? Although the apostle Paul in Romans 14:17 states that the kingdom of God does not consist of food and drink, the theme of food often ends up on the congregation's plate.

Vegetarianism and Health

In the past, there have sometimes been attempts to connect vegetarianism with a healthy lifestyle and with a disapproval of animal suffering. Both should be a characteristic of the followers of Jesus. Those who agree that humanity was only allowed to eat meat after the great flood of water by God would like to refer to the high years people lived in Genesis 5. The vegetarian Methuselah lived no less than 969 years. Even Lamech is still considered a high-year-old life at the age of 777. From this, the Jewish rabbi Yitzchak (Abarbanel, 1437–1508) took the choice for a vegetarian way of life.[34] Until now, no carnivore in history surpassed the patriarchs mentioned above in terms of age. After humans had placed their first bite in a tender piece of meat, the age expectation dropped drastically. The American George Malkmus (b. 1934) based his organization Hallelujah Acres (1976) on this interpretation. Those who followed the "Hallelujah Diet" of his organization and fed themselves consistently vegetarian with raw food and necessary supplements would avoid diseases and be allowed to enjoy a long life.[35] Health and life extension were just a plate of raw vegetables with carrot juice away from you. Of course, it was tacitly assumed that all people who lived before the great flood kept to God's food instructions in Genesis 1. None of them would have had the thought to

33. Ferrier, *Master*, 44.
34. Goldwurm, *Daniel*, 70; Neusner, *B. Sanhedrin*, 59b.
35. Malkmus, *Why Christians*; Malkmus, *God's Way*.

quench his rummy stomach by hunting and eating an animal. The basic idea of George Malkmus, to see flesh as killing poison for the body and to plead for living on vegetarian food, can also be found in other religious ideologies, such as the Seventh-day Adventist Church. They like to argue for vegetarianism because the body is a temple of God's Spirit.[36]

Vegetarianism and Animal Suffering

Others think that a stomach stuffed with delicious meat is not worth the animal suffering that precedes it. From God's image and likeness, the commission to rule over creation calls upon humans to be merciful with other creatures. "Does your momentary pleasure justify the death of an animal?" is a frequently asked question. Eating meat and fish also happened in ancient times with a different attitude than today. The life of an animal was treated with respect. There was often a natural bond between animals and humans. This caused the eating of meat to occur to a lesser extent than is the case today in the richer countries (cf. chapter 5.2.1). This attitude ensured that Jesus was not confronted with the animal suffering that we observe in the media today.

An example of this is the outbreak of the foot-and-mouth disease in 2001. In Northern European regions, this disease cost the lives of numerous animals. Because the meat and milk of infected animals were not allowed to be sold and transported for economic reasons, it was decided to kill all cattle in the vicinity of outbreaks. Only horses were left in the pastures of the areas considered infected; other cloven-hoofed animals had been culled. However, under normal circumstances, most cattle infected by foot-and-mouth disease would have recovered after a few weeks. For many, it was incomprehensible that people were allowed to exterminate cattle on such a large scale, while the disease was only temporary. Cattle farmers often thought otherwise. They had no emotional bond with their animals and only saw economic interests in it. An animal that was sick for a couple of weeks was not producing anything and was better off being culled so that it would not cause unnecessary expense. As a result, many of the conflicts took on proportions of evil against good, death against life, and darkness against light.

From this background, Christians call each other to deal responsibly with creation. The Anglican theologian Tom Wright (b. 1948) writes

---

36. White, *Testimonies for the Church*, II:70.

on Paul's reference to the rebirth of the whole creation (Rom 8) that today creation already calls us to take our responsibility.[37] Creation sighs under the evil that is done to it every day. However, creation lives in hope and is in dire straits because it realizes that a moment will soon come in which everything will be liberated. The Swiss theologian Karl Barth (1886–1968) also refers to Romans 8 in his care of animals. In his Christian doctrine, he writes that the words in Romans 8:18 ("I consider that the sufferings of this present time are not worth comparing with the glory about to be revealed to us") must be written in burning flames in every hunting lodge, slaughterhouse, and animal laboratory.[38]

13.2 VEGETARIANS AND THE FUTURE

13.2.1 Luxury Meals in the Past and Future

The biblical prophets testify that a time will come when humans and animals live in peace. At that time, the lion exchanges his carnivore's plate for an herbivore's plate, and the wolf chooses to graze with the lamb (Isa 65:25). Then comes the moment when God's will is not only in heaven but also on earth. The brutal treatment of animals with each other then comes to an end. Martin Luther (1483–1546) and many others saw in the descriptions of the original creation in Genesis 1–2 a harbinger of the time that will come.[39] In concrete terms, all people will become vegetarian when the new heaven and the new earth arrive. They will let animals live and enjoy the fruits that the tree of life produces every month (Rev 22:2).

It is particularly noteworthy that many in church history have been convinced that humans will still take in food even after the resurrection. The biblical testimonies about Jesus eating a fish and honeycomb (Luke 24:41–43) and that the Messiah would drink again from the wine cup when God's kingdom dawned (Luke 22:16) give cause for this.

At various places, the biblical testimony is heard that God will prepare a delicious feast banquet for all people. That banquet is not necessary to keep people healthy and alive. Just as in the example of the glorified Christ, who eats a fish and honeycomb, the food is also an expression of enjoying together. From this, we can discover that the party serves for

---

37. Wright, *Resurrection*, 258.
38. Barth, *Creation: The Command*, 355.
39. Ickert, "Luther and Animals," 99.

more than just consuming products. Eating also provides fun. Anyone who sees that the current food guides place wine, beer, chips, and fries in the forbidden corner doesn't immediately become cheerful. Such diagrams radiate a strict policy of discouragement and forget to tell us that enjoying food also contributes to some extent to people's mental health.

Festive meals, as we encounter them in the Bible, are therefore not uncommon in antiquity. We already find representations of this in ancient cultures, such as ancient Egypt. Such a banquet testified to great luxury. It contained exotic fruits, elaborate meat and fish dishes, varied wine, and other spirits. It was a luxurious meal in which several singers, musicians, and dancers were present. Several guests decorated themselves with flowers and perfumes.[40] In later times, the Greek poet Homer (~800–750 BC) wrote,

> For myself, I declare that there is no greater fulfillment of delight than when joy possesses a whole people, and banqueters in the halls listen to a minstrel as they sit in order due. By them, tables are laden with bread and meat, and the cup-bearer draws wine from the bowl.[41]

A well-known example of a banquet in the Bible is the wedding banquet (Judg 14:10; John 2:1–10). To have such a feast with many friends, the choice was made to let it last seven days (Gen 29:22, 27). In that week, each friend found an opportune moment to leave the work behind for a while and celebrate the wedding together with the others. Other banquet meals took place out of gratitude for the harvest. For example, the inhabitants of Shechem chose to pick the grapes in their vineyards, squeeze them out, and then hold a harvest festival in the temple of the deity (Judg 9:27).

Another example was King Solomon, who chose to lavishly celebrate the Feast of Tabernacles—which was also a harvest festival—together with many Israelites for seven days (2 Kgs 7:8). One of the most enormous feast banquets in ancient times took place in the Assyrian Empire, under the reign of Ashurnasirpal II (r. 883–59 BC). This banquet lasted ten days and was attended by 69,574 guests.[42]

---

40. King and Stager, *Life in Biblical Israel*, 356–57; Scott, "Daily Life," 30–31, 42–43.
41. Homer, *Odyssey*, IX.5–10.
42. Collon, "Banquets," 28.

Luscious Parties

The prophet Amos opposes the luxury meals of the wealthier class, who do not care about God's statutes:

> Alas for those who lie on beds of ivory, and lounge on their couches, and eat lambs from the flock, and calves from the stall; who sing idle songs to the sound of the harp, and like David improvise on instruments of music; who drink wine from bowls, and anoint themselves with the finest oils, but are not grieved over the ruin of Joseph! (Amos 6:4–6)

Such sumptuous meals can also be found among the Babylonian monarchs. King Belshazzar celebrates a feast in Babylon together with many rulers, while the armies of Persians stand in front of the walls of the city (Dan 5:1–30). These meals also occur in the Persian Empire. For example, we find no less than five different party banquets in the book of Esther. Any relationship with God or his celebration is omitted from that book. Nowadays, reliefs in Persepolis still remind us of this kind of feast.[43] One of the oldest depictions of feast banquets dates back to the fourth century BC and was found in Choghā Mīsh in present-day southwestern Iran. The image shows a person holding a barrel and offering it to a person at the party and surrounded by various musicians playing the harp and a kind of tambourine.[44]

In the Gospels, we learn that Jesus is a guest during meals several times. Hospitality and offering a meal was significant in Israel in the first century. Whoever rejected such a banquet was considered rude. That background explains the violent consequences of the rejection of God's future banquet (Matt 22:1–14). When all the guests had arrived, the doors were closed to stop intruders. During the feast banquet, the guests were usually in a U shape, and at times a distinction was made between the ranks and positions of the guests (Luke 14:10).

Because the disciples also recline during the Last Supper, Leonardo da Vinci's painting *The Last Supper*, where the disciples sit on chairs, is therefore incorrect (cf. Mark 14:15; John 13:12, 25). From the seventh century BC, it was customary for guests to lie on benches during meals. A maximum of three people could lie on a couch, and in the average dining room, the Greek *triklinos* or Latin *triclinium*, there were three couches.

---

43. Ghirshman, *Arts of Ancient Iran*, 107.
44. Collon, "Banquets," 23.

The wealthy class could sometimes have several such dining rooms in the house. However, public areas could accommodate about fifteen couches, which were placed in a U shape in the hall, so that the servants could reach each guest from the middle.[45]

Table Manners

In the Jewish tradition, table manners are known from Sirach. They call the faithful to humility and sufficiency:

> Are you seated at the table of the great? Bring to it no greedy gullet, nor say, "How much food there is here!" Remember that the greedy eye is evil. What has been created more greedy than the eye? Therefore, it weeps for any cause. Recognize that your neighbor feels as you do, and keep in mind everything you dislike. Toward what he looks at, do not put out a hand; nor reach for the same dish when he does. Eat, like anyone else, what is set before you, but do not eat greedily, lest you be despised. Be the first to stop, as befits good manners; and do not gorge yourself, lest you give offense. If there are many with you at table, do not be the first to stretch out your hand. . . . The distress of sleeplessness and of nausea and colic are with the glutton! . . . People bless one who is generous with food, and this testimony to his goodness is lasting. The city complains about one who is stingy with food, and this testimony to his stinginess is lasting. Let not wine be the proof of your strength, for wine has been the ruin of many. As the furnace tests the work of the smith, so does wine the hearts of the insolent. . . . Headache, bitterness, and disgrace is wine drunk amid anger and strife. Wine in excess is a snare for the fool; it lessens strength and multiplies wounds. Do not wrangle with your neighbor when wine is served, nor despise him while he is having a good time; Say no harsh words to him nor distress him by making demands. If you are chosen to preside at a dinner, do not be puffed up, but with the guests be as one of them; Take care of them first and then sit down; see to their needs, and then take your place, to share in their joy and receive a wreath for a job well done. (Sir 31:12—32:2)

These kinds of instructions are also found elsewhere. For example, the Babylonian Talmud allows ten cups of wine to be drunk in the house of

---

45. Yamauchi, "Banquets," 150.

sorrow.[46] And at the Purim Festival, when the Jewish people remember the events that took place in Persia, the faithful are allowed to drink wine until they no longer know the difference between the cursed enemy Haman and the blessed Mordechai.[47] This will require necessary liters of wine.

13.2.2 Isaiah and God's Future Meal

One of the most famous texts about the future festive banquet that God is offering humanity, we find with the prophet Isaiah:

> On this mountain the Lord of hosts will make for all peoples a feast of rich food, a feast of well-aged wine, of rich food filled with marrow, of well-aged wines strained clear. (Isa 25:6)

Because in this context the prophet also talks about dishes brought to the table, it is interesting to reflect on it in this chapter on eating animals.

In ancient mythology, we often hear of royal feasts celebrated on the occasion of the gods. In the Bible, we find such meals in the time of Moses, when God chooses to offer a feast on Mount Sinai together with Moses, Aaron, Nadab, Abihu, and the seventy elders (Exod 24:11). A text more familiar to most Bible readers is Psalm 23:5: "You prepare a table before me in the presence of my enemies; you anoint my head with oil; my cup overflows."

Later on, the Bible speaks several times of the relationship between God's kingdom and a feast banquet (Matt 8:11; Luke 13:29; 14:15; 22:16; Rev 19:9). The feast banquet of the prophet Isaiah is unique for our theme because it speaks more concretely about what is coming on the table. The prophet testifies that there is a luxury of food. God blesses his people with abundance and gives them the best of the best. All peoples are invited to the mountain where God dwells. At the table, God gives them delicious dishes. Because Isaiah observes in verse 8 of the same chapter that death is devoured, this feast banquet can be connected with the new heaven and earth (Isa 25:8; cf. 1 Cor 15:54).

However, does the description of Isaiah 25:6 answer our question of whether meat or fish will still be consumed in the future? After all, in addition to the aged or matured wines, there is talk of "a feast of fat things" (RSV, ASV), "a lavish banquet" (NASB), "a delicious banquet"

---

46. Neusner, *B. Ketubot*, 8b; Neusner, *B. Sotah*, 14a.
47. Neusner, *B. Megillah*, 7b.

(NLT), "a feast of choice pieces" (NKJV), or "a feast of rich food" (ESV, NRSV, TNIV). These translations give the impression that people still kill animals to eat. However, how should we interpret the "fat" (שֶׁמֶן, *shemen*) the prophet mentions? In the Bible, this Hebrew term refers to vegetable fats (Isa 1:6; 39:2; 41:19; 57:9; 61:3) or a proverbial rich and luxurious meal, a great fertility, or an enormous power and strength (5:1; 10:27; 28:1, 4).[48] There is not even a single Bible verse in which שֶׁמֶן/*shemen* is related to animal fat. For animal fat, Hebrew uses the word חֵלֶב/*chēlev*. Therefore we may not think of slaughtered animals in Isaiah 25 as "fat," but of fat olives and other vegetarian things.

More problematic is the expression "marrow" (מָחָה, *māchāh*). This word refers to both the bone marrow of animals and the marrow of plants.[49] In the Bible, the expression occurs only in Isaiah 25:6. This makes it difficult to choose between the two options. The ancient Greek translation of Isaiah does not help us in this either. The expression is missing, and we only hear about wine and perfume with which the guests enrich themselves during the meal. The reference to food that comes from animals is thus missing. Also, the Jewish Targum does not work out the meal of Isaiah 25:6. It is even interpreted as the meal of doom for the nations.

This lack of clarity leads interpreters to easily conclude from this text that people will eat meat during this rich meal. Dieter Schneider writes, for example, that Isaiah 25 points to "pieces of meat dripping from fat" (*Fett triefenden Fleischstücken*), and John Oswalt writes that we may think of "the fat portions of the meat" at this feast. According to them, it is the fat portions of the meat (חֵלֶב, *chēlev*), which the people used to sacrifice to God (Lev 3:3; 4:8–9).[50] So, people will eat meat in the afterlife.

One difficulty, however, is that the Hebrew in Isaiah 25 speaks nowhere of חֵלֶב/*chēlev*. The only indication for a possible meat meal is the presence of the "marrow" (מָחָה, *māchāh*). Furthermore, any reference to animal food is missing, as we find, for example, in the mythological coronation song for Baal:

> He slaughters both neat [and] small cattle, Fells bulls [together with] fatlings; Rams (and) one-year-ol[d] calves; Lambs . . .

---

48. Holladay, *Concise Lexicon*, 376; Gesenius and Tregelles, *Hebrew and Chaldee Lexicon*, 835.

49. Holladay, *Concise Lexicon*, 190; Gesenius and Tregelles, *Hebrew and Chaldee Lexicon*, 463.

50. Schneider, *Jesaja 1–39*, 359; Oswalt, *Isaiah 1–39*, 463.

k[i]ds ... While drinking the [wine] from flag[ons, From gold cups the blood of vines].[51]

Another possibility is to connect the meal on Mount Zion with the expectation of a future messianic peace empire. This will break out before the advent of the new heaven and the new earth and describes a not yet ideal situation. In that context also fits a feast for which animals are slaughtered because death still reigns there (Isa 65:20). Only after this realm of peace can death be conquered and tears wiped away (25:8). Before that time, there is a meal of meat and fish in the realm of peace, just as there is a meal of animal sacrifices, which the people bring to the Lord on the altar in Zion (Ezek 40:39, 42; 42:13; cf. Isa 19:21; 56:7; 60:7) or the celebration of the Passover (Ezek 45:21). Simultaneously, it makes the situation quite complicated, taking into account Isaiah's prophecy that near Mount Zion the animals will live in peace with each other (Isa 11:10–16). Near Mount Zion, according to Isaiah, there is at the same time an animal peace (11:10–16), the eating of animals (25:6), and the sacrificing of animals (19:21; 56:7; 60:7).

13.2.3 Jesus' Words at Holy Communion

Eating animals in a future realm of peace also ties in closely with Jesus' words, when he declares, "I will not eat it until it is fulfilled in the kingdom of God" (Luke 22:16). Jesus testifies with these words that he will not eat any more of the Passover until the breakthrough of the kingdom of God comes. In Luke, he pronounces these words before the meal, and in Matthew and Mark, he does so during the meal. By saying this, the approaching death and suffering become visible: "I have eagerly desired to eat this Passover with you before I suffer" (Luke 22:15). This statement is supplemented in verse 18 by not drinking any more wine: "For I tell you that from now on I will not drink of the fruit of the vine until the kingdom of God comes" (Luke 22:18; cf. Matt 26:29; Mark 14:25).

So, in the kingdom of God, Jesus eats again of the Passover.[52] This would concretely mean that lambs are still being slaughtered at the time Jesus points out. Other interpreters, however, think in the first place of the messianic realm of peace. In that time, death is still present, and

---

51. Pritchard, *Ancient Near Eastern Texts*, 134–35.

52. Butler, *Luke*, 368; Bock, *Luke 9:51—24:53*, 1721; Nolland, *Luke 18:35—24:53*, 1050; Stein, *Luke*, 541; Marshall, *Luke*, 797.

sacrifices are made in the temple of Jerusalem. In his prophecy of the time, the prophet Ezekiel also mentions the celebration of the Passover (Ezek 45:21). Jesus would then participate in a meat meal.

Those who have difficulties with such an expectation of an earthly-physical peace empire try to make these words come true in the recurring celebrations of the Lord's table in church history. Jesus would then participate in the Holy Communion or annual Easter feast of the Christians.[53] This explanation, however, is not easy to explain theologically.[54] Also, the difficulty remains that Jesus' statement about the future presupposes a consumption of animals.

Another option is to even think of the new heaven and the new earth in the words of Jesus. It must then be assumed that people still kill and eat animals in eternity and that Jesus participates in this. Because of all these difficulties, others choose to explain that Jesus expresses an intense desire that will never be fulfilled.[55] The texts that the Bible gives us about the future festive banquet do not help us say that these meals are vegetarian. The justifications for this can only be derived from a broader biblical-theological perspective. In particular, they contain the arguments we mention at the beginning of this chapter.

In any case, it can be concluded that it is not plausible for many from the original creation not to think of eating animals in the future eternal banquet chain in the new heaven and new earth. After all, death will disappear from creation forever in the future, and tears will be wiped away. This glorious promise is closely related to the future festive banquet:

> On this mountain the Lord of hosts will make for all peoples a feast of rich food, a feast of well-aged wine, of rich food filled with marrow, of well-aged wines strained clear.... He will swallow up death forever. Then the Lord God will wipe away the tears from all faces, and the disgrace of his people he will take away from all the earth, for the Lord has spoken. (Isa 25:6, 8)

At the banquets that arrive, it is possible to think of meals with vegetarian dishes from different countries. People enjoy the fat olives from Israel, the hummus from Lebanon, the kimchi from Korea, the mangos from Costa Rica, the potatoes from England, the asparagus and mushrooms from France, the cheese from Switzerland and the Netherlands, the

---

53. Stein, *Luke*, 541; Ernst, *Lukas*, 581.
54. Bock, *Luke 9:51—24:53*, 1720; Nolland, *Luke 18:35—24:53*, 1050.
55. Jeremias, *Eucharistic Words*, 207–18; Arndt, *Luke*, 438.

vegetarian sushi from Japan, and of course—the delicious fries from Belgium. All this is served with the best precious wines. We even learn about these wines in the Babylonian Talmud that they are made from grapes that have been preserved by God since the first six days of creation.[56]

In the Last Supper, which Jesus celebrated together with his disciples, Christians also look forward to the future meal that God has in mind for his children. Also, the *agapē* meals, which the first Christians shared, are often connected with this hopeful expectation.[57] With the future completion of God's kingdom, the new heaven and the new earth would become a reality. Then came the moment when the faithful would partake of God's great feast. Especially at moments of oppression, when the food the Christians had was scarce, this was an outstanding prospect. For those who clung to the physical expectation of a realm of peace that would be founded on earth by the Messiah, that prospect came even sooner. They looked forward to the great moment when Jesus Christ would return and create a feast banquet on the Temple Mount of Jerusalem. In difficult situations, they then gladly emphasized the promise of Psalm 23: "You prepare a table before me in the presence of my enemies; you anoint my head with oil; my cup overflows" (v. 5). That is the glorious prospect of those who confess Jesus Christ as Lord of lords and King of kings.

---

56. Neusner, *B. Berakhot*, 34b.
57. Yamauchi, "Banquets," 153–54.

Epilogue

Nowadays, taking care of creation is in the topicality of the media. Fortunately, there has also been a renewed attention for this subject in the church. Several designs have been made to give the theme of caring for the entire creation with all its flora and fauna a new place in Christian worship. An example of this is introducing a unique holiday in America, which bears the name Earth Day Sunday and was celebrated for the first time on April 22, 2018. Another example is the revaluation of the old World Animal Day, celebrated in the Netherlands and Belgium on October 4 every year since 1930.

In this book, it has become clear that the attention for the animals in God's creation cannot be separated from the work of salvation of Jesus Christ. The first heaven and earth and the new heaven and earth find their center in this one Person, Jesus of Nazareth. They exist only through him and are also only there for him, Paul tells us in his hymn of praise of Colossians 1:15–20. The biblical-theological reflection on eschatology helps us to get a new perspective on God's great plan with this creation. It reveals what God is doing in the totality of this reality. In this way, it offers an antithesis to a world that languishes in individualism. The own "I" is central, and the fellow creatures only serve their interests. The gospel testifies of a God who has a heart for his whole creation and does not let go of his hands' work. It testifies of a God who loves his creation so much that he gives his own Son to redeem her from the traps of evil. The testimony of the new heaven and the new earth is thus the testimony of the excellent redemption plan of this creation.

Through the instructions in the Old and New Testaments, God shows humans how to handle creation optimally. God also stands up for the animals he created. They, too, are his and are close to his heart. Thus, his instructions include all living beings and give insight into the values that live in God's heart. The prophetic proclamation expresses the dream God has in mind for this creation. This is a world characterized by the peaceful nature of God himself, a creation in which he sees the face of his beloved Son reflected. The new covenant is, therefore, not only a covenant that encompasses humanity. Like the beginning of Genesis, it extends to the totality of creation and shows how God wants to deal with his earth. From the biblical testimony, God is thus confessed as the Lord of the land. By orienting themselves to this, the righteous receive a compass that will guide them in the twenty-first century.

This book has made visible how the animals in creation long to experience their release from beginning to end. Together with the whole of creation, they are longing for the revelation of the sons of God. For creation has received hope through the work of the Messiah, because she too will be freed from the slavery of impermanence and will share in the freedom and glory given to God's sons (Rom 8:20–21). This provides the glorious Christian testimony that God does not have a hopeless end in mind for his creation, but a fantastic, endless hope.

Bibliography

Adams, Cindy L., et al. "Predictors of Owner Response to Companion Animal Death in 177 Clients from 14 Practices in Ontario." *Journal of the American Veterinary Medical Association* 217.9 (2000) 1303–9.
Adams, Edward. *The Stars Will Fall from Heaven: "Cosmic Catastrophe" in the New Testament and Its World.* Library of New Testament Studies 347. London: T.&T. Clark, 2007.
Aelianus, Claudius. *De Natura Animalium.* Edited by Manuela G. Valdés et al. Bibliotheca Scriptorum Graecorum et Romanorum Teubneriana. Berlin: De Gruyter, 2009.
Akers, Keith. *The Lost Religion of Jesus: Simple Living and Nonviolence in Early Christianity.* New York: Lantern, 2000.
Akiva ben Joseph. *Sifre Devarim.* Edited by Jacob Neusner. Midrash Halakhah. Lanham: University Press of America, 1987.
Alford, Henry. *Alford's Greek Testament: An Exegetical and Critical Commentary.* Grand Rapids: Baker Book House, 1980.
Allen, Edgar L. "The Hebrew View of Nature." In *Judaism and Environmental Ethics*, edited by Martin D. Yaffee, 80–85. Lanham: Lexington, 2001.
Allen, Leslie C. *Ezekiel 20–48.* Word Biblical Commentary 29. Dallas: Word, 1990.
———. *Psalms 101–150.* 2nd ed. Word Biblical Commentary 21. Nashville: Thomas Nelson, 2002.
Althaus, Paul. *Die letzten Dinge: Entwurf einer christlichen Eschatologie.* 4th ed. Studien des apologetischen Seminars 9. Gütersloh: Bertelsmann, 1933.
Ambrose of Milan. *Hexameron.* Translated by John J. Savage. Fathers of the Church 42. Washington: Catholic University of America, 2003.
Anderson, Hugh. *The Gospel of Mark.* New Century Bible Commentary. Grand Rapids: Eerdmans, 1981.
Aquinas, Thomas. *Summa Contra Gentiles.* 4 vols. Notre Dame: University of Notre Dame, 2009.
———. *Summa Theologiae.* Cambridge: Cambridge University, 2006.
Archer, John, and Gillian Winchester. "Bereavement Following Death of a Pet." *British Journal of Psychology* 85.2 (1994) 259–71.
Aristotle. *Politics.* Translated by Harris Rackham. Loeb Classical Library 264. Cambridge: Harvard University, 2005.
Arndt, William F. *The Gospel according to St. Luke.* Concordia Classic Commentary Series. St. Louis: Concordia, 1956.

Associated Press. "Hamster, Snake Best Friends at Tokyo Zoo." *MSNBC*, January 24, 2006.

———. "Lions Save Girl from Kidnappers." *The Guardian*, June 22, 2005.

Athanasius. *The Life of St. Antony*. Translated by Robert T. Meyer. Ancient Christian Writers 10. New York: Newman, 1978.

Athenaeus of Naucratis. *De Deipnosophists*. Translated by Charles B. Gulick. 7 vols. Loeb Classical Library. Cambridge: Harvard, 1999.

Attfield, Robin. *The Ethics of Environmental Concern*. 2nd ed. Athens: University of Georgia, 1991.

Augustine of Hippo. *The City of God, De Civitate Dei*. Edited by William S. Babcock and Boniface Ramsey. The Works of Saint Augustine 1.6. New York: New City, 2012.

———. *De Natura et Origine Animae*. Library of Latin Texts. Turnhout: Brepols, 2010.

———. *Sermons on the Liturgical Season*. Translated by Mary S. Muldowney. Fathers of the Church 38. Baltimore: Catholic University of America, 2014.

Aune, David E. *Revelation 1–5*. Word Biblical Commentary 52A. Dallas: Word, 1997.

———. *Revelation 17–22*. Word Biblical Commentary 52C. Dallas: Word, 1998.

Bacon, Francis. *Valerius Terminus: The Interpretation of Nature*. Belle Fourche: NuVision, 2003.

Bar Nafha, Yohanan, and Salomon Buber, eds. *Midrash Tehillim*. Jerusalem: Hotza'at Midrash, 1966.

Barr, James. *The Garden of Eden and the Hope of Immortality*. Minneapolis: Fortress, 1993.

———. "Man and Nature: The Ecological Controversy and the Old Testament." *Bulletin John Rylands University Library of Manchester* 55.1 (1972) 9–32.

Barth, Karl. *The Doctrine of Creation: The Command of God the Creator*. Edited by G. W. Bromiley and T. F. Torrance. Church Dogmatics, 3.4. Edinburgh: T.&T. Clark, 2009.

———. *The Doctrine of Creation: The Work of Creation*. Edited by G. W. Bromiley and T. F. Torrance. Church Dogmatics 3.1. Edinburgh: T.&T. Clark, 2009.

Basil of Caesarea. "De Hominis Structura." http://www.documentacatholicaomnia.eu.

Bauckham, Richard J. *The Fate of the Dead: Studies on the Jewish and Christian Apocalypses*. Supplements to Novum Testamentum 93. Atlanta: Society of Biblical Literature, 2008.

———. "Jesus and Animals I: What Did He Teach?" In *Animals on the Agenda: Questions about Animals for Theology and Ethics*, edited by Andrew Linzey and Dorothy Yamamoto, 33–48. Urbana: University of Illinois, 1998.

———. "Jesus and Animals II: What Did He Practise?" In *Animals on the Agenda: Questions about Animals for Theology and Ethics*, edited by Andrew Linzey and Dorothy Yamamoto, 49–60. Urbana: University of Illinois, 1998.

———. "Jesus and the Wild Animals (Mark 1:13): A Christological Image for an Ecological Age." In *Jesus of Nazareth, Lord and Christ: Essays on the Historical Jesus and New Testament Christology*, edited by Joel B. Green and Max Turner, 3–21. Grand Rapids: Eerdmans, 1994.

———. "Joining Creation's Praise of God." *Ecotheology: Journal of Religion, Nature & the Environment* 7.1 (2002) 45–59.

———. "Judgment in the Book of Revelation." *Ex Auditu* 20 (2004) 1–24.

———. *The Theology of the Book of Revelation*. Cambridge: Cambridge University Press, 1993.

Beale, Gregory K. *The Book of Revelation: A Commentary on the Greek Text*. New International Greek Testament Commentary. Grand Rapids: Eerdmans, 1999.

———. "Colossians." In *Commentary on the New Testament Use of the Old Testament*, edited by Gregory K. Beale and Donald A. Carson, 841–70. Grand Rapids: Baker Academic, 2007.

———. *John's Use of the Old Testament in Revelation*. Journal for the Study of the New Testament, Supplement Series 166. Sheffield: Sheffield Academic, 1998.

———. *A New Testament Biblical Theology: The Unfolding of the Old Testament in the New*. Grand Rapids: Baker Academic, 2011.

———. *The Temple and the Church's Mission: A Biblical Theology of the Dwelling Place of God*. New Studies in Biblical Theology 17. Leicester: Apollos, 2004.

"The Belgic Confession of Faith." In *The Three Forms of Unity*, 51–75. The Reformed Church in the United States. N.p.: PCRC, 2011. http://www.rcus.org/wp-content/uploads/2013/09/Three-Forms-of-Unity-2011-edition.pdf.

Ben Jitschaki (Rashi), Sjlomo. *Complete Tanach with Rashi*. Edited by A. J. Rosenberg. Brooklyn: Judaica, 2005.

Berkouwer, Gerrit C. *The Return of Christ*. Translated by Martin J. Van Elderen. Studies in Dogmatics 12. Grand Rapids: Eerdmans, 1972.

Bernstein, Ellen. "(Mis)Reading Genesis: A Response to Environmentalist Critiques of Judaism." In *Ecology & the Jewish Spirit: Where Nature and the Sacred Meet*, edited by Neal J. Loevinger, 32–41. Woodstock: Jewish Lights, 2000.

Beyerlin, Walter. *Near Eastern Religious Texts Relating to the Old Testament*. Old Testament Library. Pretoria: Unisa, 1999.

Bischoff, Erich. *Das Blut in jüdischem Schrifttum und Brauch nebst ausführlichen Anmerkungen: Eine Untersuchung*. Graz: Geheimes Wissen, 2009.

Bleich, J. David. "Judaism and Animal Experimentation." In *Animal Sacrifices: Religious Perspectives on the Use of Animals in Science (Ethics and Action)*, edited by Tom Regan, 61–114. Philadelphia: Temple University, 1986.

Blocher, Henri A. G. *Evil and the Cross: An Analytical Look at the Problem of Pain*. Grand Rapids: Kregel, 2004.

———. "The Theology of the Fall and the Origins of Evil." In *Darwin, Creation and the Fall: Theological Challenges*, edited by R. J. Berry and T. A. Noble, 149–72. Nottingham: Apollos, 2010.

Block, Daniel I. *The Book of Ezekiel: Chapters 25–48*. New International Commentary on the Old Testament. Grand Rapids: Eerdmans, 1998.

———. "Eden: A Temple? A Reassessment of the Biblical Evidence." In *From Creation to New Creation: Biblical Theology and Exegesis. Essays in Honor of G. K. Beale*, edited by Daniel M. Gurtner and Benjamin L. Gladd, 1–30. Peabody: Hendrickson, 2013.

Bock, Darrell L. *Luke 9:51—24:53*. Baker Exegetical Commentary on the New Testament. Grand Rapids: Baker, 1996.

Boehmer, Julius. *Neutestamentliche Parallelen und Verwandte aus altchristlicher Literatur*. Stuttgart, 1903.

Bonting, Sjoerd L. "Chaos Theology: A New Approach to the Science-Theology Dialogue." *Zygon* 34.2 (1999) 323–32.

Bornkamm, Günther, et al. *Die christliche Hoffnung und das Problem der Entmythologisierung*. Stuttgart: Evangelisches Verlagswerk, 1954.

Bouma-Prediger, Steven. *For the Beauty of the Earth: A Christian Vision for Creation Care*. Engaging Culture. Grand Rapids: Baker Academic, 2001.

Boyd, Gregory A. *Satan and the Problem of Evil: Constructing a Trinitarian Warfare Theodicy.* Downers Grove: InterVarsity, 2001.

Boyer, Paul S. *When Time Shall Be No More: Prophecy Belief in Modern American Culture.* Studies in Cultural History. Cambridge: Belknap Press of Harvard University, 1992.

Braaten, Carl E. "The Significance of Apocalypticism for Systematic Theology." *Union Seminary Review* 25.4 (1971) 480–499.

Braun, Joseph. *Tracht und Attribute der Heiligen in der deutschen Kunst.* Stuttgart: Metzler, 1943.

British Broadcasting Corporation. "Kidnapped Girl 'Rescued' by Lions." *BBC News*, June 22, 2005. http://news.bbc.co.uk.

———. "The Lioness and the Oryx." *BBC News*, January 7, 2002. http://news.bbc.co.uk.

Brueggemann, Walter. *Genesis.* Interpretation. Atlanta: Westminster John Knox, 1982.

———. *Isaiah 40–66.* Westminster Bible Companion. Louisville: Westminster John Knox, 1998.

Brunner, Emil. *Die christliche Lehre von der Kirche vom Glauben und von der Vollendung.* Dogmatik 3. Zürich: Zwingli, 1964.

———. *Das Ewige als Zukunft und Gegenwart.* Zürich: Zwingli, 1953.

Buber, Salomon, ed. *Midrash Tanhuma: Genesis.* Translated by John T. Townsend. New Jersey: KTAV, 1989.

Butler, Trent C. *Luke.* Holman New Testament Commentary 3. Nashville: Holman, 2000.

Bynum, Caroline W. "Material Continuity, Personal Survival, and the Resurrection of the Body: A Scholastic Discussion in Its Medieval and Modern Contexts." In *Fragmentation and Redemption: Essays on Gender and the Human Body in Medieval Religion.* New York: Zone, 2006.

———. *The Resurrection of the Body in Western Christianity, 200–1336.* New York: Columbia University, 1995.

Caird, George B. *The Language and Imagery of the Bible.* London: Duckworth, 1988.

———. *The Revelation of Saint John.* Harper's New Testament Commentaries 19. Peabody: Hendrickson, 1999.

Calvin, John. *Genesis.* Translated by John King. Calvin's Commentaries 1. Grand Rapids: Baker, 2009.

———. *Romans.* Translated by John Owen. Calvin's Commentaries 19b. Grand Rapids: Baker Books, 2009.

Caneday, Ardel B. "Mark's Provocative Use of Scripture in Narration: 'He Was with the Wild Animals and Angels Ministered to Him.'" *Bulletin for Biblical Research* 9 (1999) 19–36.

Carmichael, Calum M. "On Separating Life and Death: An Explanation of Some Biblical Laws." *Harvard Theological Review* 69.1–2 (1976) 1–7.

Cassuto, Umberto. *A Commentary on the Book of Genesis: Part One: From Adam to Noah.* Jeruzalem: Magnes, 1989.

———. *A Commentary on the Book of Genesis: Part Two: From Noah to Abraham.* Jerusalem: Magnes, 1964.

Chafer, Lewis S. *Systematic Theology.* 8 vols. Dallas: Dallas Theological Seminary, 1947.

Chang, Hae-Kyung. *Die Knechtschaft und Befreiung der Schöpfung: Eine exegetische Untersuchung zu Römer 8,19–22.* Reihe Bibelwissenschaftliche Monographien 7. Wuppertal: Brockhaus, 2000.

Charlesworth, James H. *The Good and Evil Serpent: How a Universal Symbol Became Christianized.* New Haven: Yale University, 2010.
Charron, Bertrand. "Escape to Sterility for Designer Fish." *New Scientist* 146 (1979) 22.
Christensen, Duane L. *Deuteronomy 21:10—34:12.* Word Biblical Commentary 6B. Nashville: Nelson, 2002.
Chrysostom, John. *Homilies on Romans.* Edited by Philip Schaff, translated by J. B. Morris et al. Nicene and Post-Nicene Fathers 16. New York: CLC, 1889.
Cicero, M. Tullius. *The Nature of the Gods [De Natura Deorum].* Translated by Harris Rackham. 2nd ed. Loeb Classical Library. Cambridge: Harvard University, 1994.
Clark, Stephen R. L. *The Moral Status of Animals.* Oxford: Oxford University, 1984.
Clement of Alexandria. *Paedagogus.* Edited by Miroslav Marcovich. Supplements to Vigiliae Christianae 61. Leiden: Brill, 2002.
Clifford, Richard J. *Creation Accounts in the Ancient Near East and in the Bible.* Catholic Biblical Quarterly Monograph Series 26. Washington: Catholic Biblical Association, 1994.
Cobb, John B. "All Things in Christ?" In *Animals on the Agenda: Questions about Animals for Theology and Ethics,* edited by Andrew Linzey and Dorothy Yamamoto, 173–80. Urbana: University of Illinois, 1998.
Cohn, Norman. *Cosmos, Chaos, and the World to Come: The Ancient Roots of Apocalyptic Faith.* New Haven: Yale Nota Bene, 2001.
Collins, C. John. *Genesis 1–4: A Linguistic, Literary, and Theological Commentary.* Phillipsburg: P&R, 2006.
———. "The Wayyiqtol as 'Pluperfect': When and Why." *Tyndale Bulletin* 46.1 (1995) 117–40.
Collon, D. "Banquets in the Art of the Ancient Near East." In *Banquets d'Orient,* edited by Rika Gyselen and Marthe Bernus-Taylor. Res Orientales 4. Bures-sur-Yvette: Groupe pour l'étude de la civilisation du Moyen-Orient, 1992.
Cooper, Lamar E. *Ezekiel.* New American Commentary 17. Nashville: Broadman & Holman, 1994.
Cowles, Kathleen V. "The Death of a Pet: Human Responses to the Breaking of the Bond." In *Pets and the Family,* edited by Marvin B. Sussman, 135–48. New York: Routledge, 2016.
Craghan, John F. "The Gerasene Demoniac." *Catholic Biblical Quarterly* 30 (1968) 522–36.
Creegan, Nicola H. *Animal Suffering and the Problem of Evil.* New York: Oxford University, 2013.
Currid, John D. *Ancient Egypt and the Old Testament.* Grand Rapids: Baker, 1997.
Dalman, Gustaf H. *Arbeit und Sitte in Palästina: Zeltleben, Vieh- und Milchwirtschaft, Jagd, Fischfang.* Vol. 6. 8 vols. Beiträge zur Förderung christlicher Theologie. Reihe 2. Sammlung wissenschaftlicher Monographien 33. Gütersloh: Bertelsmann, 1939.
Darwin, Charles. *The Correspondence of Charles Darwin: Volume 6. 1856–1857.* Edited by Frederick Burkhardt. Cambridge: Cambridge University, 1990.
———. *The Correspondence of Charles Darwin: Volume 8. 1860.* Edited by Frederick Burkhardt and Sydney Smith. Cambridge: Cambridge University, 1993.
Delio, Ilia. "Is Creation Eternal?" *Theological Studies* 66.2 (2005) 279–303.
Delling, Gerhard. "Στοιχέω, Συστοιχέω, Στοιχεῖον." In *Theological Dictionary of the New Testament,* edited by Gerhard Kittel and Gerhard Friedrich, 7:666–87. Grand Rapids: Eerdmans, 1971.

Descartes, René. *Descartes: Philosophical Letters*. Translated by Anthony Kenny. Oxford: Clarendon, 1970.

Donahue, John R., and Daniel J. Harrington. *The Gospel of Mark*. Sacra Pagina Series 2. Collegeville: Liturgical, 2002.

Dougherty, Trent. *The Problem of Animal Pain: A Theodicy for All Creatures Great and Small*. Palgrave Frontiers in Philosophy of Religion. Basingstoke: Palgrave Macmillan, 2014.

Easley, Kendell H. *Revelation*. Holman New Testament Commentary. Nashville: Broadman & Holman, 1999.

Eliade, Mircea. *Cosmos and History: The Myth of the Eternal Return*. New York: Harper, 1959.

Ellsberg, Daniel. *The Doomsday Machine: Confessions of a Nuclear War Planner*. London: Bloomsbury, 2018.

Elwood, Robert W., and Mirjam Appel. "Pain Experience in Hermit Crabs?" *Animal Behaviour* 77.5 (2009) 1243–46.

Enns, Peter. *Exodus*. NIV Application Commentary. Grand Rapids: Zondervan, 2000.

Ernst, Josef. *Das Evangelium nach Lukas*. Regensburger Neues Testament 3. Regensburg: Pustet, 1977.

Eshnunna. *The Laws of Eshnunna*. Edited by Reuven Yaron. 2nd ed. Jerusalem: Hebrew University, 1988.

Eve, Eric. *The Jewish Context of Jesus' Miracles*. Journal for the Study of the New Testament. Supplement Series 231. London: Sheffield Academic, 2002.

Faro, Ingrid. "The Question of Evil and Animal Death before the Fall." *Trinity Journal* 35 (2015) 193–213.

Farrer, Austin M. *Love Almighty and Ills Unlimited*. Fontana Library: Theology and Philosophy. London: Collins, 1966.

Fekkes, Jan, III. *Isaiah and Prophetic Traditions in the Book of Revelation: Visionary Antecedents and Their Development*. Sheffield: Sheffield Academic, 1994.

Fensham, F. Charles. "Liability of Animals in Biblical and Ancient Near Eastern Law." *Journal of Northwest Semitic Languages* 14 (1988) 85–90.

Ferrier, J. Todd. *The Master: His Life and Teachings*. London: Order of the Cross, 1925.

Feuerbach, Ludwig Andreas. *The Essence of Christianity*. New York: Prometheus, 1989.

Field, Nigel P., et al. "Role of Attachment in Response to Pet Loss." *Death Studies* 33.4 (2009) 334–55.

Fisher, Loren R. "Creation at Ugarit and in the Old Testament." *Vetus Testamentum* 15.3 (1965) 313–24.

Fitzmyer, Joseph A. *The Gospel according to Luke I-IX*. Anchor Bible 28. Garden City: Doubleday, 1981.

Fletcher-Watts, Vivienne J. *A Study of Deuteronomic and Priestly Legislation with Particular Reference to Clean and Unclean Foods*. Berrien Springs: Andrews University, 1982.

Ford, J. Massyngberde. *Revelation*. Anchor Bible 38. Garden City: Doubleday, 1975.

France, Richard T. *The Gospel of Mark: A Commentary on the Greek Text*. New International Greek Testament Commentary. Grand Rapids: Eerdmans, 2002.

Frear, George L., Jr. "Caring for Animals: Biblical Stimulus for Ethical Reflection." In *Good News for Animals? Christian Approaches to Animal Well-Being*, edited by Jay B. McDaniel and Charles R. Pinches, 3–11. Eugene, OR: Wipf & Stock, 1993.

Freedman, Harry, and Simon Maurice, eds. "Midrash Rabbah: Ecclesiastes." In *Midrash Rabbah: Ruth and Ecclesiastes*. Midrash Rabbah 8. London: Soncino, 1983.
———, eds. *Midrash Rabbah: Exodus*. Midrash Rabbah 3. London: Soncino, 1983.
———, eds. *Midrash Rabbah: Genesis*. 2 vols. Midrash Rabbah 1–2. London: Soncino, 1983.
———, eds. *Midrash Rabbah: Leviticus*. Midrash Rabbah 4. London: Soncino, 1983.
Fretheim, Terence E. *God and World in the Old Testament: A Relational Theology of Creation*. Nashville: Abingdon, 2005.
———. "The Plagues as Ecological Signs of Historical Disaster." *Journal of Biblical Literature* 110.3 (1991) 385–96.
Froom, LeRoy E. *The Prophetic Faith of Our Fathers: The Historical Development of Prophetic Interpretation*. 4 vols. Washington: Review and Herald, 1946–54.
Garrett, Duane A. *Rethinking Genesis: The Sources and Authorship of the First Book of the Bible*. Grand Rapids: Baker Book House, 1991.
Garrett, Duane A. and Walter C. Kaiser. *NIV Archaeological Study Bible: An Illustrated Walk through Biblical History and Culture*. Grand Rapids: Zondervan, 2005.
Garroway, Joshua. "The Invasion of a Mustard Seed: A Reading of Mark 5.1–20." *Journal for the Study of the New Testament* 32.1 (2009) 57–75.
Geisler, Annette M. "Companion Animals in Palliative Care: Stories from the Bedside." *American Journal of Hospice and Palliative Medicine* 21.4 (2004) 285–88.
Gerwolls, Marilyn K., and Susan M. Labott. "Adjustment to the Death of a Companion Animal." *Anthrozoös* 7.3 (1994) 172–87.
Gesenius, Wilhelm, and Samuel Prideaux Tregelles. *Gesenius' Hebrew and Chaldee Lexicon to the Old Testament*. Baker Book House, 1979.
Ghirshman, Roman. *The Arts of Ancient Iran from Its Origins to the Time of Alexander the Great*. Arts of Mankind. New York: Golden, 1964.
Giamatti, A. Bartlett. *The Earthly Paradise and the Renaissance Epic*. New York: Norton, 1989.
Gibson, Jeffrey B. *The Temptations of Jesus in Early Christianity*. Journal for the Study of the New Testament. Supplement Series 112. Sheffield: Sheffield Academic, 1995.
Gill, John. *The New John Gill's Exposition of the Entire Bible*. London: Woodward, 1763.
Gilmour, Michael J. *Eden's Other Residents: The Bible and Animals*. Eugene, OR: Cascade, 2014.
Gindi, Joseph. *Greening the Torah: The Use of Classical Texts in Jewish Environmentalist Literature*. Ann Arbor: ProQuest, 2011.
Gleason, Kathryn. "Gardens in Preclassical Times." In *The Oxford Encyclopedia of Archaeology in the Near East*, edited by E. Meyers, 2:383–85. New York: Oxford University, 1997.
Goldingay, John. *Old Testament Theology: Volume One: Israel's Gospel*. Downers Grove: IVP Academic, 2015.
Goldwurm, Hersh. *Daniel*. ArtScroll Tanach Series. Brooklyn: Mesorah, 2006.
Gordon, Cyrus H. *Ugarit Handbook*. Analecta Orientalia 25. Roma: Pontificium Institutum Biblicum, 1965.
Graf, G. Robert. *Moral Dimensions of Animal Life in the Old Testament*. Dallas: Dallas Theological Seminary, 2010.
Gregory of Nyssa. *De Anima et Resurrectione*. Gregorii Nysseni Opera Online 15. Leiden: Brill, 2017.
Guelich, Robert A. *Mark 1–8:26*. Word Biblical Commentary 34A. Nashville: Thomas Nelson, 1989.

Gundry, Robert H. *Mark: A Commentary on His Apology for the Cross*. Grand Rapids: Eerdmans, 1993.

Gunkel, Hermann. *Genesis*. Göttinger Handkommentar zum Alten Testament. Göttingen: Vandenhoeck & Ruprecht, 1964.

Gunton, Colin E. *Christ and Creation*. Grand Rapids: Eerdmans, 1993.

———. *The Triune Creator: A Historical and Systematic Study*. Edinburgh Studies in Constructive Theology. Edinburgh: Edinburgh University, 1998.

Habermas, Gary R., and James P. Moreland. *Beyond Death: Exploring the Evidence for Immortality*. Eugene, OR: Wipf & Stock, 2004.

Habig, Marion A. *St. Francis of Assisi: Writings and Early Biography*. Cincinnati: Anthony Messenger, 2008.

Hagencord, Rainer. *Gott und die Tiere: Ein Perspektivenwechsel*. Regensburg: Pustet, 2008.

Hamilton, Victor P. *The Book of Genesis: Chapters 1–17*. New International Commentary on the Old Testament. Grand Rapids: Eerdmans, 1990.

Hammurabi. *The New Complete Code of Hammurabi*. Edited by Heinz-Dieter Viel. Lanham: University of America, 2012.

Happ, Heinz. *Die Scala naturae und die Schichtung des Seelischen bei Aristoteles*. Berlin: De Gruyter, 1969.

Haran, Menahem. "Seething a Kid in Its Mother's Milk." *Journal of Jewish Studies* 30.1 (1979) 23–35.

Harland, Peter J. *The Value of Human Life: A Study of the Story of the Flood (Genesis 6–9)*. Supplements to Vetus Testamentum 64. Leiden: Brill, 1996.

Harrison, Lucy, and Richard Harrington. "Adolescents' Bereavement Experiences: Prevalence, Association with Depressive Symptoms, and Use of Services." *Journal of Adolescence* 24.2 (2001) 159–69.

Harrison, Peter. "Descartes on Animals." *The Philosophical Quarterly* 42.167 (1992) 219–27.

Hartl, Gregory. "The Environment: Where's the Risk, and Where Are Children Safe?" World Health Organization. Last modified 2004. https://www.who.int/mediacentre/news/releases/2004/pr43/en/.

Hartog, John. *Sin, Redemption, and the Animal Kingdom*. Winona Lake: Grace Theological Seminary, 1978.

Hausoul, Raymond R. "Eine Eschatologie aus der Protologie: Genesis 1–2 und die christliche Hoffnung." *Biblisch erneuerte Theologie: Jahrbuch für theologische Studien* 3 (2019) 11–29.

———. "An Evaluation of Jürgen Moltmann's Concept of Time and Space in the New Creation." *Journal of Reformed Theology* 7.2 (2013) 137–59.

———. "The Land in the Books of Exodus, Leviticus and Numbers." In *The Earth and the Land: Studies about the Value of the Land of Israel in the Old Testament and Afterwards*, edited by Hendrik J. Koorevaar and Mart-Jan Paul, 65–95. Edition Israelogie 11. Berlin: Lang, 2018.

———. *The New Heaven and New Earth: An Interdisciplinary Comparison between Jürgen Moltmann, Karl Rahner, and Gregory Beale*. Eugene, OR: Wipf & Stock, 2020.

———. "Theology and Cosmology: A Call for Interdisciplinary Enrichment." *Zygon* 54.2 (2019) 324–36.

Heil, John P. "Jesus with the Wild Animals in Mark 1:13." *Catholic Biblical Quarterly* 68.1 (2006) 63–78.
Hick, John. *Evil and the God of Love*. 2nd ed. Basingstoke: Palgrave Macmillan, 2010.
Hilbrands, Walter. "Ein veraltetes Weltbild im biblischen Schöpfungsbericht? 'Raqia' im Alten Testament." In *Genesis, Schöpfung und Evolution: Beiträge zur Auslegung und Bedeutung des ersten Buchs der Bibel*, edited by Junker Reinhard, 191–94. Studium Integrale Theologie, 2015.
Hildenbrand, Michael D. *Structure and Theology in the Holiness Code*. BIBAL Dissertation Series 10. North Richland Hills: Bibal, 2004.
Hillers, Delbert R. "A Study of Psalm 148." *Catholic Biblical Quarterly* 40.3 (1978) 323–34.
Hoekema, Anthony A. *The Bible and the Future*. Grand Rapids: Eerdmans, 1994.
Holladay, William L. *A Concise Hebrew and Aramaic Lexicon of the Old Testament*. Grand Rapids: Eerdmans, 2000.
Homer. *The Iliad*. Translated by Peter Green. Oakland: University of California, 2015.
———. *The Odyssey*. Translated by Ian C. Johnston. 2nd ed. Arlington: RRP, 2007.
Horrell, David G., and Dominic Coad. "'The Stones Would Cry out' (Luke 19:40): A Lukan Contribution to a Hermeneutics of Creation's Praise." *Scottish Journal of Theology* 64.1 (2011) 29–44.
Houston, Walter. "What Was the Meaning of Classifying Animals as Clean or Unclean?" In *Animals on the Agenda: Questions about Animals for Theology and Ethics*, edited by Andrew Linzey and Dorothy Yamamoto, 18–24. Urbana: University of Illinois, 1998.
Hütterman, Aloys. *Am Anfang war die Ökologie: Naturverständnis im Alten Testament*. Freiburg: Herder, 2004.
———. *The Ecological Message of the Torah: Knowledge, Concepts, and Laws Which Made Survival in a Land of "Milk and Honey" Possible*. South Florida Studies in the History of Judaism 199. Atlanta: Scholars, 1999.
Hyrkanos, Elieser. *Pirkê de Rabbi Eliezer*. Translated by Gerald Friedlander. 4th ed. Judaic Studies Library 6. Breinigsville: Nabu, 2011.
Ickert, Scott. "Luther and Animals: Subject to Adam's Fall?" In *Animals on the Agenda: Questions about Animals for Theology and Ethics*, edited by Andrew Linzey and Dorothy Yamamoto, 90–99. Urbana: University of Illinois, 1998.
Irenaeus of Lyon. *Adversus Haereses*. Translated by Norbert Brox. 5 vols. Fontes Christiani 8. Freiburg: Herder, 2001.
Jacob, Benno. *The Second Book of the Bible: Exodus*. Jerusalem: KTAV, 1992.
Jaki, Stanley L. *Genesis 1: Through the Ages*. 2nd ed. Royal Oak: Real View, 1998.
Jauhiainen, Marko. *The Use of Zechariah in Revelation*. Wissenschaftliche Untersuchungen Zum Neuen Testament. 2. Reihe 199. Tübingen: Mohr Siebeck, 2005.
Jenson, Robert W. *Systematic Theology: The Works of God*. Volume 2. 2 vols. Oxford: Oxford University, 2001.
Jeremias, Joachim. *The Eucharistic Words of Jesus*. New York: Scribner, 1990.
Jerome. *Letters and Select Works*. Translated by William G. Martley, George Lewis, and W. H. Fremantle. Nicene and Post-Nicene Fathers, Second Series 6. Grand Rapids: Eerdmans, 2007.
Johnson, Elizabeth A. *Ask the Beasts: Darwin and the God of Love*. London: Bloomsbury, 2015.

Johnston, Gordon H. "Genesis 1 and Ancient Egyptian Creation Myths." *Bibliotheca Sacra* 165.658 (2008) 178–94.

Kaiser, Otto. "Die ersten und die letzten Dinge." *Neue Zeitschrift für systematische Theologie und Religionsphilosophie* 36.1 (1994) 75–91.

Kant, Immanuel. "The End of All Things." In *On History*, edited by Lewis W. Beck. Library of Liberal Arts 162. New York: Macmillan, 1985.

Kara, Simeon. *Yalkut Shimoni: Midrash Al Torah, Neviim u-Khetuvim*. Edited by Abraham A. Gombiner. 2 vols. Yerushalayim: Makor, 1990.

Kärkkäinen, Veli-Matti. *Creation and Humanity. A Constructive Christian Theology for the Pluralistic World* 3. Grand Rapids: Eerdmans, 2015.

———. *Hope and Community. A Constructive Christian Theology for the Pluralistic World* 5. Grand Rapids: Eerdmans, 2017.

Kaufman, Kenneth R., and Nathaniel D. Kaufman. "And Then the Dog Died." *Death Studies* 30.1 (2006) 61–76.

Keel, Othmar. *Das Böcklein in der Milch seiner Mutter und Verwandtes: Im Lichte eines altorientalischen Bildmotivs*. Orbis Biblicus et Orientalis 33. Göttingen: Vandenhoeck & Ruprecht, 1980.

———. *The Symbolism of the Biblical World Ancient Near Eastern Iconography and the Book of Psalms*. London: SPCK, 1978.

Keil, Carl F., and Franz J. Delitzsch. *The Pentateuch*. Commentary on the Old Testament 1. Grand Rapids: Eerdmans, 1988.

Keiter, Sheila T. "Noah and the Dove: The Integral Connection between Noah and Jonah." *Jewish Bible Quarterly* 40.4 (2012) 5.

Kelly, Stewart E. "The Problem of Evil and the Satan Hypothesis." *Sophia* 36.2 (1997) 29–42.

King, Philip J., and Lawrence E. Stager. *Life in Biblical Israel*. Library of Ancient Israel. Louisville: Westminster John Knox, 2011.

Kistemaker, Simon J. *Exposition of the Book of Revelation*. New Testament Commentary. Grand Rapids: Baker Academic, 2001.

Kline, Meredith G. *Images of the Spirit*. Baker Biblical Monograph. Grand Rapids: Baker Book House, 1980.

———. *Kingdom Prologue: Genesis Foundations for a Covenantal Worldview*. Eugene, OR: Wipf & Stock, 2006.

Knauf, Ernst A. "Zur Herkunft und Sozialgeschichte Israels: 'Das Böckchen in der Milch seiner Mutter.'" *Biblica* 69 (1988) 153–69.

Koch, Klaus. "Gestaltet die Erde, doch heget das Leben! Einige Klarstellungen zum dominium terrae in Genesis 1." In *Spuren des hebräischen Denkers: Beiträge zur alttestamentlichen Theologie*, edited by Klaus Koch, 223–37. Gesammelte Aufsätze 1. Neukirchen-Vluyn: Neukirchener Verlag, 1991.

Kornfeld, Walter. "Die unreinen Tiere im Alten Testament." In *Wissenschaft im Dienste des Glaubens: Festschrift für Abt. Dr. Hermann Peichl*, edited by Josef Kisser. Wien: Wiener Katholische Akademie, 1965.

Kowalski, Beate. *Die Rezeption des Propheten Ezechiel in der Offenbarung des Johannes*. Stuttgarter biblische Beiträge 52. Stuttgart: Katholisches Bibelwerk, 2004.

Küng, Hans. *Eternal Life? Life after Death as a Medical, Philosophical, and Theological Problem*. Eugene, OR: Wipf & Stock, 2002.

Kurz, Gary. *Cold Noses at the Pearly Gates: A Book of Hope for Those Who Have Lost a Pet*. 2nd ed. New York: Citadel, 2008.

Labuschagne, Casper J. "'You Shall Not Boil a Kid in Its Mother's Milk': A New Proposal for the Origin of the Prohibition." In *The Scriptures and the Scrolls: Studies in Honour of A. S. van Der Woude*, edited by Florentino G. Martínez et al., 6–17. Supplements to Vetus Testamentum 49. Leiden: Brill, 1992.

Ladd, George E. *A Commentary on the Revelation of John*. Grand Rapids: Eerdmans, 1972.

———. *A Theology of the New Testament*. 2nd ed. Grand Rapids: Eerdmans, 1993.

Landau, Yehezkel. "The President and the Bible: What Do the Prophets Say to Our Time?" *Christianity and Crisis* 12 (1983) 474–75.

Lane, William L. *The Gospel according to Mark: The English Text with Introduction, Exposition, and Notes*. New International Commentary on the New Testament. Grand Rapids: Eerdmans, 1974.

———. *Hebrews 1–8*. Word Biblical Commentary 47A. Dallas: Word, 1991.

Larwood, Gilbert P., ed. *Extinction and Survival in the Fossil Record*. Systematics Association Special Volume 34. Oxford: Systematics Association Clarendon, 1987.

Lawee, Eric. "The Reception of Rashi's 'Commentary on the Torah' in Spain: The Case of Adam's Mating with the Animals." *The Jewish Quarterly Review* 97.1 (2007) 33–66.

———. "The Sins of the Fauna in Midrash, Rashi, and Their Medieval Interlocutors." *Jewish Studies Quarterly* 17.1 (2010) 56–98.

Le Goff, Jacques. *Medieval Civilization 400–1500*. Oxford: Blackwell, 1992.

Lehmann, Ulrich. *Paläontologisches Wörterbuch*. 4th ed. Berlin: Springer Berlin, 2015.

Lenski, Richard C. H. *The Interpretation of the Epistles of St. Peter, St. John and St. Jude*. Minneapolis: Augsburg, 1966.

Levenson, Jon D. *Creation and the Persistence of Evil: The Jewish Drama of Divine Omnipotence*. San Francisco: Harper & Row, 1988.

Lewis, Clive S. *The Problem of Pain*. Collected Letters of C. S. Lewis. New York: HarperCollins, 2009.

Lewis, Jack P. "The Days of Creation: An Historical Survey of Interpretation." *Journal of the Evangelical Theological Society* 32.4 (1989) 433–55.

Lichtheim, Miriam, ed. *Ancient Egyptian Literature: The New Kingdom*. Ancience Egyptian Literature 2. Berkeley: University of California, 2006.

Lichtheim, Miriam, and Antonio Loprieno, eds. *Ancient Egyptian Literature: The Old and Middle Kingdoms*. Ancience Egyptian Literature 1. Berkeley: University of California, 2006.

Lietzmann, Hans. *Geschichte der Alten Kirche 4: Die Zeit der Kirchenväter*. Berlin: De Gruyter, 1944.

Linzey, Andrew. *Animal Theology*. London: SCM, 1996.

Lloyd, Michael. "Are Animals Fallen?" In *Animals on the Agenda: Questions about Animals for Theology and Ethics*, edited by Andrew Linzey and Dorothy Yamamoto, 147–60. Urbana: University of Illinois, 1998.

Lohfink, Norbert. "'Macht euch die Erde untertan'?" In *Studien zum Pentateuch*, edited by Norbert Lohfink, 11–28. Stuttgarter biblische Aufsatzbände 4. Stuttgart: Verlag Katholisches Bibelwerk, 1988.

Luomanen, Petri. "Nazirenes." In *A Companion to Second-Century Christian "Heretics,"* edited by Antti Marjanen and Petri Luomanen, 279–314. Leiden: Brill, 2008.

Luzzatto, Samuel D. *The Book of Genesis: A Commentary by ShaDaL*. Edited by Daniel A Klein. Northvale: Aronson, 1998.

MacDonald, Nathan. "Food and Diet in the Priestly Material of the Pentateuch." In *Eating and Believing: Interdisciplinary Perspectives on Vegetarianism and Theology*, edited by Rachel Muers and David Grumett, 17–30. London: T.&T. Clark, 2008.

Maimonides, Moses. *The Guide of the Perplexed*. Chicago: University of Chicago, 1963.

Malkmus, George H. *God's Way to Ultimate Health: A Common Sense Guide for Elimination of Sickness through Nutrition*. Shelby: Hallelujah Acres, 1996.

———. *Why Christians Get Sick*. Eidson: Hallelujah Acres, 2016.

Manson, William. *The Gospel of Luke*. Moffatt New Testament Commentary 3. New York: Harper, 1930.

Marcus, Joel. *Mark 1–8: A New Translation with Introduction and Commentary*. Anchor Bible 27. New York: Doubleday, 2000.

Marshall, I. Howard. *The Gospel of Luke*. New International Greek Testament Commentary. Grand Rapids: Eerdmans, 1978.

Mathews, Kenneth A. *Genesis 1–11:26*. New American Commentary 1A. Nashville: Broadman & Holman, 1996.

Mathewson, David. *A New Heaven and a New Earth the Meaning and Function of the Old Testament in Revelation 21.1—22.5*. Journal for the Study of the New Testament, Supplement Series 238. London; New York: Sheffield Academic, 2003.

Matthews, Gary. "Augustine and Descartes on the Souls of Animals." In *From Soul to Self*, edited by M. James C. Crabbe, 89–107. London: Routledge, 1999.

McCabe, Robert V. "A Defense of Literal Days in the Creation Week." *Westminster Theological Journal* 62 (2000) 113–20.

McDonagh, Sean. *The Greening of the Church*. Maryknoll: Orbis, 1990.

———. *Passion for the Earth: The Christian Vocation to Promote Justice, Peace and the Integrity of Creation*. Quezon City: Claretian, 1995.

McFague, Sallie. *Metaphorical Theology: Models of God in Religious Language*. London: SCM, 1983.

McGrath, Alister E. *A Brief History of Heaven*. Malden: Blackwell, 2003.

Meijer, Fik. *De hond van Odysseus: Het dier in de oudheid*. Amsterdam: Athenaeum-Polak & Van Gennep, 2009.

Methodius of Olympus. "From the Discourse on the Resurrection." In *The Writings of the Fathers down to A.D. 325*, edited by Cleveland Coxe, translated by William Clark, 364–78. Ante-Nicene Fathers 6. Buffalo: CLC, 1886.

Middleton, J. Richard. *The Liberating Image: The Imago Dei in Genesis 1*. Grand Rapids: Brazos, 2005.

Milgrom, Jacob. "Blood." In *Encyclopedia Judaica*, edited by C. Roth and G. Wigoder, Vol. 4. Jerusalem: Keter, 1972.

Mitchell, A. "Three Lions Save Girl." *The Scotsman*, June 22, 2005.

Moberly, R. Walter L. "Why Did Noah Send out a Raven?" *Vetus Testamentum* 50.3 (2000) 345–56.

Moloney, Francis J. *The Gospel of Mark: A Commentary*. Peabody: Hendrickson, 2002.

Moltmann, Jürgen. *Erfahrungen theologischen Denkens: Wege und Formen christlicher Theologie*. Systematischen Beiträge zur Theologie 6. München: Kaiser, 1999.

———. *In der Geschichte des dreieinigen Gottes: Beiträge zur trinitarischen Theologie*. München: Kaiser, 1991.

———. *Gott in der Schöpfung: Ökologische Schöpfungslehre*. Systematischen Beiträge zur Theologie 2. München: Kaiser, 1985.

———. *Das Kommen Gottes: Christliche Eschatologie*. Systematischen Beiträge Zur Theologie 5. München: Kaiser, 1995.

———. "Liebe—Tod—Ewiges Leben: Entwurf einer personalen Eschatologie." In *Im Angesicht des Todes: Ein interdisziplinäres Kompendium*, edited by Hansjakob Becker, Bernhard Einig, and Peter-Otto Ullrich, 2:837–54. Pietas Liturgia 4. St. Ottilien: EOS, 1987.

———. *"Sein Name ist Gerechtigkeit": Neue Beiträge zur christlichen Gotteslehre*. Gütersloh: Gütersloher Verlagshaus, 2008.

———. *Der Weg Jesu Christi: Christologie in messianischen Dimensionen*. Systematischen Beiträge zur Theologie 3. München: Kaiser, 1989.

———. "Is the World Coming to an End or Has Its Future Already Begun?" In *The Future as God's Gift: Explorations in Christian Eschatology*, edited by Marcel Sarot and David Fergusson, 129–38. Edinburgh: T.&T. Clark, 2000.

Moo, Douglas J. "Nature in the New Creation: New Testament Eschatology and the Environment." *Journal of the Evangelical Theological Society* 49.3 (2006) 449–88.

Moo, Jonathan. "The Sea That Is No More: Rev 21:1 and the Function of Sea Imagery in the Apocalypse of John." *Novum Testamentum* 51.2 (2009) 148–67.

Morley, Brian. *God in the Shadows: Evil in God's World*. Ross-shire: Christian Focus, 2006.

Morris, Leon. *The Book of Revelation*. 2nd ed. Tyndale New Testament Commentaries 20. Grand Rapids: Eerdmans, 1987.

Mounce, Robert H. *The Book of Revelation*. The New International Commentary on the New Testament. Grand Rapids: Eerdmans, 1998.

Mouw, Richard J. *When the Kings Come Marching in: Isaiah and the New Jerusalem*. Grand Rapids: Eerdmans, 2002.

Mundia, Wilberforce O. *The Existence of the Devil*. Boston: Boston University, 1994.

Murphy, Nancey C., and George F. R. Ellis. *On the Moral Nature of the Universe: Theology, Cosmology, and Ethics*. Cambridge: International Society for Science and Religion, 2007.

Murray, Michael J. *Nature Red in Tooth and Claw: Theism and the Problem of Animal Suffering*. Oxford: Oxford University, 2011.

Murray, Robert. *The Cosmic Covenant: Biblical Themes of Justice, Peace, and the Integrity of Creation*. London: Sheed & Ward, 1992.

Murti, Vasu. "Loaves and Fishes." https://www.all-creatures.org/murti/art-loaves-fishes.html.

Neusner, Jacob, ed. *B. 'Abodah Zarah*. Translated by Jacob Neusner. The Babylonian Talmud: A Translation and Commentary 17. Nashville: Hendrickson, 2011.

———, ed. *B. Baba Batra*. Translated by Jacob Neusner. The Babylonian Talmud: A Translation and Commentary 15. Nashville: Hendrickson, 2011.

———, ed. *B. Berakhot*. Translated by Jacob Neusner. The Babylonian Talmud: A Translation and Commentary 1. Nashville: Hendrickson, 2011.

———, ed. *B. Gittin*. Translated by Jacob Neusner. The Babylonian Talmud: A Translation and Commentary 11. Nashville: Hendrickson, 2011.

———, ed. *B. Hagigah*. Translated by Jacob Neusner. The Babylonian Talmud: A Translation and Commentary 7. Nashville: Hendrickson, 2011.

———, ed. *B. Hullin*. Translated by Tzvee Zahavy. The Babylonian Talmud: A Translation and Commentary 20. Nashville: Hendrickson, 2011.

———, ed. *B. Ketubot*. Translated by Jacob Neusner. The Babylonian Talmud: A Translation and Commentary 9. Nashville: Hendrickson, 2011.

———, ed. *B. Megillah*. Translated by B. Barry Levy. The Babylonian Talmud: A Translation and Commentary 7. Nashville: Hendrickson, 2011.

———, ed. *B. Pesahim*. Translated by Jacob Neusner. The Babylonian Talmud: A Translation and Commentary 4. Nashville: Hendrickson, 2011.

———, ed. *B. Qiddushin*. Translated by Jacob Neusner. The Babylonian Talmud: A Translation and Commentary 12. Nashville: Hendrickson, 2011.

———, ed. *B. Sanhedrin*. Translated by Jacob Neusner. The Babylonian Talmud: A Translation and Commentary 16. Nashville: Hendrickson, 2011.

———, ed. *B. Sotah*. Translated by Jacob Neusner. The Babylonian Talmud: A Translation and Commentary 11. Nashville: Hendrickson, 2011.

———, ed. *B. Tamid*. Translated by Peter Haas. The Babylonian Talmud: A Translation and Commentary 22. Nashville: Hendrickson, 2011.

———, ed. *B. Yebamot*. Translated by Jacob Neusner. The Babylonian Talmud: A Translation and Commentary 8. Nashville: Hendrickson, 2011.

———. "M. Hullin." In *Mishnah*. New Haven: Yale University Press, 1988.

———. "M. Qiddushin." In *Mishnah*. New Haven: Yale University Press, 1988.

———. "M. Sanhedrin." In *Mishnah*. New Haven: Yale University Press, 1988.

———. "T. Sanhedrin." In *Tosefta*. New Haven: Yale University Press, 1981.

Neville, Richard. "Differentiation in Genesis 1: An Exegetical Creation Ex Nihilo." *Journal of Biblical Literature* 130.2 (2011) 209–26.

Nolland, John. *Luke 18:35—24:53*. Word Biblical Commentary 35C. Dallas: Word, 1993.

Olley, John. "Mixed Blessings for Animals: The Contrasts of Genesis 9." In *The Earth Story in Genesis*, edited by Norman C. Habel and Shirley Wurst, 2:130–39. The Earth Bible 2. Sheffield: Sheffield Academic, 2000.

Origen of Alexandria. *Origen: Contra Celsum*. Translated by Henry Chadwick. Cambridge: Cambridge University, 1980.

Osborne, Grant R. *Revelation*. Baker Exegetical Commentary on the New Testament. Grand Rapids: Baker Academic, 2002.

Oswalt, John N. *The Book of Isaiah: Chapters 1–39*. New International Commentary on the Old Testament. Grand Rapids: Eerdmans, 1986.

———. *The Book of Isaiah: Chapters 40–66*. New International Commentary on the Old Testament. Grand Rapids: Eerdmans, 1998.

Otto, Eckart. *Theologische Ethik des Alten Testaments*. Theologische Wissenschaft 3.2. Stuttgart: Kohlhammer, 1994.

Ouro, Roberto. "The Earth of Genesis 1:2: Abiotic or Chaotic? Part I." *Andrews University Seminary Studies* 36.2 (1998) 6.

Ouweneel, Willem J. *Die Offenbarung Jesu Christi*. Bibelstudien über das Buch der Offenbarung. Bielefeld: CLV, 1997.

Park, Kyung-Chul. *Die Gerechtigkeit Israels und das Heil der Völker: Kultus, Tempel, Eschatologie und Gerechtigkeit in der Endgestalt des Jesajabuches (Jes 56,1–8; 58,1–14; 65,17–66,24)*. Beiträge zur Erforschung des Alten Testaments und des antiken Judentums 52. Frankfurt: Lang, 2003.

Pascal, Blaise. *Pascal's Pensées*. Edited by H. F. Stewart. Routledge Revivals. London: Routledge, 2020.

Patterson, Paige. *Revelation*. New American Commentary 39. Nashville: Broadman & Holman, 2012.

Patton, Kimberley C. "'He Who Sits in the Heavens Laughs': Recovering Animal Theology in the Abrahamic Traditions." *Harvard Theological Review* 93.4 (2000) 401–34.

Philo of Alexandria. "On the Creation: De Opificio Mundi." In *The Works of Philo*, translated by Charles D. Yonge, 1–24. Peabody: Hendrickson, 2005.

———. "Questions on Genesis II: Quaestiones in Genesim II." In *The Works of Philo*, translated by Charles D. Yonge, 814–40. Peabody: Hendrickson, 2005.

———. "On Rewards and Punishments: De Praemiis et Poenis." In *The Works of Philo*, translated by Charles D. Yonge, 664–681. Peabody: Hendrickson, 2005.

Plato. *Republic*. Edited by Chris Emlyn-Jones and William Preddy. Loeb Classical Library 5–6. London: Harvard University, 2013.

Pliny the Elder. *Naturalis Historia*. Edited by Karl Mayhoff. 2 vols. Bibliotheca Scriptorum Graecorum et Romanorum Teubneriana. Monachii: Saur, 2002.

Plummer, Alfred. *A Critical and Exegetical Commentary on the Gospel according to St. Luke*. International Critical Commentary. Edinburgh: T.&T. Clark, 2004.

Plutarch. *Moralia VII*. Edited by Phillip De Lacy and Benedict Einarson. Loeb Classical Library 405. Cambridge: Harvard University, 1958.

Polkinghorne, John C. *Science and the Trinity: The Christian Encounter with Reality*. New Haven: Yale University, 2006.

Possidius of Calama. *The Life of Saint Augustine: A Translation of the Sancti Augustini Vita*. Translated by Herbert T. Weiskotten. Christian Roman Empire Series 6. Merchantville: Evolution, 2008.

Pritchard, James B. *Ancient Near Eastern Texts Relating to the Old Testament*. Princeton: Princeton University, 1969.

Procksch, Otto. *Die Genesis*. Kommentar zum Alten Testament 1. Leipzig: Deichertsche, 1942.

Quackenbush, James. "The Death of a Pet: How It Can Affect Owners." *The Veterinary Clinics of North America, Small Animal Practice* 15.2 (1985) 395–402.

Raabe, Paul R. "'Daddy, Will Animals Be In Heaven?' The Future New Earth." *Concordia Journal* 40.2 (2014) 148–60.

Rahner, Karl. "Auferstehung des Fleisches." In *Schriften zur Theologie*, edited by Karl Rahner, 2:211–25. Einsiedeln: Benziger, 1955.

———. *Auferstehung des Fleisches: Können wir noch daran glauben?* Kevelear: Butzon & Bercker, 1962.

———. "Einheit von Geist und Materie." *Neues Forum* 16.160–61 (1967) 337–40.

———. "Eschatologie." In *Sacramentum Mundi*, edited by Karl Rahner, 1:1184–92. Freiburg: Herder, 1967.

———. "Die ewige Bedeutung der Menschheit Jesu für unser Gottesverhältnis." In *Schriften zur Theologie*, edited by Karl Rahner, 3:47–60. Einsiedeln: Benziger, 1956.

———. *Hörer des Wortes: Schriften zur Religionsphilosophie und zur Grundlegung der Theologie*. Edited by Albert Raffelt. Sämtliche Werke 4. Freiburg: Herder, 1997.

———. "Immanente und transzendente Vollendung der Welt." In *Schriften zur Theologie*, edited by Karl Rahner, 8:593–609. Einsiedeln: Benziger, 1967.

———. "Der Leib in der Heilsordnung." In *Schriften zur Theologie*, edited by Karl Rahner, 12:407–27. Einsiedeln: Benziger, 1975.

———. "Theologische Prinzipien der Hermeneutik eschatologischer Aussagen." In *Schriften zur Theologie*, edited by Karl Rahner, 4:401–28. Einsiedeln: Benziger, 1960.

———. "Über die Theologische Problematik der 'Neue Erde.'" In *Schriften zur Theologie*, edited by Karl Rahner, 8:580–92. Einsiedeln: Benziger, 1967.

Ratzinger, Joseph. *In the Beginning: A Catholic Understanding of the Story of Creation and the Fall*. Ressourcement. Edinburgh: T.&T. Clark, 2005.

Raven, Charles E., and Joseph Needham. *The Creator Spirit: A Survey of Christian Doctrine in the Light of Biology, Psychology and Mysticism*. Hulsean Lectures, Cambridge, 1926-27. London: Hopkinson & Co, 1932.

Rendtorff, Rolf. "Some Reflections on Creation as a Topic of Old Testament Theology." In *Priests, Prophets, and Scribes: Essays on the Formation and Heritage of Second Temple Judaism in Honour of Joseph Blenkinsopp*, edited by Joseph Blenkinsopp and Eugene Ulrich. Journal for the Study of the Old Testament. Supplement Series 149. Sheffield: JSOT, 1992.

Richter, Sandra. "Environmental Law in Deuteronomy: One Lens on a Biblical Theology of Creation Care." *Bulletin for Biblical Research* 20.3 (2010) 355-76.

Riede, Peter. *Im Spiegel der Tiere: Studien zum Verhältnis von Mensch und Tier im alten Israel*. Orbis Biblicus et Orientalis 187. Göttingen: Vandenhoeck und Ruprecht, 2002.

Rienecker, Fritz. *Das Evangelium des Matthäus*. Wuppertaler Studienbibel. Wuppertal: Brockhaus, 1953.

Roloff, Jürgen. *The Revelation of John*. Continental Commentary. Minneapolis: Fortress, 1993.

Rolston, Holmes, III. "Does Nature Need to Be Redeemed?" *Zygon* 29.2 (1994) 205-29.

Roop, Eugene F. *Genesis*. Believers Church Bible Commentary. Scottdale: Herald, 1987.

Rosner, Fred. "Eating Fish and Meat Together: Is There a Danger?" *Tradition: A Journal of Orthodox Jewish Thought* 35.2 (2001) 36-44.

Sailhamer, John. *Genesis Unbound: A Provocative New Look at the Creation Account*. Colorado Springs: Dawson Media, 2011.

Samuelson, Norbert M. *Judaism and the Doctrine of Creation*. Cambridge: Cambridge University, 2010.

Sandy, Brent. *Plowshares and Pruning Hooks: Rethinking the Language of Biblical Prophecy and Apocalyptic*. Westmont: InterVarsity, 2013.

Sanford, Charles L. *The Quest for Paradise: Europe and the American Moral Imagination*. New York: AMS, 1979.

Sarfati, Jonathan D. *Refuting Evolution 2: Updated and Expanded*. 3rd ed. Atlanta: Creation Book, 2013.

Sarna, Nahum M. *Genesis [Bereshit]: The Traditional Hebrew Text with New JPS Translation*. JPS Torah Commentary. Philadelphia: JPS, 1989.

Schaeffer, Francis A. *Pollution and the Death of Man*. Wheaton: Tyndale, 1970.

Schenderling, Jacques. *Mens en dier in theologisch perspectief: Een bijdrage aan het debat over de morele status van het dier*. Zoetermeer: Boekencentrum, 1999.

Schlatter, Adolf. *Der Evangelist Matthäus: Seine Sprache, sein Ziel, seine Selbständigkeit. Ein Kommentar zum 1. Evangelium*. Stuttgart: Calwer, 1929.

Schneemelcher, Wilhelm. *New Testament Apocrypha: Gospels and Related Writings*. Edited by R. McL. Wilson. Cambridge: Clarke & Co., 1991.

Schneider, Dieter. *Der Prophet Jesaja: Kapitel 1-39*. Wuppertaler Studienbibel. Wuppertal: Brockhaus, 1997.

Schochet, Elijah J. *Animal Life in Jewish Tradition: Attitudes and Relationships: Attitudes and Relationships*. New York: Ktav, 1984.

Schulze, Wilhelm August. "Der Heilige und die wilden Tiere." *Zeitschrift für die neutestamentliche Wissenschaft und die Kunde der älteren Kirche* 46.3-4 (1955) 280-83.

Schwartz, Richard H. *Judaism and Vegetarianism*. New York: Lantern, 2001.

———. "Tsa'ar Ba'alei Chayim—Judaism and Compassion for Animals." In *Judaism and Animal Rights: Classical and Contemporary Responses*, edited by Roberta Kalechofsky, 59–70. Marblehead: Micah, 2002.

Scott, Nora E. "The Daily Life of the Ancient Egyptians." Repr. 1997. *Metropolitan Museum of Art Bulletin* 31.3 (1973) 1–52.

Scott, Walter. *Exposition of the Revelation of Jesus Christ*. Westwood: Revell, 1968.

Seely, Paul H. "The Firmament and the Water Above." *Westminster Theological Journal* 53 (1991) 227–40.

Sharkin, Bruce S., and Donna Knox. "Pet Loss: Issues and Implications for the Psychologist." *Professional Psychology: Research and Practice* 34.4 (2003) 414–21.

Shaw, Teresa M. "Vegetarianism, Heresy, and Asceticism in Late Ancient Christianity." In *Eating and Believing: Interdisciplinary Perspectives on Vegetarianism and Theology*, edited by David Grumett and Rachel Muers, 75–95. Edinburgh: T.&T. Clark, 2011.

Skillen, James W. "The Seven Days of Creation." *Calvin Theological Journal* 46 (2011) 111–39.

Sneddon, Lynne U. "The Evidence for Pain in Fish: The Use of Morphine as an Analgesic." *Applied Animal Behaviour Science* 83.2 (2003) 153–62.

Snyder, Barbara W. *Combat Myth in the Apocalypse: The Liturgy of the Day of the Lord and the Dedication of the Heavenly Temple*. California: University of California at Berkeley, 1992.

Southgate, Christopher. *The Groaning of Creation: God, Evolution, and the Problem of Evil*. Louisville: Westminster John Knox, 2008.

———. "Protological and Eschatological Vegetarianism." In *Eating and Believing: Interdisciplinary Perspectives on Vegetarianism and Theology*, edited by Rachel Muers and David Grumett, 247–65. London: T.&T. Clark, 2008.

Spencer, Colin. *Vegetarianism: A History*. Havertown, PA: Grub Street, 2016.

Stein, Robert H. *Luke*. New American Commentary 24. Nashville: Broadman & Holman, 1993.

Stek, John H. "What Says the Scriptures?" In *Portraits of Creation: Biblical and Scientific Perspectives on the World's Formation*, edited by Howard J. van Till, 203–65. Grand Rapids: Eerdmans, 1990.

Stipp, Hermann-Josef. "'Alles Fleisch hatte seinen Wandel auf der Erde verdorben' (Gen 6,12): Die Mitverantwortung der Tierwelt an der Sintflut nach der Priesterschrift." *Zeitschrift für die alttestamentliche Wissenschaft* 111.2 (1999) 167–86.

———. "Dominium Terrae: Die Herrschaft der Menschen über die Tiere in Gen 1,26.28." In *Alttestamentliche Studien: Arbeiten zu Priesterschrift, Deuteronomistischem Geschichtswerk und Prophetie*, edited by Hermann-Josef Stipp, 53–94. Beihefte zur Zeitschrift für die alttestamentliche Wissenschaft 442. Berlin: De Gruyter, 2013.

Sweeney, Emmet. *The Pyramid Age 2: Ages in Alignment Series*. New York: Algora, 2007.

Swinburne, Richard. *The Existence of God*. 2nd ed. Oxford: Clarendon, 2004.

Templeton, Charles. *Farewell to God: My Reasons for Rejecting the Christian Faith*. Toronto: McClelland & Stewart, 1999.

Tertullian, Quintus. "On Fasting in Opposition to the Psychics." In *Hippolytus, Cyprian, Caius, Novatian*, edited by Cleveland Coxe, Alexander Roberts, and James Donaldson, translated by S. Thelwall, 102–16. Ante-Nicene Fathers 4. Buffalo: CLC, 1885.

Teugels, Lieve M., trans. *Aggadat Bereshit*. Jewish and Christian Perspectives Series 4. Boston: Brill, 2001.

Thiel, John E. "For What May We Hope? Thoughts on the Eschatological Imagination." *Theological Studies* 67.3 (2006) 517–41.

Thiselton, Anthony C. "The Future of Biblical Interpretation and Responsible Plurality in Hermeneutics." In *The Future of Biblical Interpretation: Responsible Plurality in Hermeneutics*, edited by Stanley E Porter and Matthew R. Malcolm, 11–27. Downers Grove: IVP Academic, 2013.

Thurneysen, Eduard. "Christus und seine Zukunft: Ein Beitrag zur Eschatologie." *Zwischen den Zeiten* 9 (1931) 187–211.

Tigay, Jeffrey H. *Deuteronomy: The Traditional Hebrew Text with the New JPS Translation*. JPS Torah Commentary. Philadelphia: JPS, 1996.

Trethowan, Illtyd. *An Essay in Christian Philosophy*. London: Longmans Green and Co., 1954.

Tsumura, David T. *The Earth and the Waters in Genesis 1 and 2: A Linguistic Investigation*. Journal for the Study of the Old Testament. Supplement Series 83. Sheffield: Sheffield Academic, 2009.

Twain, Mark. *Letters from the Earth: Uncensored Writings*. Edited by Bernard De Voto. New York: Perennial Classics, 2004.

Vaclavik, Charles P. *The Vegetarianism of Jesus Christ: Pristine Christianity's Dietary Testimony*. Three Rivers: Kaweah, 1986.

Van de Beek, A. (Bram). *God doet recht: Eschatologie als christologie*. Spreken over God, 2.1. Zoetermeer: Meinema, 2008.

Van der Poll, Evert. *Sacred Times for Chosen People: Development, Analysis and Missiological Significance of Messianic Jewish Holiday Practice*. Zoetermeer: Boekencentrum, 2008.

Van Leeuwen, Raymond C. "Cosmos, Temple, House: Building and Wisdom in Mesopotamia and Israel." In *Wisdom Literature in Mesopotamia and Israel*, edited by Richard J. Clifford, 67–90. Society of Biblical Literature Symposium Series 36. Leiden: Brill, 2007.

Von Rad, Gerhard. *Genesis: A Commentary*. 2nd ed. Louisville: Westminster John Knox, 1973.

Waddell, Helen. *Beasts and Saints*. Grand Rapids: Eerdmans, 1996.

Walker, Pamela J. *Pulling the Devil's Kingdom Down: The Salvation Army in Victorian Britain*. Berkeley: University of California, 2001.

Waltke, Bruce K. "Kingdom Promises as Spiritual." In *Continuity and Discontinuity: Perspectives on the Relationship between the Old and New Testaments*, edited by John S. Feinberg, 263–87. Westchester: Crossway, 1988.

———. *An Old Testament Theology: An Exegetical, Canonical, and Thematic Approach*. Grand Rapids: Zondervan, 2008.

Walton, John H. *Ancient Israelite Literature in Its Cultural Context: A Survey of Parallels between Biblical and Ancient Near Eastern Texts*. Library of Biblical Interpretation. Grand Rapids: Regency Reference Library, 1989.

Ward, Keith. *The Concept of God*. Glasgow: Collins, 1977.

———. *Pascal's Fire: Scientific Faith and Religious Understanding*. New York: Oneworld, 2013.

———. *Rational Theology and the Creativity of God*. Oxford: Basil Blackwell, 1985.

Webb, Barry G. *The Message of Isaiah: On Eagles' Wings*. Bible Speaks Today. Leicester: InterVarsity, 1996.

Webb, Stephen H. *Good Eating*. Christian Practice of Everyday Life. Grand Rapids: Brazos, 2001.

Wenham, Gordon. *Genesis 1–15*. Word Biblical Commentary 1. Dallas: Word, 1987.
Wenkel, David H. "Wild Beasts in the Prophecy of Isaiah: The Loss of Dominion and Its Renewal through Israel as the New Humanity." *Journal of Theological Interpretation* 5.2 (2011) 251–64.
Wesley, John. "Sermon 60: The General Deliverance." In *First Series of Sermons (40–53). Second Series Begun (54–86)*, 3rd ed. Works of John Wesley 6. Grand Rapids: Baker, 2007.
Wessels, Marc A. "The Spiritual Link between Humans and Animals." *Prism* 5.2 (1990) 25–36.
Westermann, Claus. *Genesis 1–11: A Continental Commentary*. Translated by John J. Scullion. Minneapolis: Fortress, 1994.
White, Ellen G.H. *Education*. Oakland: Pacific, 1903.
———. *Testimonies for the Church*. 4th ed. 9 vols. Mountain View: Pacific, 1948.
White, Lynn T. "The Historical Roots of Our Ecologic Crisis." *Science* 155.3767 (1967) 1203–7.
Wildberger, Hans. "Das Abbild Gottes." *Theologische Zeitschrift* 21 (1965) 481–501.
Wilkinson, David. *Christian Eschatology and the Physical Universe*. London: T.&T. Clark, 2010.
Williams, J. Rodman. *Systematische Theologie aus charismatischer Sicht*. Vol. 1. Wuppertal: One-Way, 1995.
Williams, Norman P. *The Ideas of the Fall and of Original Sin: A Historical and Critical Study*. London: Longmans, Green and co., 1927.
Wirzba, Norman. *The Paradise of God: Renewing Religion in an Ecological Age*. Oxford: Oxford University, 2007.
Wiseman, Donald J. "Mesopotamian Gardens." *Anatolian Studies* 33 (1983) 137–44.
Witherington, Ben. *The Gospel of Mark: A Socio-Rhetorical Commentary*. Grand Rapids: Eerdmans, 2001.
Wright, Christopher J. H. *The Mission of God: Unlocking the Bible's Grand Narrative*. Westmont: InterVarsity, 2013.
Wright, N. T. *The Resurrection of the Son of God*. Christian Origins and the Question of God 3. London: SPCK, 2003.
Yamauchi, Edwin M. "Banquets in the Biblical World." *Proceedings, Eastern Great Lakes and Midwest Biblical Societies* 22 (2002) 147–57.
Yeatts, John R. *Revelation*. Believers Church Bible Commentary. Scottdale: Herald, 2003.
Zahn, Theodor. *Das Evangelium des Lucas*. Kommentar zum Neuen Testament 3. Leipzig: Deichert, 1913.
Zenger, Erich. *Gottes Bogen in den Wolken: Untersuchungen zu Komposition und Theologie des priesterschriftlichen Urgeschichte*. Stuttgarter Bibelstudien 112. Stuttgart: Verl. Kath. Bibelwerk, 1987.
Zimmerli, Walther. *Old Testament Theology in Outline*. Translated by David E. Green. Edinburgh: T.&T. Clark, 2000.
Zlotowitz, Meir. *Bereishis 1:1—28:9*. ArtScroll Tanach Series. New York: Mesorah, 2007.

Subject Index

Adam and Eve, nakedness, 73–74
Animal suffer, 2, 49–55, 78–88
Animal welfare, 2–3, 83, 109–11, 206
Animals in human history, 78–88

Balaam, 45–48, 198
Biblical Theology, 4, 8, 12, 61, 207
Breastplate of the high priest, 72

Creation story, 7–19
Crown of creation, 18–19

Eden, 4, 18, 27, 20–29, 38–39, 43–48, 59–66, 71–75, 100, 129–30, 160, 167, 202, 207
Enuma Elish, 22–23, 60
Eschatology of Genesis 1–3, 20–29
European gods, 14
Ex nihilo, x, 21, 144

Firstborn of creation, 11, 26, 157

Gnosticism, 28, 149–50, 160, 205

Heavenly Jerusalem, 11, 142, 148, 177–78

Interpretation of prophecy, 136–69

Jewish Feasts, 26–27, 216
Leviathan, 15, 68, 70

Macrocosmic-microcosmic temple, 12, 22, 73, 196, 214–16

Mesopotamian religions, 14, 18, 22–23, 82
Messiah, reign, 11, 24–28, 121–33, 157–69
Messianic Kingdom, 121–28, 148, 194–96

New creation, 5–6, 19–20, 24–28, 127–29, 140–63, 188–201
Nicea-Constantinople confession, 20
Noah, story of, 89–107
Noah's ark, 94–96

Old and new clothes, 76–77

Paradisiacal Conditions 7–29
Plagues of Egypt, 38, 117–20, 173–75, 179, 201

Rainbow, 104–5, 138

Sabbath, seventh day of creation, 9, 19, 26–27, 37–38, 108–11, 160, 200, 209
Serpent, 43–45, 126
Sons of God, 59–60, 89, 90–92, 100, 137, 192, 225
Spirit of God, 10, 20–21, 26, 50, 153–55
Subdue the earth/land, 30–47

Tree of knowledge, 43, 47, 61, 66, 74–75
Two trees in the Garden, 60–61

Vegetarian, 2, 203–21

Author Index

Adams, Cindy, 186
Adams, Edward, 171
Aelianus, Claudius, 133
Akers, Keith, 211–12
Akiva ben Joseph, 210
Alford, Henry, 197
Allen, Edgar, 18
Allen, Leslie, 139
Althaus, Paul, 161
Ambrose of Milan, 204
Anderson, Hugh, 167
Appel, Mirjam, 51
Aquinas, Thomas, 3, 158, 188–89
Archer, John, 186
Aristotle, 32, 189
Arndt, William, 222
Athanasius, 204
Athenaeus of Naucratis, 83
Attfield, Robin, 143
Augustine of Hippo, 53, 71, 189, 203, 205
Aune, David, 181, 197

Bacon, Francis, 33
Bar Nafha, Yohanan, 20, 70
Barr, James, 31, 36, 61
Barth, Karl, ix, 4, 215
Basil of Caesarea, 204–5
Bauckham, Richard, 130, 167, 177, 181, 199
Beale, Gregory, 61, 72–73, 139, 146, 181–82, 197
Ben Jitschaki (Rashi), Sjlomo, 10, 12, 14–15, 18, 120
Ben Josef, Akiva, 17

Berkouwer, Gerrit, 161
Bernstein, Ellen, 33
Beyerlin, Walter, 198
Bischoff, Erich, 101
Bleich, David, 110
Blocher, Henri, 51–52
Block, Daniel, 73, 139
Bock, Darrell, 221–22
Boehmer, Julius, 166
Bonting, Sjoerd, 21
Bornkamm, Günther, 151
Bouma-Prediger, Steven, 34
Boyd, Gregory, 59, 63, 68
Boyer, Paul, 170
Braaten, Carl, 137
Braun, Joseph, 133
Brueggemann, Walter, 105, 196
Brunner, Emil, 142–43
Buber, Salomon, 10, 20, 70, 92
Buber, Samuel, 20, 70
Butler, Trent, 221
Bynum, Caroline, 144

Caird, George, 141, 146, 174
Calvin, John, 40, 65, 71, 192, 207
Caneday, Ardel, 129
Carmichael, Calum, 114
Cassuto, Umberto, 39, 97, 105
Chafer, Lewis, 145
Chang, Hae-Kyung, 58
Charlesworth, James, 44
Charron, Bertrand, 91
Christensen, Duane, 112
Chrysostom, John, 189
Cicero, M. Tullius, 32

Author Index

Clark, Stephen, 190
Clifford, Richard, 13
Coad, Dominic, 199
Cobb, John, 211
Cohn, Norman, 22
Collins, C. John, 39, 60
Collon, D., 216–17
Cooper, Lamar, 139
Cowles, Kathleen, 185
Craghan, John, 167
Currid, John, 22

Dalman, Gustaf, 113
Darwin, Charles, 49–50
Delio, Ilia, 21
Delitzsch, Franz, 70, 90, 97, 207
Delling, Gerhard, 148
Descartes, René, 33
Donahue, John, 130
Dougherty, Trent, 51, 59

Easley, Kendell, 197
Eliade, Mircea, 122
Ellis, George, 53
Ellsberg, Daniel, 174
Elwood, Robert, 51
Enns, Peter, 117
Ernst, Josef, 222
Eshnunna, 116
Eve, Eric, 167

Faro, Ingrid, 55, 61
Farrer, Austin, 52
Fekkes, Jan, 182
Fensham, F. Charles, 101
Ferrier, J. Todd, 213
Feuerbach, Ludwig, 33
Field, Nigel, 185
Fisher, Loren, 12
Fitzmyer, Joseph, 166
Fletcher-Watts, Vivienne, 93
Ford, J., 181
France, Richard, 129
Frear, George, 211
Freedman, Harry, 11, 13, 15, 18, 25–26,
    39, 41–42, 45, 74, 92, 110, 173,
    207
Fretheim, Terence, 61, 91, 103, 117

Froom, LeRoy, 124

Garrett, Duane, 23, 44
Garroway, Joshua, 169
Geisler, Annette, 184
Gerwolls, Marilyn, 185
Gesenius, Wilhelm, 220
Ghirshman, Roman, 217
Giamatti, A. Bartlett, 31
Gibson, Jeffrey, 129
Gill, John, 171
Gilmour, Michael, 167
Gindi, Joseph, 33
Gleason, Kathryn, 82
Goldingay, John, 8, 12
Goldwurm, Hersh, 213
Gordon, Cyrus, 113
Graf, G. Robert, 143
Gregory of Nyssa, 155–56, 163
Guelich, Robert, 130
Gundry, Robert, 129
Gunkel, Hermann, 32
Gunton, Colin, 6, 21, 192

Habermas, Gary, 190
Habig, Marion, 187
Hagencord, Rainer, 190
Hamilton, Victor, 34, 91, 207
Hammurabi, 116
Happ, Heinz, 189
Haran, Menahem, 114
Harland, Peter, 91
Harrington, Daniel, 130
Harrison, Lucy, 186
Harrison, Peter, 33
Hartl, Gregory, 87
Hartog, John, 190
Hausoul, Raymond, ix–xi, 5, 11, 67, 73,
    111, 128, 137, 144, 146, 152,
    154, 160–61
Heil, John, 129
Hick, John, 67
Hildenbrand, Michael, 111
Hillers, Delbert, 198
Hoekema, Anthony, 146–47
Holladay, William, 220
Homer, 46, 216
Horrell, David, 199

Author Index

Houston, Walter, 93
Hütterman, Aloys, 111–12
Hyrkanos, Elieser, 74–75

Ickert, Scott, 215
Irenaeus of Lyon, 21, 66, 146, 155–56, 158–59, 163–64, 205

Jacob, Benno, 77–79, 113
Jaki, Stanley, 12
Jauhiainen, Marko, 182
Jenson, Robert, 59
Jeremias, Joachim, 222
Jerome, 71, 133
Johnson, 59
Johnston, Gordon, 22

Kaiser, Otto, 44, 129
Kant, Immanuel, 143
Kara, Simeon, 10, 75
Kärkkäinen, Veli-Matti, ix–xi, 4, 191
Kaufman Nathaniel, 185
Kaufman, Kenneth, 185
Keel, Othmar, 114, 198
Keil, Carl, 70, 90, 97, 207
Keiter, Sheila, 98
Kelly, Stewart, 68
King, Philip, 217
Kistemaker, Simon, 197
Kline, Meredith, 12, 73
Knauf, Ernst, 114
Koch, Klaus, 34
Kornfeld, Walter, 93
Kowalski, Beate, 182
Küng, Hans, 137
Kurz, Gary, 190

Labuschagne, Casper, 113
Ladd, George, 161, 197
Landau, Yehezkel, 170
Lane, William, 25, 166–67
Larwood, Gilbert, 94
Lawee, Eric, 41, 93
Le Goff, Jacques, 75
Lehmann, Ulrich, 94
Lenski, Richard, 146
Levenson, Jon, 24, 68
Lewis, Clive, 9, 64, 196

Lewis, Jack, 9
Lichtheim, Miriam, 46
Lietzmann, Hans, 134
Linzey, Andrew, 206, 212
Lloyd, Michael, 59
Lohfink, Norbert, 34
Loprieno, Antonio, 46
Luomanen, Petri, 212
Luzzatto, Samuel, 207

MacDonald, Nathan, 207
Maimonides, Moses, 14, 122, 192–93
Manson, William, 166
Marcus, Joel, 130
Marshall, Howard, 221
Mathews, Kenneth, 16, 60
Mathewson, David, 182
Matthews, Gary, 33
Maurice, Simon, 11, 13, 15, 18, 25–26, 39, 41–42, 45, 74, 92, 110, 173, 207
McCabe, Robert, 9
McDonagh, Sean, 212
McFague, Sallie, 141
McGrath, Alister, x
Meijer, Fik, 133
Methodius of Olympus, 155–56, 159
Middleton, Richard, 23
Milgrom, Jacob, 101
Mitchell, A., 135
Moberly, R. Walter, 98
Moloney, Francis, 130
Moltmann, Jürgen, ix, 67, 140, 152, 158, 164–65
Moo, Douglas, 144
Moo, Jonathan, 181–82
Morley, Brian, 51
Morris, Leon, 197
Mounce, Robert, 181
Mouw, Richard, 124
Mundia, Wilberforce, 68
Murphy, Nancey, 53
Murray, Michael, 59
Murray, Robert, 36
Murti, Vasu, 212

Nathan the Babylonian, 16–17
Needham, Joseph, 50

Author Index

Neusner, Jacob, 10, 12, 15, 18, 24, 32, 41, 71, 75, 92, 111, 113, 115, 207, 209, 213, 219, 223
Neville, Richard, 16
Nolland, John, 221–22

Olley, John, 3
Origen of Alexandria, 71, 146, 155–56, 159
Osborne, Grant, 181, 197
Oswalt, John, 122–23, 194, 220
Otto, Eckart, 100
Ouro, Roberto, 10
Ouweneel, Willem, 172

Park, Kyung-Chul, 123
Pascal, Blaise, 161
Patterson, Paige, 197
Patton, Kimberley, 199
Philo of Alexandria, 23, 97, 125–26
Plato, 203–4
Pliny the Elder, 85, 133–34
Plummer, Alfred, 166
Plutarch, 180, 204
Polkinghorne, John, 201
Possidius of Calama, 205
Pritchard, James, 221
Procksch, Otto, 32
Pythagoras of Samos, 2,3 203

Quackenbush, James, 185

Raabe, Paul, 146
Rahner, Karl, x, 138–39, 159–60, 164
Ratzinger, Joseph, 28
Raven, Charles, 50
Rendtorff, Rolf, 4
Richter, Sandra, 87
Riede, Peter, 42
Rienecker, Fritz, 167
Roloff, Jürgen, 181
Rolston, Holmes, 53
Roop, Eugene, 26
Rosner, Fred, 209

Sailhamer, John, 60
Samuelson, Norbert, 9, 11, 15, 17, 25
Sandy, Brent, 138–39

Sanford, Charles, 31
Sarfati, Jonathan, 64
Sarna, Nahum, 91, 97
Schaeffer, Francis, 33
Schenderling, Jacques, 133, 187
Schlatter, Adolf, 166
Schneemelcher, Wilhelm, 131
Schneider, Dieter, 220
Schochet, Elijah, 112
Schulze, Wilhelm, 133
Schwartz, Richard, 110, 208
Scott, Nora, 216
Scott, Walter, 146
Seely, Paul, 13
Sharkin, Bruce, 185–86
Shaw, Teresa, 204
Sjlomo Yitzchaki (Rashi), 9, 10, 12–15, 18, 41, 120
Skillen, James, 12
Sneddon, Lynne, 51
Snyder, Barbara, 182
Southgate, Christopher, 59, 191, 206, 211
Spencer, Colin, 210
Stager, Lawrence, 217
Stek, John, 23
Stipp, Hermann-Josef, 91, 93
Sweeney, Emmet, 118
Swinburne, Richard, 68

Templeton, Charles, 50
Tertullian, Quintus, 204
Teugels, Lieve, 209
Thiel, John, 143
Thiselton, Anthony, 138
Thurneysen, Eduard, 160–61
Tigay, Jeffrey, 112
Trethowan, Illtyd, 50
Tsumura, David, 22, 60
Twain, Mark, 54

Vaclavik, Charles, 211–12
Van de Beek, A. (Bram), 155, 164
Van der Poll, Evert, 26
Van Leeuwen, Raymond, 12
Von Rad, Gerhard, 10

Waddell, Helen, 134

Walker, Pamela, 210
Waltke, Bruce, 61, 159, 207
Walton, John, 22
Ward, Keith, 191
Webb, Barry, 123
Webb, Stephen, 211–12
Wenham, Gordon, 10, 26, 73, 91, 97
Wenkel, David, 124
Wesley, John, 188, 192, 205
Wessels, Marc, 199
Westermann, Claus, 6, 33–34, 76
White, Ellen, 205, 210, 214
White, Lynn, 30–31, 33
Wildberger, Hans, 36
Wilkinson, David, 137
Williams, Norman, 59

Williams, Rodman, 9
Winchester, Gillian, 186
Wirzba, Norman, 111
Wiseman, Donald, 82
Witherington, Ben, 167
Wright, Christopher, 36
Wright, Tom, 144, 214–15

Yamauchi, Edwin, 218, 223
Yeatts, John, 197

Zahn, Theodor, 166
Zenger, Erich, 105
Zimmerli, Walther, 4
Zlotowitz, Meir, 10, 12–16, 77

Ancient Document Index

OLD TESTAMENT/ HEBREW BIBLE

Genesis

Reference	Pages
1–11	6
1–3	62, 67, 92, 124
1–2	5, 27, 48, 59, 62–63, 65–66, 98, 128, 137, 152, 160, 183, 202, 207, 209, 215
1	7–20, 30–37, 39–40, 60, 63–64, 76, 93, 95, 98, 105, 183, 213
1:1	6, 25, 59
1:2	10, 21, 24, 60, 96–97, 173, 181
1:3	11, 20
1:5	25
1:6	13, 20
1:7	20
1:8	12, 25
1:9–10	98
1:9	20
1:10	13–14, 17
1:11	20
1:12	13–14, 17
1:13	25
1:14	20, 26
1:15	10, 20
1:17	13
1:19	25
1:20–21	15
1:20	20
1:21	15, 190
1:22	16, 20, 160
1:23	25
1:24–30	200
1:24	8, 15, 18, 20, 190
1:25	16–17
1:26–29	20
1:26–28	30–34
1:26	15, 17, 20, 30, 33, 37, 76, 101
1:28	15, 17, 20, 27, 29, 32, 35, 40, 59–60, 76–77, 92, 98, 102, 124, 160–61
1:29–30	37, 65, 206
1:29	18, 20, 65, 206
1:30	15, 20, 65, 190
1:31	25, 61, 90, 103
2–3	44, 74
2	38–42, 61, 65, 105
2:1–24	75
2:3	18, 20, 25
2:4–7	60
2:4–6	74
2:4	9, 18
2:5–6	105
2:5	38
2:7–24	74
2:7–8	43
2:7	6, 15, 18, 39, 190
2:8–9	73
2:9	43, 73–74
2:10	73

Genesis (*cont.*)

2:15	39, 43, 59–60, 68, 73, 124
2:16–17	74, 98
2:19–20	42, 100, 200, 206
2:19	6, 15, 18, 39, 190
2:20	41
2:23	41
2:25	44, 73, 74–75
3	14, 17–18, 42–48, 55–59, 61–68, 70–71, 76–77, 90, 92–93, 100, 102–3, 124, 183, 207–8
3:1	28, 43–44, 46, 59–60, 66, 75
3:6	43
3:7	99
3:8	73–74
3:10	74, 99
3:13	44
3:14–19	48
3:14	45, 58, 127, 195
3:15	77, 99
3:16	62
3:17–21	75
3:17–18	58
3:17	38, 56, 62
3:18	45
3:20	44
3:21	70
3:22–24	202
3:22–23	62
3:22	61, 76
3:23	93
3:24	47, 73
4–6	103
4	45, 90, 101–2
4:1–23	102
4:1	102
4:7	60
4:8–11	101
4:8	45
4:9	101
4:10–12	102
4:12	38, 58, 93
4:15	103
4:16	93
4:19	92
4:23–24	92, 102
4:26	103
5	213
5:22–24	89
5:29	58
6–9	91, 103
6–8	117
6	59–61, 67, 90, 92–93, 100, 103
6:1–12	200
6:1–4	59, 89, 92
6:2	92
6:4	90
6:5	59, 60, 90, 92–93
6:6	119
6:7	103
6:8	89–90, 103
6:11–13	91, 101
6:11–12	90, 93
6:11	92
6:12	91, 103
6:13	91–92
6:15	95
6:16	95
6:17	91
6:18–20	100, 103, 200
6:19	91
7	93
7:2	119
7:4	119
7:8–9	65
7:9	119
7:11–12	12
7:11	97
7:12	91, 119
7:15–16	91
7:17	119
7:21	91
8	98
8:1	96–98, 119
8:4	96
8:6	119
8:7	97
8:9	97
8:14	119

8:21	90, 103, 209	2:16	79
8:22	104	3:1	79
9	92, 101–3, 105	3:13–14	118
9:1–7	102	7:18	117
9:1	76, 98, 102, 104	7:20	173
9:2	67, 100	7:21	117
9:2–6	93	8:1–18	117
9:3–4	208	9:3–4	117
9:3	100, 213	9:10	117
9:4	93, 99	9:23–25	172
9:5	68, 91	11–15	118
9:5–6	102, 116	11:5–7	117–18
9:6	101	12:7–13	117
9:7	17, 102, 104	13:2	118
9:8–17	91, 106, 200	16:22–30	20
9:9–10	104, 106	19:13	116
9:11	91, 104	19:16	175
9:15–16	105	20:8–11	108–9, 200
9:15	91	20:10	160
9:22–25	99	20:11	197
9:22–23	73	20:18	175
9:25	99	20:10	37
9:26–27	99	20:11	9
10:8–9	90	20:13	101
10:9	77	20:26	73
12:16	78	21:10	76
13:10	27	21:13	102
13:5	78	21:28–32	101, 108, 116
13:6	78	21:28–29	68
14:5	90	21:28	116
15:5	17	22:1–2	102
20:14	78	23:1–2	114
24:35	78	23:4–5	108, 114
26:14	79	23:4	166
27:15	77	23:7–9	114
27:28	159	23:12	37, 109
28:16–17	22	23:18	113
29:22	216	23:19	108, 112–13
29:27	216	23:26	18
30:43	79	23:29	37
32:6	79	24:11	219
41:42	77	24:16	9
		25:8–40	73
Exodus		26:7	71
		27:9–16	73
1:8–22	175	28:42–43	74
1:11	116	30:34–36	72
1:16	116	31:17	9

Exodus (cont.)

34:3	116
34:26–27	112–13
34:29	24
39:3	12

Leviticus

3:3	220
3:17	101
4:8–9	220
7:26–27	101
10:10	8
11:1–47	207
11:7–8	167
11	44, 93, 209
11:4	93
11:6	93
11:11	91
11:46–47	8
17:10	101
17:14	93, 101
18:6–10	73
18:23	41
19:26	101
20:15–16	101, 116
20:17–19	73
23:9–14	97
25:1–7	111, 160
25:23	111
25:43	35
25:46	35
25:53	35
26:3–12	48
26:6	37, 48, 106, 126
26:9	17
26:12	48
26:17	35
26:21–22	17
26:22	83
26:43	38
26:45	106

Numbers

3:7–8	73
8:25–26	73
11:4	209
11:5	210
11:20	209
11:34	209
13:21–33	90
13:33	90
22:22–35	45–46, 47–48
23:10–24	48
24:5–17	48
32:22–29	35, 59
35:6–34	102

Deuteronomy

2:10–11	90
2:20–21	90
3:11–13	90
4:31	106
5:16	112, 114
7:14	18
9:2	90
11:15	111
11:25	100
12:16–24	101
12:20–21	210
14	44, 93
14:1–21	207, 209
14:21	113
19:1–13	102
19:15	102
20:19–20	112
21:1–9	115
21:18–21	209
22:1–4	108, 114
22:4	166
22:6–7	108–11
22:9–11	115
22:10	108, 115
25:4	37, 108–10
32:11	97
32:22	145
32:24	83
32:42	104

Joshua

6:21	117
7:24	117
5:12	97

11:21–22	90	**1 Chronicles**	
12:4	90	20:4–8	90
13:12	90	22:18	35, 59
14:12	90		
14:15	90	**2 Chronicles**	
15:8	90	8:10	35
15:14	90	28:10	35
17:5	90	36:21	38
18:1–2	35, 59		
18:16	90	**Nehemiah**	

Judges

1:20	90	5:5	35, 59
9:8	45	5:17–18a	80
9:27	216	9:6	197
14:10	216	9:28	35

Esther

1 Samuel

14:32–34	101	7:8	35
15:3	117		
22:19	117	**Job**	
25:2	79	1:3	79
		1:6	89
		2:1	89

2 Samuel

8:11	35, 59	7:12	68
21:16–18	90	9:13	68
		11:8–9	197
		26:12–13	68

1 Kings

3:9	61	34:10	52
4:23	78, 80	37:18	12
4:24	35	38–41	37
5:2–3	79	38–40	55
5:30	35	38:6–11	68
6:18	73	38:7	45, 89
6:29–35	73	38:35	45
7:18–20	73	38:39–41	55
8:63	79	39:30	55
9:23	35	41:1–34	68
21	210	41:17	71

Psalms

2 Kings

		7:2–3	123
7:8	216	8:5	36
6:17	22	8:6	38
17:25	37	8:9	15
28:10	59	14:1	19

Psalms (cont.)

19:1	13, 45
18:7–15	175
22:7–22	123
23:5	219, 223
29:1	89
49:13	18
49:21	18
33:8–9	20
36:6	200
36:9	11
50:10–11	37, 200
57:5	123
58:7	123
69:34	197
72:8	35
74:10–17	68
74:12–14	175
74:14	68
84:3–4	196
89:7	89
89:9–10	68
91:11–13	129
92:1	70
96:11–13	198
98:7–9	198
102:26–28	149
104	37, 40, 55
104:2	12, 20
104:5	147
104:7–9	68
104:21	55, 200
104:24–26	55
104:24	199
104:27–28	200
104:27	55
104:29	18
104:30	18
104:31	200
105:28–38	118
106:9	181
110:2	35, 194
121:2	4
132:11–14	195
146:6	197
148	198
148:6	147
148:7	131
145:4	18
145:9	18
145:15	37
147	55
147:9	55
148:4	12
148:5	20
150:1	12
150:6	198

Proverbs

8:27–29	68
12:10	37, 80, 115
15:17	210

Ecclesiastes

3:19–21	18

Isaiah

1:3	131
1:6	220
2:13	171
2:20	123
3:1–7	124
5:1	220
5:29	123
9:7a	128
10:26	182
10:27	220
11	63, 123–24, 126–28, 130, 132, 134, 195, 200
11:6–9	104
11:1–5	123
11:1–2	122
11:5	122
11:6–10	159
11:6–9	121, 123–24
11:6	201
11:9	126
11:10–16	221
11:11	126
11:15	182
12:1–6	128
13:21–22	123

Ancient Document Index

14:2	35
14:6	35
14:12–15	173
17:2	123
18:6	124
19:21	221
23:13	124
25	220
25:6	219–22
25:8	194, 219, 221–22
26:6–9	194
26:19	159
27:1	68
27:10	124
28:1	220
28:4	220
29:6–7	175
30:6	124
30:7	175
31:22	6
32:14	124
34:4	145
34:11	60, 124
34:13–15	124
35:7	124
35:9	124–25
39:2	220
40:22	12
41:19	220
42:9	6
43:1–2	6
43:16	182
43:19	6
43:20	124, 197
45:6–7a	24
45:7	54
45:8	148
45:12	6
51:3	27
53:7	71
54:6–10	104
50:17	123
51:10	182
56:7	221
56:9	124
57:9	220
58:8	24
59:11	123
60:1	11, 24
60:7	221
60:19–20	27
60:19	24
61:3	220
61:11	148
65	63, 127–28, 130, 132, 134, 182, 188, 194–96, 200
65:13	126
65:16	195
65:17–25	126–27, 194, 196
65:17	127, 188, 193–95
65:18–19	194
65:18	195
65:19–23	159
65:19	195
65:20–21	195
65:20	194–95, 221
65:22–23	195
65:23	194–95
65:24	195
65:25	104, 125–27, 132, 159, 188, 195, 206, 215

Jeremiah

2:15	123
4:7	123
4:23	60
34:11	35, 59
34:16	35, 59
46:7–8	175
51:34	123

Ezekiel

1:22	12
1:26–28	24, 105
10:1	12
22:31	176
26:19–21	181
28:13–14	72
28:13	42
28:25–26	159
29:3–5	175
29:15	35

Ezekiel (cont.)

32:2–8	175
32:2	123
34:4	35
34:25–31	104
34:25	37, 106, 125
36:35	27
37:26	104
38:20	15
39:3	138
40:39	221
42	221
42:13	221
45:21	221–22
47:1–12	73

Daniel

5:1–30	217
6:23	132
7	173, 183

Hosea

2:12	106
2:18	104, 105, 195
2:23–25	106
4:3	15, 38

Joel

1:16–20	81
2:2	183
2:31	183
3:13	30

Amos

2:9	90
3:6	54
6:4–6	217
6:4	79
8:9	183

Jonah

1:4	119
1:9	199
2:1–2	120
2:1	199
2:10	119
3:4–10	119
4:7	199
4:8	119
4:11	119, 199–200

Micah

7:16–17	127

Habakkuk

3:2	131
3:9–11	104

Zephaniah

1:3	15
1:15	183

Haggai

2:6–7	175

Zechariah

9:14	104
10:11	182
11:2	171
14:8–9	73

NEW TESTAMENT

Matthew

5:45	56
6:10	165
6:26	211
6:29	165
8:11	219
8:16–17	168
8:19	168
8:21	169
8:23–34	166
8:29	167
8:31–32	167–68
10:29	168, 211
11:19	211
12:11	109

12:43	168
13:25	60
19:28	151
19:29	159
22:1–14	217
23:37	211
24:8	171
24:35	149
26:29	159, 221
27:45–51	75

Mark

1:13	129–30, 132, 160
2:15	211
3:14	130
5:1–20	166
5:3–5	166
5:13	168–69
5:15–17	166–67
5:18	130
5:34	168
6:38–43	211
14:15	217
14:25	221
14:67	130
16:33	183

Luke

4:6	68
5:3–10	211
7:36	211
8:31	167
8:32–33	168–69
8:37	168
8:39	168
11:24	168
11:37	211
12:6	211
12:24	55, 165
13:29	219
14:1	211
14:5	109, 168
14:10	217
14:15	219
19:5	211
22:15	221
22:16	215, 219, 221
22:18	221
22:24	211
24:16	162
24:31	162
24:39	162
24:41–43	211, 215

John

1:1–4	21
1:29	29, 56, 191
1:31	137
2:1–10	216
2:1	14
3	191
3:3	6
3:8	21
3:16–17	29
3:16	191
9:5	11
12:31	68
14:30	68
16:11	68
13:12	217
13:25	217
20:1	162
20:14–16	162
20:25–27	161–62

Acts

1:6	152
3:1–26	143
3:21	143, 147, 152
10–11	212
15:20	101
17	143
17:32–33	144
17:32	28
26:18	68

Romans

4:17	20
5	58
5:12	57–58, 62
5:15	57
5:19	58

Romans (cont.)

5:21	58
8	144, 151, 215
8:12–17	150
8:18–22	125, 150–51, 157, 192, 215
8:19	151
8:20–21	29, 58, 106, 225
8:20	151
8:21	151, 191–92
8:22	151
8:23–24	137, 150–51
8:26	151
14:14	212
14:17	206, 213
14:20–21	204

1 Corinthians

2:14–15	153
3:2	66
7:31	149
10:25–26	212
10:25	204
15	143
15:14	29
15:21	62
15:32	134
15:35–38	153
15:42–44	153–54
15:48	154
15:53	154
15:54	219

2 Corinthians

4:4	68
5:1–4	154
5:14–17	157
5:17	6

Galatians

2:1–10	212
3:27	77
3:29	77

Ephesians

1:9–10	192
2:2	68

Philippians

2:7	36
2:7–8	50
2:10–11	197

Colossians

1	144
1:15–20	148, 224
1:15–18	157
1:16–20	144, 189
1:18–20	192
1:15–17	11
1:20	54
2:9	29
3	77
3:9–10	77

1 Timothy

4:3	212

Hebrews

2:14	62
11:3	20

1 Peter

5:8	68

2 Peter

1:4	146
2:4	60
3	145, 147
3:3–7	146
3:10–13	145–46
3:13	201
3:14	146
3:16	146

1 John

1:5	11

2:28	137	8:7–9	171–72
3:2	137	8:8–11	173
3:8	146, 168	8:8–9	171, 180–81
5:19	68	8:9	173, 177, 180
		8:10–11	171
Jude		8:12	171
		9:1–11	181
1:6–7	89	9:1–5	172–74
1:6	60, 183	9:21	9
1:7	92	10:1—11:13	178
1:13	183	10:1	9
		10:6	180, 197
Revelation		11:2	182
1:8	177	11:3	177
2:7	63, 177, 201	11:7	180
2:26	177	11:13	9, 171
3:9	177	11:14–19	9
3:14	27	11:18	146, 176
3:21	177	11:19	175
4	182	12–13	175, 180
4:5	175	12:9	44, 68
4:6	182	12:12	180
5	175, 197	13	139, 173, 183
5:3	197	13:1	180
5:6	172	13:5–7	174
5:8–10	197	14–15	174
5:8	178	15–16	175
5:11	197	15:1–8	178
5:13	69, 180, 197	15:1	174
6:1–17	9	15:2	182
6:1–9	174	15:3	176
6:9–10	178	15:7—16:21	174
6:12–14	171	16:1–12	9
6:14–15	147	16:1	174
6:14	171	16:3–4	171
6:16	172, 175	16:3	171, 173, 180, 190
7:1–17	9, 178	16:4	171
7:1–3	174	16:5	176
7:3	171	16:6–7	176, 178
7:17	173, 177	16:8	174
8–10	175	16:15	9
8	174	16:17	9
8:1	9	16:18	171, 175
8:2—11:19	174	16:19	175
8:3	178	16:21	175
8:5	175	17:8	180
8:6	9	17:12	174
		17:15	181

Revelation (cont.)

17:16	174
18–21	142
18:4	179
18:5	176
18:8	176
18:17–19	173
18:20	176, 179
18:21	181
18:24	179
19:2	176, 178
19:9	219
19:11	176
20	194
20:1–3	181
20:11	147
20:13	181
21–22	5, 28, 63, 142, 144, 160, 183, 196
21	182, 194
21:1	147, 179–82
21:4	142, 177, 179, 182, 202
21:6	173, 177–78
21:23	11, 24
22:1	173
22:2	63, 201, 215
22:3	77, 182
22:5	182
22:14	78
22:18–19	177

EARLY JEWISH AND CHRISTIAN WRITINGS

1 Enoch

6:1	100
6–19	60, 89
7:1–3	100
21	60, 89
86–88	60, 89

2 Enoch

25:3	23

2 Maccabees

7:28	21

4 Ezra

4:11–12	56
6:40	23
10:1—11:3	57

Gospel of Pseudo-Matthew

18:2	131
19:2	132

Jesus Sirach

7:22	110
31:12—32:2	218
39:26–27	212

Jubilees

3:26–27	72
4:15	60, 89
4:22	60, 89
5:1	60, 89
7:27	100
50:9	26

Sibylline Oracles

3:788–95	125
5:158–60	173

Testaments of the Twelve Patriarchs

5:1–2	111

Wisdom of Solomon

1:13	56
11:15–16	117

www.ingramcontent.com/pod-product-compliance
Lightning Source LLC
Chambersburg PA
CBHW071243230426
43668CB00011B/1570